Praise for

Nancy Kress's *Dynamic Characters*

"Nancy Kress has written an invaluable book on characterization here . . . a wonderfully systematic and easy-to-apply approach to what is essential in all good fiction: good characters. Let Nancy Kress help you make your characters as powerful and convincing as they can be. You'll be grateful you did."
—Mike Magnuson, author of *The Right Man for the Job* and the forthcoming *The Fire Gospels*, both from HarperCollins

"Nancy Kress's *Dynamic Characters* is full of intelligent, savvy advice on what makes characters come to life vividly on the page, and is especially useful for the careful way it delineates how character intertwines with plot. I recommend it highly."
—John Kessel, college professor and award-winning author of *Another Orphan* and *Corrupting Dr. Nice*

"This impressive work is definitely a 'must have' . . . for anyone who is interested in how convincing, multidimensional characterization is accomplished. It stands among the best of instructional manuals—and the published author will benefit as well as the beginner. Highly recommended!"
—Miriam Monfredo, author, Seneca Falls/Glynis Tryon historical mysteries

"Aspiring screenwriters, novelists, short-story writers, and students of any kind of creative fiction will find *Dynamic Characters* an essential resource. Buy this book, keep it on hand and refer to it often. You'll be glad you did."
—Claudia Bishop, author of the Hemlock Falls series

Dynamic Characters

How to create personalities that keep readers captivated

Nancy Kress

WRITER'S DIGEST BOOKS
CINCINNATI, OHIO

This hardcover edition of *Dynamic Characters* features a "self-jacket" that eliminates the need for a separate dust jacket. It provides sturdy protection for your book while it saves paper, trees and energy.

Other fine Writer's Digest Books are available from your local bookstore or direct from the publisher.

02 01 00 99 98   5 4 3 2 1

Library of Congress Cataloging-in-Publication Data

Kress, Nancy.
    Dynamic characters / by Nancy Kress.
        p.   cm.
    Includes index.
    ISBN 0-89879-815-9 (alk. paper)
    1. Fiction—Technique. 2. Characters and characteristics in literature. I. Title.
PN3383.C4K74   1998
808.3'97—dc21   97-50356
                                                                           CIP

Editors: Jack Heffron and Roseann S. Biederman
Production Editor: Nicole R. Klungle
Interior Designer: Brian Roeth
Cover Designer: Angela Lennert Wilcox

Excerpts from *Higher Education* by Charles Sheffield and Jerry Pournelle are reprinted by permission of the authors. Copyright © 1996 by Charles Sheffield and Jerry Pournelle.

Portions of this book have previously appeared as "Fiction" columns in *Writer's Digest* magazine.

Nancy Kress is the author of over a dozen books of fiction, including *Beggars in Spain*, which won both the Hugo and Nebula awards. She is a regular columnist for *Writer's Digest* magazine, and her short fiction frequently appears in *Omni* magazine. She also teaches fiction-writing classes for universities and writing conferences.

For my children, Kevin and Brian,
who don't want to be writers
but are pretty terrific anyway.

table of contents

Creating Strong and Believable Characters: The Externals 7

Creating Strong and Believable
Characters: The Internals 82

part three

Character and Plot

WHO ARE THESE PEOPLE, AND WHO NEEDS THEM?

"Character is plot."

So said novelist Henry James, master of both, a hundred years ago. Unfortunately, in an uncharacteristic burst of taciturnity, James stopped there, leaving several crucial points unexplained. *Why* is character plot? *How* do you use your characters to move your plot forward? *What* kind of characters must you create to make that happen, and *how* do you create them? And *why* are characters such a pivotal concern anyway? If you have really exciting events, can't you just plug in people with enough characterization to carry those events out? After all, how much characterization do most best-sellers actually have?

Good questions, all of them. This book will address them in reverse order, starting with: Do you really need strong, complex, original characters to write a book that might sell?

The honest answer to this has to be "No." Pick up certain

best-selling authors—I name no names—and you can't help but notice that their characters have all the depth of wallpaper. And yet the books are dazzling successes, at least in terms of sales. So why labor over creating believable and original characters?

Four reasons, ranging from the cynical to the idealistic. The most cynical reason first.

PUT AS MANY BEST FEET FORWARD AS YOU CAN

Novels that sell to editors—and then to readers—must have at least one strongly appealing characteristic. In books where the plot is all and the characters characterless, that appeal is the exciting events. Some editor bought the book because the events are different, fast-paced, gripping. Readers read it for the same reason. Both editor and readers stick with the book not *because* the characters are flat, but *despite* that fact.

So why not give your book more than one quality to catch an editor's interest? A terrific plot earns you one point. A terrific plot plus fascinating characters earns you two. A terrific plot plus fascinating characters plus an eloquent style . . . but you get the idea.

I said this was a cynical reason for concentrating on characterization. It is. It assumes that your only interest in writing a book is the eventual sales volume. In fact, however, that is almost never true. Writing a novel is a major undertaking, consuming anywhere from several months to several decades, and few people can last through the marathon of writing one if their only motivation is a large print run. Which brings us to the second reason for concentrating on characterization.

WELL, *I* LIKED HIM!

Those authors with sketchy, hackneyed characters in best-selling books don't *believe* they're sketchy or hackneyed. I've seldom met a writer who didn't think his protagonist felt very real. The most simpering and savorless romance heroine, stereotyped tough-guy detective, purely evil black-hatted villain—it doesn't matter. Their creators see in them depth and interest and reality.

The point of this is not that there are a lot of deluded writers out there (although there probably are). The point is that in order to create a character—think him up, animate him, stick with him for five hundred pages—a writer has to be enthusiastic about that character. Even if not everybody else is.

Which means you must believe in your characters. Be convinced of their solidity. Feel a quickening of interest as you decide what they'll do next. Care about their fates.

All this is much easier if you have created original, complex, individual characters in the first place, rather than simply plugging in stock characters from other people's fiction (or, worse, from TV). Your interest will come through in the writing. We'll discover more depth in the characters—because *you* have.

THE MULTIFACETED CHARACTER: MANY THINGS TO MANY PEOPLE

We all have different friends for different occasions. With John we share a love of discussing politics. We go to the movies mostly with Karen. Bill is the one we turn to when we're in trouble. Nobody is as good as Terry at organizing interesting vacations.

Characters are like that, too. Some are fitted for only one function: the classic "spear carriers" who walk on stage, deliver one line and exit. That's fine, for bit players.

But main characters are another story. Like that wonderful multifaceted friend—the one we can talk with, rely on *and* vacation with— major characters need to participate in many different kinds of events. To do so believably, they need to have enough complexity so that readers accept them in these multiple roles.

Let's consider an example.

You're writing a book about a man—we'll call him Roger—who goes through several kinds of hell before he finally realizes that he cannot be responsible for the welfare of his five grown children. You conceive of Roger as a good man, kind and generous. What kinds of events will he participate in during the course of the book?

- He will be manipulated by a selfish daughter who plays on his guilt as a parent to get him to support her while she spends her life drinking.
- He will face a tough decision about whether to bail out of jail a teenage son who has stolen a car—or let him take the consequences of his own act.

- He will experience a close bond with one daughter, his favorite child—and also experience grief over her death in childbirth.
- He will undertake to raise that daughter's infant—and be appalled at how much resentment he feels toward this helpless mite who caused her mother's death.
- He will love a woman—and lose her because he can't seem to make enough time for her while preoccupied with his children's problems.

Do you see what's happening here? Roger will have to grow—or, rather, your initial conception of him will. Simply thinking of Roger as "a good man, kind and generous" is not going to be enough. Your readers must believe him as a man who also experiences guilt, indecision, grief, resentment and passion—not to mention poor judgment. If all we ever see of Roger is his kindness and generosity, the other events of the story won't seem convincing. "No," we'll say, "I don't believe this guy would really do *that*."

In order to believe that yes, he *would* do that, we need to be given up front a more complex, conflicted and multiply motivated Roger. A man who may indeed be kind and generous, but whose kindness is sometimes misplaced (when?) and whose generosity may have other motives than just benevolence. Perhaps he needs to be in control of everyone around him. Perhaps he can't separate his own self-worth from how good a "showing" his children make in life. Perhaps he unconsciously needs them to be weak, so he can be strong. We need to be shown which of these possibilities motivates this particular Roger. We need, in short, a real human being.

A character with genuine, tangled, messed-up, mixed-bag characterization. Just like all of us.

This is what Henry James meant by "Character is plot." Characterization is not divorced from plot, not a coat of paint you slap on after the structure of events is already built. Rather, characterization is inseparable from plot. What characters do, how they react to story events, must grow naturally out of their individual natures. After all, a Roger who was *not* kind and generous would react entirely differently to his adult kids' difficulties. So would a Roger who *was* kind and generous, but not also driven by guilt and self-doubt—a Roger with more confidence and better judgment.

And why *doesn't* Roger have these qualities? Do you know?

Creating a character with depth and complexity takes time and effort. But the effort pays off in making the character's response to events more believable and interesting.

It works the other way, as well: Once you know a complex character down to his core, then that knowing can help you generate plot ideas. Roger, for instance, is driven by a deep, pervasive fear that he isn't really a good person or a good father. He will do anything to put that anxiety to rest, to reassure himself that yes, he's a good parent because—look!—his kids are fine. Who realizes that about him, consciously or not? His daughter who drinks? Yes. His son in jail? No. The daughter who died? Yes. Each of these people will then react to Roger in terms of what they know (or think they know) of his character.

And their reactions, in turn, create more plot complications.

In short, paying concentrated attention to characterization is useful to you, the writer. It means you end up with stronger and fresher plots. This is not only true of novels concerned, as is Roger's, with exploring psychological dilemmas. It's true whether your story is romance, science fiction, action-adventure, whatever. What characters do must grow out of who they are, and who they are is, in turn, influenced by what you make happen to them. Two sides of the same solid gold coin. This is the best reason for putting effort into characterization.

Well, maybe not the best. There's one reason more.

YOU ARE WITH ME ALWAYS

Huckleberry Finn. Jane Eyre. Sydney Carton. Jay Gatsby. Marianne Dashwood. Sherlock Holmes.

There are characters in fiction so real, so palpable, that we can reach out and touch them our whole lives. See them, hear them, sometimes even smell them. They have a solidity and a humanity that calls up answering emotions in us, and we know we would have been much poorer if we'd never met them.

Hester Prynne. Sam Spade. Philip Carey. Ellen Olenska. Rhett Butler. Lady Brett Ashley.

The chance of creating such a character is the best reason of all for giving characterization everything you've got. "Character is

5

plot"—but it's also so much more. It's the reason books are not only read but reread, not only praised but loved.

Jo March. Quentin Compton. Becky Sharp. Fagin. Jean Brodie. Lord Peter Wimsey.

Hey, as they say in New York about the state lottery, you never know.

BLOOD, SWEAT, TEARS AND PRINTER TONER

One reason you never know is that no one says creating wonderful characters is surefire. Nor is it easy (and if anyone says it is, don't listen). Nor is it, by definition, formulaic. There is no software you can download, type character parameters into and command to crunch out interesting protagonists (and don't believe anyone who says *that*, either). You create characters out of everything that *you* are: your perceptions, emotions, beliefs, history, lifelong reading, desires, dreams. It's not a mappable process, or a simple one, or a straight-line one. You need patience, and insight, and trial and error.

And even then the balky imaginary so-and-sos sometimes won't cooperate.

However, there *are* some techniques you can experiment with in your trial-and-error approach to characterization. That's why this book exists—to explain such techniques. Part one focuses on police-report externals that contribute to characterization: appearance, dress, environment, name(s), place of birth, job, spoken dialogue. Part two is concerned with what goes on inside your character's head: her thoughts, attitudes, fears, loves and dreams. Part three applies these external and internal aspects of character to creating a plot: how to use each to show your protagonist initiating action, reacting to others, making critical decisions, changing over the course of your novel. Finally, we discuss how characterization contributes—or doesn't—to your book's overall theme.

People are endlessly fascinating, endlessly surprising, endlessly strange; just pick up a newspaper. Any newspaper. If you start with people—characters—as you feel your way into your novel, it, too, can become fascinating, surprising and strange.

In short—real.

Let's get started.

part one

Creating Strong and Believable Characters: The Externals

chapter one

BEAUTY AND/OR THE BEAST
Choosing Descriptive Details

One of the first encounters your reader has with your character will probably come from the outside, especially if your novel is told in third person. Someone will observe the character's appearance, clothes, manner. This someone may be the author, or another character, or even the protagonist himself. Whoever does the observing, the description will be related to us readers, and we will get our first chance to form an impression of this person we're going to spend five hundred pages with. Readers pay a lot of (mostly unconscious) attention to this first impression. They want to know if they're looking at a beauty, a beast or something in between.

Thus, you must make the reader's first encounter with your character sharp and memorable. The key is to choose your first descriptive details carefully. These details should:

- create a visual image, so we can picture the character in some important way(s)
- tell us something about the person inside the visual image
- convey an impression of individuality, of someone unique and interesting, whom we will want to know more about

What you don't want is the kind of description that turns up in police reports: "Caucasian male, twenty-seven years old, six feet, 170 pounds, short brown hair, blue eyes." That could describe thousands of men, none of them memorably. It's not individual, it's not evocative of personality, and it's not interesting. Such a description has detail, all right, but not the *right* detail.

So what kind of details are right? Ones that grab the reader's attention.

I NOTICED YOU RIGHT AWAY . . .

One way to grab your reader's attention, of course, is to create a character so bizarre that the reader *can't* look away:

> Bethany, an inch short of seven feet high, had lost her bikini top again. The blue-sequined bottom spanned her generous hips, with a hole cut on the left side for the growing calcium deposit, now the size of a golfball. But on top her 40D breasts flapped free, hidden only by the cascading tresses of greenish-black hair.

We'll notice Bethany. But not every book is the kind of story in which Bethany would have a legitimate place (in fact, very few are). And even in the right novel, a string of Bethanys would become tiresome. When everyone is bizarre, nobody seems really weird.

So what descriptive details both feel "normal" and succeed in creating a strong first impression of your character's physical appearance? Let's consider some examples.

THREE TERRIFIC DESCRIPTIONS

The following are introductory descriptions of a wide variety of characters, from wildly disparate books of different genres. (I know this is a lot of examples to throw at you all at once, but we're going to analyze them throughout this whole chapter.) The characters have nothing in common with each other—except that all arouse interest:

> He was a lank, tall, bearded man in a shaggy brown suit that might have been cut from blankets, and on his head he wore a red ski cap—the pointy kind with a pom-pom at the tip. Masses of black curls burst out from under it. His beard was so wild and black and bushy that it was hard to tell how old he was. Maybe forty? Forty-five? At any rate, older than you'd expect to see at a puppet show, and no child sat next to him.
>
> —MORGAN GOWER, IN ANNE TYLER'S *MORGAN'S PASSING*

> Carrie stood among [the girls in the locker room] stolidly, a frog among swans. She was a chunky girl with pimples on her neck and back and buttocks, her wet hair completely without color. It rested against her face with dispirited sogginess and she simply stood, head slightly bent, letting the water splat against her flesh and roll off. She looked the part of the sacrificial goat, the constant butt, believer in left-handed monkey wrenches, perpetual foul-up, and she was.
>
> —CARRIE WHITE, IN STEPHEN KING'S *CARRIE*

> Solid, rumbling, likely to erupt without prior notice, Macon kept each member of his family awkward with fear. His hatred of his wife glittered and sparkled in every word he spoke to her. The disappointment he felt in his daughters sifted down on them like ash, dulling their buttery complexions and choking the lilt out of what should have been girlish voices. Under the frozen heat of his glance they tripped over door sills and dropped the salt cellar into the yolks of their poached eggs.
>
> —MACON DEAD, IN TONI MORRISON'S *SONG OF SOLOMON*

Each of these descriptions creates a vivid picture (can't you just *see* Morgan Gower, or Carrie White?) But each also does more; it links appearance to personality, letting us glimpse the person underneath. We not only visualize Morgan, we sense his exuberant, childlike eccentricity. We are convinced that Carrie White is passive and Macon Dead is dangerous. And all from descriptions of less than a hundred words.

HOW DO THEY DO THAT?

These authors and the others quoted throughout this chapter achieve so much with visual description because they choose and present details that suggest more than their literal meaning. You, too, can choose from several categories of details that accomplish this. Consider the following as a literary smorgasbord, to sample as you wish.

Use Appearance to Indicate Personality

The technique is to choose details that match your character's inner self, and then to use language that makes that connection clear. There are hundreds of details that could be cited about anyone's appearance. Stephen King chose to describe Carrie's blemished skin, passive posture and colorless hair because they suggest an unattractive person, a victim. This suggestion is reinforced by King's word choices: *stolidly, dispirited, sogginess, letting* the water run off her—even the word *splat* to describe the water hitting her, since *splat* is usually a sound associated with someone being hit, rather than someone enjoying a hot shower. The facts that Carrie is plain and overweight would not, by themselves, indicate a victim—there are plenty of plain, overweight, feisty fighters in the world. It's King's diction that transforms a collection of physical details into a memorable impression.

Similarly, Margaret Mitchell selects some details over others in describing Scarlett O'Hara in *Gone With the Wind*:

> Scarlett O'Hara was not beautiful, but men seldom realized it when caught by her charm as the Tarleton twins were. In her face were too sharply blended the delicate features of her mother, a Coast aristocrat of French descent, and the heavy ones of her florid Irish father. But it was an arresting face, pointed of chin, square of jaw. Her eyes were pale green without a touch of hazel, starred with bristly black lashes and slightly tilted at the ends. Above them, her thick black brows slanted upward, cutting a startling oblique line in her magnolia skin. . . .

By focusing on Scarlett's square jaw, aggressive eyebrows and feminine skin and lashes, Mitchell emphasized the contradictions within Scarlett's nature: a delicate Southern belle with a will of steel.

Use a Character's Own Reaction to
His Appearance to Indicate Personality

This is Sylvie Fisher, from Marilynne Robinson's novel *Housekeeping*:

> After a while they would turn on the radio and start brushing Sylvie's hair, which was light brown and hung down to her waist. The older girls were expert at building it into pompadours with ringlets at ears and nape. Sylvie crossed her legs at the ankles and read magazines. When she got sleepy she would go off to her room and take a nap, and come down to supper with her gorgeous hair rumpled and awry. Nothing could induce vanity in her.

From this we learn that Sylvie has long, thick brown hair. This helps us visualize her, but we actually learn more about Sylvie from her reaction to her own beauty. She is unimpressed. Rather than participate, she passively lets her sisters fiddle with her hair. She destroys their efforts carelessly, preferring sleep to vanity. Sylvie, for the entire length of Robinson's novel, remains careless and unimpressed.

How does your character feel about her own appearance? Proud? Indifferent? Dissatisfied (if so, why)? Insanely jealous of people with more attractive exteriors? Would including her reaction to another's appearance give us vital information about her? If so, do it.

Use Appearance to Indicate a Temporary Situation

In this case, you choose physical details that apply to how the character is feeling at the moment, rather than as indicators of permanent personality. This description of teen Conrad Jarrett occurs early in Judith Guest's *Ordinary People*:

> He does a quick look in the mirror. The news isn't good. His face, chalk-white, is plagued with a weird, constantly erupting rash. This is not acne, they assured him. What it was, they were never able to discover. Typical. He tries to be patient as he waits for his hair to grow out. . . . Everything's okay, he's here, wearing his levis, boots, and jersey shirt, just like everybody else, all cured, nobody panic.

From Guest's wording, we understand that Conrad didn't always have acne, hacked-up hair and an intense concern with dressing "normal."

Rather, these are temporary conditions, and Guest has chosen to emphasize them because they reflect Conrad's current situation: uncertain, still damaged from mental illness, hacked up inside.

Even in a romance novel, where the heroine's beauty is usually fulsomely dwelt on, you can introduce her with a focus on temporary disadvantages rather than permanent prettiness. Meet Hero Wantage, from Georgette Heyer's *Friday's Child*:

> The Viscount looked her over. She was a very young lady, and she did not at this moment appear to advantage. The round gown she wore was of an unbecoming shade of pink, and had palpably come to her at secondhand, since it seemed to have been made originally for a larger lady. . . . In her hand she held a crumpled and damp handkerchief. There were tear stains on her cheeks, and her wide grey eyes were reddened and a little blurred. Her dusky ringlets, escaping from a frayed ribbon, were tumbled and very untidy.

Hero's reddened eyes, tear-stained cheeks and messy hair are not indicative of her usual state. She is currently very unhappy. The description thus accomplishes two goals at once: letting us visualize the basic facts of Hero's appearance (young, small, dark-haired) and giving us her temporary state of mind.

If you decide to introduce your character to us at a moment of high emotion, pick details that do double duty.

Use Dress to Indicate Personality

Because a character can choose his clothes—or at least his reaction to them—clothing details are a good way to tell us about your character's personality. Note Jenny Fields's reactions to her own clothing:

> In Jenny's opinion, her breasts were too large; she thought the ostentation of her bust made her look "cheap and easy." . . . She liked her simple, no-nonsense [nurse's] uniform; the blouse of the dress made less of her breasts; the shoes were comfortable, and suited to her fast pace of walking.
>
> —JOHN IRVING, *THE WORLD ACCORDING TO GARP*

Jenny likes her sensible shoes and relatively sexless nursing uniform because *she* is sensible and sexless.

Dominique Francon, from Ayn Rand's best-selling *Atlas Shrugged*, chooses much different clothing:

> She had gray eyes that were not ovals, but two long, rectangular cuts edged by parallel lines of lashes; she had an air of cold serenity and an exquisitely vicious mouth. Her face, her pale gold hair, her suit seemed to have no color, but only a hint, just on the verge of the reality of color, making the full reality seem vulgar.

Dominique's subtle suit, which makes actual colors look "vulgar," tells us that she is elegant and disdainful.

Look back at the description of Morgan Gower. He wears a child's pom-pom hat, pointed like an elf's cap, in bright red. To see how truly dress can indicate personality, picture Dominique in Morgan's hat. Or Scarlett O'Hara in Jenny Fields's sexless uniform. No, no.

What clothes does *your* character prefer? Sharply creased slacks? Jeans? Designer dresses? Shapeless ones? His military uniform? Give this some thought. Then show us.

Use Dress to Indicate a Temporary Situation

On the other hand, Hero Wantage's shabby cloak and made-over, ill-fitting gown don't indicate her basic personality any more than do her reddened eyes. The frumpy clothes clearly have been forced on her by necessity, and so serve to tell us more about her current situation (poor relation) than her own taste. Do this when you wish to put your character's current situation in the foreground, so you can change it later (Hero becomes rich and well dressed).

Use Details of the Home to Indicate Personality

Among the first things we learn about Kinsey Millhone, Sue Grafton's popular detective, is that Kinsey lives sparsely:

> My name is Kinsey Millhone. I'm a private investigator, licensed by the state of California. I'm thirty-two years old, twice divorced, no kids. . . . My apartment is small but I like living in a cramped space. I've lived in trailers most of

my life, but lately they've become too elaborate for my taste, so now I live in one room, a "bachelorette." I don't have pets. I don't have houseplants.

—'A' Is for Alibi

Note that this apartment contains nothing living that might shackle its occupant. Kinsey has chosen this environment. Beyond letting us visualize setting, this is Grafton's way of alerting us that Kinsey is a loner, not materialistic, wary of close bonds. And so she is.

Use Personal Tastes to Indicate Personality

Just as homes can illustrate character, so can anything else that your character chooses: car, food, drink, music, books, vacation spots. Ian Fleming suggested quite a lot about James Bond with Bond's precise specifications for his martinis ("shaken, not stirred"). Is your character more likely to drive a Ford Escort, a Mercedes-Benz or a pickup truck? Conservative black, or gold with racing stripes? With or without bumper stickers? What do the bumper stickers say? What's in the back seat: decaying McDonald's wrappers, a complete first-aid kit, a change of clothes and toothbrush (just in case), fishing gear from last summer, broken toys? When was the car last serviced? Washed? Is it usually driven on a familiar round of home-work-mall, or has it seen both Acapulco and Anchorage?

The man with volumes of Nietzsche beside his bed is not the same man with *Turkey Grower Monthly* beside his. Or maybe he *is* (interesting). Show us. Not everything, of course. Just two or three personal tastes that indicate a lot about who this character really is.

Use Mannerisms to Indicate Personality

Jenny Fields walks fast, swinging her arms. Carrie White stands with her head bent. Other characters may chew on their hair, endlessly jiggle one foot or carefully fold all pieces of paper into precise thirds before throwing them away. Such mannerisms—habitual physical gestures—tell us something about the inner life of each character.

Some mannerisms, such as lighting a cigarette to show nervousness, have been so overused that they're now clichés. But the *idea* of using mannerisms is still viable. Search for fresh gestures that let us visualize what your character is doing while telling us something significant about her personality.

Use Description to Indicate Relationships With Others

Look again at the description of Macon Dead. We don't actually learn anything about what Macon looks like. What author Morrison does instead is use minimal physical description as a jumping-off place for authorial exposition about how Macon Dead relates to other people.

Philip Roth uses the same technique in *Goodbye, Columbus*. Here is the narrator, Neil, describing his new girlfriend's mother:

> I did not like Mrs. Patimkin, although she was certainly the handsomest of all of us at the table. She was disastrously polite to me, and with her purple eyes, her dark hair, and large, persuasive frame, she gave me the feeling of some captive beauty, some wild princess, who had been tamed and made the servant to the king's daughter—who was Brenda.

The actual visual details about Mrs. Patimkin are pretty generic: handsome, purple eyes, dark hair, large frame. That's because the visual details aren't the point. They're merely a springboard for the narrator's observations about the family's social dynamics.

But, you might ask, isn't that just abstract *telling* rather than *showing*? Not the way Morrison and Roth do it. Both use command of the English language to create vivid metaphors, word pictures striking enough to replace descriptions of their characters' bodily appearance. Macon Dead's hatred is a physical thing; it "glitters" and "sparkles." His disappointment, too, is physical: "like ash, dulling [his daughters'] buttery complexions and choking" them. His glance is "frozen heat"; its effects are described in the specific physical images of his daughters tripping over door sills and dropping salt cellars into poached eggs (more specificity: poached, not scrambled or over-easy—nothing in Macon Dead's house is easy). Attitudes have been translated into strong and original metaphors that show us Macon Dead as well as— or better than—a direct description.

Similarly, Roth gives us a striking metaphor for Mrs. Patimkin's relationship with her family. She's a captive princess forced to serve a younger woman, "disastrously polite" in her impotent rage. This is such a startling metaphor to evoke about a mother-daughter relationship that it serves as a memorable description of Mrs. Patimkin. She's fixed in our minds.

This works best if you allow us to first glimpse your character when he's in the presence of other people. Visualize the scene carefully before you write. Where is everybody standing? What do body language and facial expressions say about these people's relationships? When you're sure *you* know, search for an interesting way to convey that information to *us*.

Use Other Senses to Indicate Personality

Although none of the above descriptions employ the other senses, this technique can be very effective. Describe your character in terms of a characteristic sound, smell, feel or perhaps even taste. Think of F. Scott Fitzgerald's Daisy Buchanan, whose "voice was full of money." Of John Steinbeck's Tom Joad, day after day tasting dust. Of Sandra Cisneros's Lucy, "who smells like corn." Does your character always feel warm to the touch, radiating body heat? Smell of cinnamon, or manure? Talk in a voice so shrill it sounds like fingernails scraping a blackboard? What can you imply about her inner self through such sensory details?

COMBINING TYPES OF DETAILS: BUBBA'S PLACE

Your descriptions, of course, don't have to be confined to only one of the above techniques. Look again at John Irving's description of Jenny Fields. It combines details of physical appearance, dress and mannerisms, plus Jenny's own opinion of all these. Mix and match.

However, one important caveat: Don't get carried away. Too many details are as bad as too few. Paragraph after paragraph of descriptive details, no matter how brilliantly evocative, will overwhelm your reader. He'll burn out from sensory overload—and all you'll have done so far is introduce the character!

So how many details are too many? As with nearly everything else in writing, there's no simple answer. It depends on the book's length, purpose, voice and overall tone. But as a rule of thumb, a half-dozen details are plenty. If you choose carefully, that's usually more than enough. (For more on leaving out details, see chapter seven.)

To see just how much the right details can contribute to your reader's picture of a character, consider the following three descriptions. The action is exactly the same in all three, but the details of environment and diction make all the difference:

> When I stormed into Bubba's trailer, the Carson-Akabar fight was playing on the TV. Bubba was nowhere to be seen, but that didn't stop me. Nothing could stop me. I tore past the beer cans and the Harley, racing through the trailer until I found him taking a crap in the bathroom. "You bastard! I've got something to give you!"

> When I sauntered into Serge's, *Tosca* was playing on the stereo. Serge was nowhere to be seen, but that didn't stop me. Nothing could stop me. I strolled past the library and the dining room, making my way through the mansion until I found him repotting violets in the conservatory. "You sly dog, I have a message for you."

> When I crept into Daddy's, some old-timey music was playing on the radio. Daddy was nowhere to be seen, but that didn't stop me. Nothing could stop me. I sneaked past all the women's clothes on the living room floor and past the closed bedroom door, tiptoeing through the house until I found him in the garage. "D-Daddy, listen, *please*, I've got to tell you something!"

It's all in the details. You can have Beauty or the beast—as long as you choose your specifics carefully.

SUMMARY: THE KEYS TO SUCCESSFUL DESCRIPTION

- Choose details that create strong visual images.
- Choose details that add up to an accurate, coherent impression of your character's personality.
- Use word choices that further reinforce this impression.
- Don't choose too many details. Quality is more effective than quantity.
- Use your effective details the first time we encounter your character, so we will want to keep on reading.

chapter two

WHAT'S IN A NAME?
Using Monikers to Convey Character

You have this person inhabiting your head, soon to be a person inhabiting your page. You can see him, hear him, feel him. As yet, he's nameless. To you he's already a very real, distinct entity, but to everyone else he will need a name. How do you choose one?

Some writers think of the name first, and the name suggests their character's personality. Some writers can't even begin to write until their character has the exactly right name; others change their minds four times during the writing of the first draft, as they make decisions about characters' actions and reactions. Some create elaborate family trees to the fourth generation; others seem to resent the necessity of naming and use the same names over and over in unrelated books. But all these writers—and you—have one thing in common: Characters have to be called *something*.

And since they do, you may as well get more mileage out of names than simply a tag before "said" or "walked to the store" or "killed the sniper with his Beretta 92F at an unbelievable seventy-five yards." You may as well make your names contribute to world building, characterization and plot development.

THE NAME YOU CHOOSE FOR A CHARACTER

Surnames, and sometimes first names as well, indicate ethnic background. A character called Reginald Fitzsimmons III comes from a different ancestry than one called Salah Mahjoub—and readers will have different expectations of him. You may choose to work with these expectations or deliberately flout them, but you should realize they're there. If Reginald is not descended from British aristocrats, you will have to account for his aristocratic name (maybe his dirt-poor, unwed, sixteen-year-old mother wanted to give him *something* fancy). And if Salah is not Muslim but a Presbyterian deacon, you will have to explain why. The rule of thumb is: The farther you move from the commonly accepted background suggested by ethnic names, the more explaining you must do.

On the other hand, since America is not the equal melting pot we might wish it were, not all ethnic names carry the same evocation of family background. European immigrants have now been here for so many generations that most readers will not automatically equip a character named Robert Olson with a religion, class, occupation, or accent. Instead, Robert Olson (or Sam Carter or Jack Romano) is a blank slate, and you will have to do all the work of drawing him well.

An additional point about ethnic names: This is a diverse world. Some stories have a "closed" setting, in which nearly all the names are logically Anglo-Saxon (John Cheever's Shady Hill), or Jewish (Chaim Potok's novels about the Hasidim), or Chinese (Amy Tan's *The Joy Luck Club*). Others use an ethnic mix that reflects a given reality. Ed McBain's earliest novels of the Eighty-Seventh Precinct featured a lot of Italian and Irish names, in keeping with the makeup of the New York City police force at that time. Think about who is likely to inhabit your fictional world, and reach for an appropriate ethnic mix.

Your character's name will also reflect her parents' personal choices, which in turn characterizes her family life. Parents who name their child Susan Mary are not implying the same worldview as those who pick Bernadette Chantelle. Did your character's parents want a name that will blend in? That will stand out? That will emphasize a heritage (perhaps a grandfather's first name)? That will disguise a heritage? Serious? Flowery? Trendy? The child named Rainbow Sweetgrass Smith by sixties' flower-child parents is being handed more than words to someday sign on her checks. So are the children named Malcolm X Smith and George Patton Smith. How a character reacts to such freighted names may even suggest plot developments. Does she like her name? Hate it? Spend the whole book trying to escape whatever it means to her?

What about using a name whose meaning either characterizes the person or reflects your theme? There are two dangers here: pretentiousness and obscurity. John Bunyan may have gotten away with naming his protagonist Christian to stand for the entire Western world, but contemporary audiences find this heavy-handed. On the other hand, *you* may know that *Elizabeth* means *oath of God* and that her name is a thematic comment, but don't expect your reader to know it.

Sometimes writers call their characters after people they know. This can be a useful device for helping yourself to visualize a character, to "feel" him as you're writing the first draft. But change the name before you submit the story anywhere, to avoid not only hurt feelings but possible legal problems. (More on this in chapter eight.)

Names can also plant a character in a given generation. Jennifer and Jessica have been popular names in the last twenty years; their mothers' generation ran more toward Sue and Karen. And their grandmothers included a lot of Dorothys and Bettys.

Don't give characters in the same story similar names (Jean and June); it can be confusing. The exception to this is when you want it to be confusing, such as when parents with a terminal case of cuteness have named their triplets Mike, Mac and Mick.

Finally, the name by which you refer to your character should be consistent. If his name is Fred Potter, use his full name the first time he's on stage. After that, refer to him in narration as either Fred or Potter. Don't worry about overusing a name; it's exempt from the usual rules about redundancy. The reader won't notice.

THE NAME A CHARACTER CHOOSES FOR HIMSELF

The ways your character modifies her birth name can also be used as a characterizing device. Bernadette Chantelle, for instance, may decide to call herself Bernie. She might do this because she thinks of herself as a no-frills person, or because she likes having a name that sounds male, or because it annoys her mother, or because her husband's name is also Bernie and she thinks the match is just darling. Each of these motivations suggests a very different person. Similarly, the thirty-year-old who does *not* change Rainbow Sweetgrass Smith to Rainie, but instead insists on the whole moniker, is very confident, very flamboyant or very into environmental politics. You decide.

An interesting example here is Marge Piercy's protagonist in her wonderful novel of radical politics, *Vida*. Born Davida Witherspoon, the character first shortens her name to Vida to fit in with other children. She then goes by Vida Asch, a symbolic choosing of her stepfather Sanford Asch over her father Tom Witherspoon; this choice fills her with both satisfaction and guilt. She marries twice, but does not take either of her husbands' surnames because she values her own independence. When she goes underground after a political bombing, she chooses the name Peregrine, after the falcon. When she's older, however, Vida finds this choice too romantic and regrets it. One of her pleasures is calling her sister Natalie by her real name, thus reaffirming Vida's right to have a family even though she's been in hiding, cut off from mainstream life, for over ten years. Piercy got a lot of plot and thematic mileage out of this changing roadway of names.

Ask yourself: What did my character choose to be called as a child? A teenager? At college? In the army? When he was part of a gang? In prison? After the divorce? In social situations? In professional ones? The man who insists that even his wife refer to him as "the senator" is characterizing himself loud and clear.

THE NAME OTHERS CHOOSE FOR A CHARACTER

The names others call your protagonist without his permission can also be used to create characterization, tension and plot developments. How will the child dubbed Stinky react? By running away? Laughing at his tormentors? Beating the shit out of anyone he can catch alone?

Names imposed on others say something about the relationship. The woman who calls her mother-in-law "Sally" is assuming a different relationship than the one who calls her "Mom," or "Mrs. Jones." Consider what your character is called by his parents, children, children's friends, personal friends, enemies, colleagues, neighbors, lovers, the press and the local cops. Then consider whether these names might change over the course of the relationship. The man who is "Bobby" to his mistress but "Robert" when the affair is over has swapped a breezy, playful name for a more formal one. On the other hand, the man who is called Robert during the affair and Bobby when it's over has just been demoted to a child.

Finally, as with names bestowed on a birth certificate, consider how your character feels about his or her nicknames. Is the business-woman who usually goes by Elizabeth secretly delighted by the lover who dubs her Kitten? Does the high-school kid glory in being referred to as Slash? How far will he go to live up to that name?

Here's Vida Asch again, in a striking illustration of just how much names matter:

> Joel grinned. "I recognized you immediately. Vida Asch."
>
> He seemed to enjoy saying her name, while she experienced an automatic spurt of cold along her arteries. In contrast, he had been flattered when she called him by name—not frightened or at least startled as she had expected. That had not given her the commanding edge she had anticipated, but rather had eliminated some small advantage she had not been aware of.
>
> —MARGE PIERCY, *VIDA*

There is power in names. That is why some cultures reveal true names only to highly trusted intimates. But even in our informal American culture, eager to seize on the first names of total strangers, what we call each other has meaning. Exploit it.

SUMMARY: NAMING YOUR CHARACTERS
- Choose surnames that reflect your fictional world's ethnic diversity (or lack of it).
- Choose first names that tell us something about this character's family's worldview, hopes and/or generation.
- Choose nicknames that show us how the character is viewed by others.
- Show us how the character reacts to her names and nicknames.
- Use her reactions to fuel action—and so generate plot developments.

chapter three

ZIP CODE, PLEASE
The Role of Setting
in Creating Character

So now your character has an appearance, a name, some personal tastes. Let's go back in time. He also has a background, a specific place he grew up and first encountered the world—which was, of course, only the version of the world accepted in his particular family in his particular hometown. This chapter will consider that hometown and the marks it has inescapably left on your protagonist. Even if he himself has left town, the town has left its mark on his character. It does on all of us. Place of birth is a lot more than just a phrase on your driver's license application. It's a clue to character.

It can also be a surprisingly effective way to approach plotting.

"There are three rules for writing a novel," said the great novelist and short-story writer W. Somerset Maugham. "Unfortunately, nobody knows what they are." Another piece of Maugham's advice—about as useful as the first—is, "Devise incidents." Well, OK, fine. A novel consists of incidents; probably not even the deconstructionists would dispute this. But *which* incidents? What are they supposed to do? And how do you think them up?

One way is to think about the conflicts inherent in your character's background. And there *will* be conflicts. No matter where she's from or how idealistic her childhood was, there's no place on earth that is Eden. Not anymore. And even if there were, would Eden be the best preparation for climbing on the school bus and encountering the rest of the less-than-perfect world?

Background, in other words, can contribute to both characterization and plot. So before you even begin your story, spend some time thinking about your protagonist's hometown. This chapter explores why you should do that—and how.

EXTERNAL CHARACTERIZATION: I RECOGNIZE YOU

Your character was born in Salt Lake City. Or East Harlem. Or rural Iowa. Or southern California. She spent, say, the first eighteen years of her life there, before joining the army and being shipped to Fort Polk, Louisiana, for basic training.

Each of these four birthplaces has its own subculture. The recruit from East Harlem and the one from southern California are going to speak differently, dress differently, wear their hair and makeup differently, judge others differently. If you, the author, are mindful of these differences, you can use them to enrich your protagonist's believability.

The differences are of two kinds: the simpler external signs of origin, and the more complex inner worldview. Tackle the externals first. Ask yourself the following questions:

- Where was my character born?
- How long did she live there?
- What social class did she grow up in within that setting? (This is vital; the girl living in New York in nanny/private-school/summers-in-the-Hamptons privilege may be less than half a mile from the girl living on struggling-to-pay-the-rent welfare, but their formative experiences will be radically different.)
- Does she have an accent? What kind? Does it indicate class as well as geography? How pronounced is it?

- How old is she now? Has she had time to leave behind the tastes and fashions of her childhood setting, or is she still following them? Has she had time to leave them behind but is still following them anyway? (That says something about her right there.)
- Does her background influence the way she dresses? Wears her hair? Uses makeup? (The girl from Iowa wears jeans. So does the girl from East Harlem. But the Iowan's jeans are worn with a sweater, sneakers and small gold earrings. The East Harlemite is sitting on the subway in her jeans, high-heeled lace-up boots, leotard top and four-inch earrings heavy enough to distend her earlobes.)
- Does her background influence her tastes in music, food, leisure activities? What does she like to do for fun, and where does she like to do it?
- What was she taught to do as a child, by her family or older kids or professional lessons? Surfing? Ballet? Basketball? Violin? Blues guitar? Horseback riding? Housework? Embroidery? Carpentry?
- What are the political attitudes of her region? Does she share them?

We've departed from externals. In a minute, we'll consider the internal qualities your character may have absorbed from her birthplace. But first let's look at a few objections often raised about this entire process.

STEREOTYPES: I RECOGNIZE YOU TOO EASILY

But, goes one objection to this process, if I create a character this way, won't I end up with a stereotype? The blonde, air-headed, California surfer? The New York black girl in her midriff-baring top, baggy jeans and feisty attitude who says, "You *go*, girl"? The Iowa farm girl raising chickens for her 4-H project?

Yes, you'll end up with a stereotype if background is the *only* means by which you create a character. But it won't be (or at least, it shouldn't). Background is where you start. Then you consider how this individual, this specific person, has reacted to his background. There are a number of possibilities:

He's rejected his background, deliberately re-creating himself on some other model. This is the entire premise of Margaret Drabble's wonderful novel *Jerusalem the Golden*. Clara, from working-class north

England, meets Clelia at college. Clelia's background is upper-class arts/intellectual, and Clara is so entranced she immediately adopts Clelia's family, speech, tastes and judgments.

Other famous rejecters of their background, whose rejection ends up shaping their personalities, include Jay Gatsby (*The Great Gatsby*, by F. Scott Fitzgerald), Becky Sharp (*Vanity Fair*, by William Makepeace Thackeray), and Rudolph Jordache (*Rich Man, Poor Man*, by Irwin Shaw).

He's embraced his background, to the point of exaggerating its outer signs. The businessman who wears the boots, Stetson and hearty accent of his native Texas, even though he now lives in Philadelphia. The Frenchwoman whose accent, after thirty years in Boston, is more Parisian than Parisians' living on the Champs-Elysées. The South Dakotan who's never left Sioux Falls, never will, and belongs to the same civic organizations her mother did. Check out Scotty Hoag, in Herman Wouk's *Youngblood Hawke*, who does multimillion-dollar real estate deals all over the country, yet sounds and acts like a good ol' boy who never left the Kentucky hills.

What motivates such people? Pride, or contentment, or homesickness, or inertia, or lack of imagination, or lack of pretentiousness, or deliberate camouflage. You decide.

He's ambivalent about his background, and so vacillates between erasing its signs and clinging to them. For a more complex portrait than Scotty Hoag, consider Wouk's hero in the same novel. Youngblood Hawke, a famous novelist, is from the Kentucky hills but now lives in Manhattan. His success has given him entrée to upper-class social circles. Hawke, who's only twenty-six, buys expensive suits and shoes like those he sees on New Yorkers at parties. He also clings fiercely to his Kentucky accent. He buys an East Side brownstone, but ends up living in its cramped attic, which is "much like his bedroom in his mother's house." He pursues a sophisticated concert manager who seems to him the epitome of the "New York woman," but falls in love with a small-town girl of working-class parents. In short, he fumbles his way out of, back into, halfway out of his background—like most of us engaged in the lifelong process of growing up.

Using a character's background to help create him does not have to lead to stereotypes. Not if you use your imagination to go beyond the obvious.

A DIFFERENT OBJECTION TO BACKGROUND WORK

Another objection to this process goes like this: OK, well and good, my character does indeed have to come from somewhere, but for the book I have in mind, her background doesn't matter. It's a book about (pick one) the FBI solving crimes/the military chasing foreign subs/ the spaceship crew trading with Deneb Four. There's a lot of action, and no time for explaining characters' earlier lives. All that matters is who they are *now*. There's no point in my inventing a geographical and social background, because I just won't use the information for anything. Right?

Only half right.

It's true that there are good books in which we never get a hint about where the protagonist comes from. Not a geographical name, not a whiff of accent, not a single childhood recollection. That's fine. It doesn't have to be in the book, or in your character's mind. But it should nonetheless be in *your* mind, because even if it's never mentioned, it will still influence the way you write him. And if you don't have some sense of his background, you are far more likely to write a bland, colorless, generic sort of protagonist. Yes, the fast-paced and ingenious action might compensate for that—but wouldn't it be better to have both? What can you lose? No book was ever harmed by having interesting, layered characters—but many are never published because they don't have them.

To see how much background can add to a book in which it's not the main concern, read Kim Stanley Robinson's *Red Mars*, possibly the best novel ever written about colonizing Mars. The colonization is an international effort, and the characters, although never stereotypes, are solidly rooted in their backgrounds: Maya Toitovna, the brilliant and volatile Russian, growing up in a socialist matriarchy. Nadia Cherneshevsky, used to the self-sufficiency and hardships of Siberia. Hiroko Ai, with her Japanese dislike of direct confrontation and her Shintoism. John Boone, the easy-going American, accustomed to open friendliness. Selim el-Hayil, from an Arab nation used to being slighted by the West and to settling political problems by assassination. The novel is about terraforming Mars, but the characters are about themselves, the selves that their backgrounds have made them, and the effect is to immeasurably enrich the action.

No matter what kind of book you're writing, take the time to think your way into your characters' pasts—even if you never directly mention their backgrounds. The effort will pay off in deeper, more plausible characterization. It can also, as we'll discuss next, help you to construct stronger plots.

STAYING PUT: USING BACKGROUND TO GENERATE PLOT

Once you know where your character is from, there are two possibilities. Either he's still there, or he's not. In each case, your strategy will differ for making use of the background you've invented.

First, let's consider staying put. Your character has never moved away from her hometown, and neither will the action of your novel. This is important because the whole point of any novel is to create difficulties for your character. That's what plot is. Stories in which the characters sail along happily, without having things made tough for them, are boring. Stories are about conflict. In fact, every story is a war, with battles and artillery and winners and losers. War, as General Sherman remarked, is tough (or words to that effect). So you want to seek out conflicts for your characters.

The usual advice on how to do this goes something like this: Every protagonist has to want something. So first figure out what your character wants. Then figure out what is preventing him from getting it, what obstacles stand in the way. Then show how the character struggles to overcome the obstacles, and succeeds. Or doesn't. Hamlet, for instance, wants to avenge his father; the obstacle is his reluctance to kill his own uncle and his own mother. Jay Gatsby wants Daisy; the obstacle is their differing social classes. The detective wants to solve the murder; the obstacle is that the murderer does not wish him to do this and so has tried to cover his traces.

Background comes into all this when you begin to work out the specifics of both desire and obstacle. The setting of your story holds all the larger forces that will in turn shape the specific ones at work inside your character, which in turn will determine what he *perceives* as both desire and obstacle (one person's desire is another's nightmare). By considering setting first, you are going right to the source. The wellspring of what makes your protagonist who he is. The context which provides the forces ranged for and against him. Out of the interaction of those forces can come the specific incidents of the plot.

This might be easier to see in examples.

THERE'S NO PLACE LIKE HOME

- Example one: Start with a Southern tidewater town in which status is everything, and the pull of the tides an almost mystical force. This is the setting that has shaped your protagonist's mother. What does she want? How does that impact what her son wants?
- Example two: Start with a quiet upper-class prep school during World War II. The young men here, on the verge of draft age, have been raised with the values of success, athleticism and competition. What does an ambitious student want?
- Example three: Start with the Texas border right after World War II, when the big ranches are being broken up or swallowed up by agribusiness, and the smaller ones are nearly all gone. Take a desolate, isolated ranch. What does the teenage boy who has grown up on it want?

Probably you found you could not answer those questions without deciding on the specific personality of your young mother, your preppy student, your teenage Texan. In these settings, different people will want different things. So the next step is to think about where your character fits within the setting, and how she reacts to it.

If the mother in your tidewater, status-conscious town is poor white trash, and she desperately wants to not be, she will push her children to bolster her own respectability. And one or more of those children may resist: through anger, through rebellion, through madness. Through intense identification with the magnificent natural world around them. Pat Conroy used this background to generate plot for *The Prince of Tides*.

If your prep-school student has always had the best of everything and has been raised to competition and success, he may want to *be* the best in everything. He may even be prepared to go to violent lengths to do this, spurred on by the awareness of the violence of war just beyond graduation. This logical extension of the values inherent in the setting fuels John Knowles's classic *A Separate Peace*.

If your teenage boy regrets the passing of his way of life on the Texas border, and he is a strong-willed and adventurous kid, he will run away south, to Mexico, where that way of life still exists, as

Cormac McCarthy showed in the National Book Award winner *All the Pretty Horses*.

Note, too, that when you start with setting and character, the obstacles grow as naturally out of the setting as do the desires. This is because every setting in the galaxy will favor some character types and provide hardships for others. (I use *in the galaxy* advisedly; science fiction has long known the value of starting with setting.) If, for instance, the mother in *The Prince of Tides* had been a different sort of mother, or even from a different social class, she would not have put the same pressures on her three children, and Tom's and Luke's and Savannah's stories would have been much different.

If Gene Forrester of *A Separate Peace* had not been such a personally driven kid, the competitiveness encouraged in his time, place and class might not have reached such murderous intensity.

If John Grady Cole had said, "Oh, I don't care that the ranch is sold, I'm eager for city life in Austin," Cormac McCarthy would have generated for him much different incidents.

Setting, then, is the actual birthplace for desire, character, obstacles—all the things that cause conflict for your characters and hence generate plot. Any character who stays in his hometown may experience conflict between the setting and his own personality. Use that conflict to build plot.

A warning: To serve this function, your setting must be real. That doesn't mean it has to exist in the actual world (I write science fiction, after all). But it *does* have to exist complete in your mind, with not only physical features but also prevailing values, beliefs, class structure, economics and social customs. To do you any good as a generator of incidents, a setting must be as complex as real-life settings are.

This is why it's not sufficient, when asked where your novel takes place, to say simply, "Rochester, New York." There are many Rochesters. The mansions along East Avenue are not artsy Park Avenue is not the working-class suburb of Spencerport is not the academic-heavy neighborhoods around the University of Rochester is not the northwest quadrant, parts of which have a higher per-capita murder rate than Manhattan. Nor is there one Boston, one St. Louis, one Prairie View, Arkansas. Even if these places are invented, you must invent them *completely*. Not just physically, but sociologically and economically as well.

Fiction is not sociology. But fiction, like sociology, is about human behavior. If you answer some of the same questions as sociologists, you will get a fuller picture of your setting.

And when you do, you'll find you have helped yourself enormously with both character and plotting. Because from your knowledge of what is prevalent and expected in this place, what is valued and believed, you can generate characters at odds with some aspect of your setting. They might be at odds because, like John Grady Cole, they want something different. Or because, like Gene Forrester, they want what everybody else wants but with much more intensity. Or, like Tom and Luke and Savannah, what somebody else wants for them is screwing up their lives.

LEAVING HOME: USING BACKGROUND TO GENERATE PLOT

The essential process is the same for the character who leaves his hometown: Look for the conflicts between setting and personality. Here, however, you have even more choices, because you have more settings. There are at least two settings: the place the character comes from and the place she is now. Plus many different personalities to interact with them.

Suppose, for example, that our New York girl newly inducted into the army (remember her?) has just arrived at Fort Polk. Let's call her Lisa. She is feisty, street-smart, suspicious, self-reliant, cosmopolitan—all characteristics with high survival value in Harlem. Louisiana, however, is laid-back, friendly, slow-paced and provincial. Things are done by tradition. Members of the black community rely heavily on each other to live their lives. Sarcasm is not, as it is in New York, an art form. Lisa can adjust all right to basic training, but the culture shock of Louisiana is causing conflict whenever she has leave in town.

You have a good opportunity to generate plot incidents from the clash between the character, holding onto her old-setting values, and the new setting.

Or take a different Lisa. This one also comes from New York, but she reacted to her hometown by becoming very self-protective. Silent, withdrawn, almost always fearful but self-trained not to show it. A stoic. In Louisiana, however, she finds a slower, more open culture—and she loves it. She flourishes here. She's happy. But when she goes back to New York, everyone there expects her to be who she was before. She is unhappy and miserable.

This version of Lisa lets you plot from her internal conflict between the characteristics of old and new settings.

Or—a third Lisa. She loves Louisiana as much as the second Lisa. However, she's a stronger character. When her hitch in the army is over, she moves to Louisiana and cuts all ties with New York. She renounces her frantic, violent, shiftless family. She starts over. But gradually, over a lifetime, she realizes how many good things there were in her seemingly awful background. Her grandmother's loving endurance. Her brother's colorful scheming. The willingness to try different things. Lisa eventually comes to a reconciliation of her two settings.

Actually, this is a common plot structure. A character turns her back on the culture of her childhood and chooses a much different setting—geographical or class-based or ethnic. But as time goes on, the character either returns to the values of her childhood or else learns to integrate two different ways of life.

Thus, Marjorie Morgenstern rebels against her immigrant Jewish background but eventually returns to keeping a kosher household (*Marjorie Morningstar*, by Herman Wouk). Doug Gardner moves back to his childhood Brooklyn and opens an antique store, leaving behind Manhattan corporate life (*Fifty*, by Avery Corman). And Michel Duval, a long way from his home of Provence, France (he's on Mars), is first numbingly homesick, and later learns to translate his feeling for Provence into a similar feeling for the much different landscapes of an alien planet (*Red Mars*, by Kim Stanley Robinson).

Whether your character leaves home, stays put or returns home, your setting can be a rich source of both characterization and plot. Setting can do so many things: furnish motivation, illuminate internal conflicts, bolster the plausibility of action, provide a larger context for choices. But, of course, setting can do these things only if you take the time and imagination to explore its implications in your own mind, in order to decide which aspects of a particular setting you wish to emphasize in your fiction.

Then send us there.

SUMMARY: A CHECKLIST TO
START THINKING ABOUT SETTING

- Who lives in this place? How do they make their living? How stable is the economic situation? What does a household usually consist of? How stable are most households?
- What values are held in the community as a whole about material possessions? Religion? Children? Patriotism? Education? Crime? Sex? Working? Leaving? Newcomers? Privacy? Loyalty to kin?
- Who has status here—who is looked up to? For what reasons? Are high-status people treated differently from low-status people? How? How hard is it to change social groups? (Contrast Edwardian England, where it was *very* hard, with contemporary Los Angeles, where one good movie deal opens all doors.)
- How are little boys expected to behave? Little girls? Teenagers? Young adults? Wives? Husbands? Community leaders? Old people? What usually happens if each of these people violates behavioral expectations?
- What is the best personal future most of the people in this setting can imagine? The worst? The best community future? The worst?
- How does your protagonist match—or differ from—the general community answers to the above questions? What are his preferences in dress, hair, books, music, food, etc.? Which of the prevailing cultural values does he share, which does he reject, which is he ambivalent about?
- What plot incidents might result from mismatches between character and setting?

chapter four

WHAT DID YOU SAY YOU DO?
Using the World of Work to Enhance Characterization

Work is important.

Of course, you already believe that, or else why are you reading this book, and why are you trying to write fiction in the first place? But I'm not talking now about your work in creating characters. I'm talking about *their* work. In the words of that perennial cocktail-party question, "What do you do?"

And even more important, "Why and how do you do it?"

Knowing the answers to these three questions—really knowing them, in detail—can give your novel a tremendous boost.

THE CASE FOR CHARACTER EMPLOYMENT

In a short story, it may not matter how a protagonist earns his living. A successful short story is pared down and tight, with everything extraneous to the plot and theme left out, which may include careers.

In Irwin Shaw's much-anthologized short story, "The Girls in Their Summer Dresses," we never find out what the two characters, Michael and Frances, do when they're not having a Sunday stroll on Fifth Avenue. It doesn't matter. The story is concerned with a powerful moment in the deceptions and desires that make up a marriage, and not with anything else. As far as we readers are concerned, Michael and Frances are eternally walking Fifth Avenue.

Novels are different. When we spend five hundred pages with a character, we want more than a powerful moment. We want to know this person.

That's why occupation is important. It lets us see how your protagonist spends his days, structures his time, invests his energies, realizes his dreams. Or doesn't. A job can be many things, and sometimes a paycheck is the least important aspect.

The right job for your character can do three things for your novel:

- characterize the protagonist
- gain credibility for the author
- provide plot ideas

However, it must be the *right* job. What job is that?

THE PRE-EMPLOYED PROTAGONIST

In some novels, you don't really have a choice. The job *is* the novel. If P.D. James's protagonist, Adam Dalgliesh, weren't a detective, he wouldn't have murders to solve. If Herman Wouk's Willie Keith weren't an officer aboard the U.S.S. *Caine*, he couldn't have participated in *The Caine Mutiny*. In such books, employment comes tightly bound to the original idea.

However, employment can still be used to characterize. What is most important about a job is not just what a person works at but why, how and with what results. Did your character choose his job? Is he doing it from financial necessity, because it's the only work he could find, because his parents wanted him to, only temporarily while he qualifies for something else, or as the realization of a lifelong dream?

Does he like his work? Hate it? Regard it as a necessary but boring interruption to the parts of his life he really likes? Resent it because he considers it beneath him? A fourth-grade teacher who wakes up every morning eager to rush to the classroom is a different person from the fourth-grade teacher who loathes the very sight of a chalkboard.

Is he good at it? Mediocre? Downright terrible? Does he care? How much of his ego is bound up in his work?

Dramatizing answers to questions like these can show us a lot more about your protagonist than merely telling us he works as a salesman, or a lathe operator, or a doctor. Some examples:

• Charles Paris, the recurring amateur sleuth in Simon Brett's mystery series, is a British actor. But Olivier he's not. We see Charles appearing in a string of bad productions, knowing they're bad, yet taking comfort in the fact that his small parts give him plenty of time backstage to drink Bell's whiskey. When he's supposed to be a corpse, hidden on-stage during the whole first act, he can't keep from giggling. Yet, touchingly, he collects his own reviews, which are usually of the type, "Also appearing in the cast was Charles Paris." Through his attitudes toward his lamentable parts, we come to know Charles's real interests (drinking), his detached but acute powers of perception, his acceptance of his own mediocrity and his nearly dead traces of failed hope.

• The unnamed, second-person protagonist of Jay McInerney's novel *Bright Lights, Big City* has a different attitude. He works in the "Department of Factual Verification" of a national magazine. His job is to verify facts in articles by big-name authors. He hates the job and hates his boss. As his life unravels, so does his work performance. McInerney uses job details to illuminate his character's confusion about the world, himself and his future. Had we known this protagonist only in social settings, we wouldn't have known him nearly as well, nor realized the full extent of his personal crisis.

• Violet Clay, in Gail Godwin's eponymous novel, is similarly confused. Violet knows what she wants to do: paint. But she expects easy success, and when it doesn't come, she panics. She turns instead to painting covers for trashy paperback books, because there she can be a star. Violet's career is only one aspect of her self-centered attitude (she also expects love and money to be instantly available to her), but an important one. When she finally grows up, she starts making the sacrifices necessary to genuinely learn her art.

• At the opposite end of the attitude scale, Adam Silverstone, in Noah Gordon's medical novel *The Death Committee*, is totally

37

committed to his profession. Chief resident in a great Boston hospital, he has always wanted to be a doctor, has struggled against great economic odds to realize his dream and knows he is talented. Author Gordon uses Silverstone's committed, professional attitude toward his work as a counterpoint to his halfway, ungiving attitude toward human relationships. Silverstone is a wonderful doctor, but must learn to become an ethical human being.

A JOB WITH CLASS

A second way that a job characterizes your protagonist is to locate him in the socioeconomic structure. This can be a convenient shorthand for conveying information about background, because readers will make certain assumptions about certain jobs. If, for instance, your character teaches Greek at Yale, most readers will make certain assumptions about her: She's educated, her salary allows middle-class living, she is not going to say "ain't" or "I give her three dollars for that hat." Starting from your readers' basic assumptions about professors (or doctors, or drug dealers, or NBA stars), you can then expend your wordage on individualizing your character and differentiating her from type.

Or, you can play it another way. You can use our socioeconomic preconceptions to play *against* type, surprising us with intriguing anomalies. Show us your character on the job as a dishwasher—and then show us that he also collects reproductions of pre-Columbian art and reads the great French poets in the original. We'll be fascinated to learn this guy's background, including his reasons for choosing the work he has.

Judith Rossner did this very well in her novel *Looking for Mr. Goodbar.* Her protagonist is an elementary-school teacher from a respectable family, who habitually picks up rough and dangerous men at bars. Eventually, one of them kills her. Because our expectations about primary-school teachers don't include this behavior, Rossner gets our immediate attention. What made this particular young woman behave so contrary to her class?

A note of caution, however: When you play strongly against occupational type, you must spend time convincing us that your character really would do this sort of work. We have no trouble accepting that smart, ambitious Adam Silverstone would choose to be a doctor. You will have to work hard to show us why an art collector and admirer of French poets is employed as a dishwasher.

POSITION WANTED:
THE NOT-YET-EMPLOYED CHARACTER

So much for the novel in which the job and the basic novel structure arrive in your mind in a single package. Detectives in mystery novels, doctors in medical thrillers, platoon leaders in war novels—piece of cake. But suppose you don't know *what* your character does?

Then you have a marvelous opportunity to employ him. Don't reach unthinkingly for those staples of TV sitcoms: architect, advertising copywriter, waitress. Be more imaginative. He could be an antique dealer, a ballet dancer, a costumer, a diemaker, an engineer, a forger, a gunsmith. . . . You get the idea. The possibilities are wide.

Wide, but not infinite. The right job for your character must fit in with both the rest of your novel and your own abilities. You couldn't, for instance, employ a major character in *Looking for Mr. Goodbar* as a circus clown. The book has no need for a circus clown; it would seem artificial. Descriptions of circus-clown duties would add nothing to Rossner's story, and might compete against its thematic concerns and general atmosphere.

So employ your protagonist—and the major secondary characters as well—carefully. As you choose jobs for them, keep five criteria in mind: self-image, worldview, natural abilities, class and credibility.

GIVE HIM A JOB THAT TELLS US
SOMETHING ABOUT HIS SELF-IMAGE

Did your protagonist choose to become a successful scientist, spending eight years in college and fifteen in intense research on plasma physics? This man is focused, disciplined, intelligent—and he knows it. Perhaps modestly, perhaps egotistically. Either way, he trusts himself to set a goal and follow through until he's achieved it.

Similarly, the forty-year-old man who in the past two years has worked as a salesclerk, handyman, busboy, truck driver, day laborer, telemarketer and petty thief—and none of them for more than four months at a stretch—has a different self-image. He sees the world as hostile ("Look what they did to me now!") and himself as a fundamental loser. Is he? Maybe that's what your novel is about.

On the other hand, a string of jobs is normal for a twenty-year-old still searching for his place in the world. Before he becomes a doctor, W. Somerset Maugham's Philip Carey (*Of Human Bondage*) tries out accountant, artist and floorwalker. He is confused about himself, his talents and his desires, and his confusion is beautifully dramatized by his wildly disparate jobs.

GIVE HIM A JOB THAT TELLS US ABOUT HIS IMAGE OF THE WORLD

This may come less from his choice of job than from his attitude toward its permutations. He's a cop: Is he the type who prefers to work with troubled kids or the type who prefers to break down doors and get rough with perps? She's a fashion designer: Does she fawn on rich customers, or enjoy adapting pretty clothes for the average female figure? He's an accountant—does he genuinely enjoy the work, or did he choose it because it's a secure job, with regular hours and no physical danger, in a frightening world? Show us.

GIVE HIM A JOB THAT LETS US ASSESS HIS TALENTS

This comes partly from how well he succeeds at different aspects of his profession. Is he organized? Clumsy? Hopeless with people? Persuasive? Punctual? Patient? Persistent? Show us, through how he handles work duties.

GIVE HIM A JOB THAT FITS THE NOVEL'S SOCIAL CIRCUMSTANCES

I recall a recent, let-it-be-nameless romance in which a woman was supposedly paying the rent on a New York penthouse apartment and supporting two kids on her salary as an art-gallery assistant. She also dressed superbly and sent a lot of roses. People familiar with art-gallery salaries and New York prices howled with derisive laughter. If you need your character to have lots of money and he hasn't inherited it, stolen it or married it, give him a job where he can earn it.

The same goes for more intangible acquisitions. If your character has impressive political connections, either have her born into a political family (à la the Kennedys) or employ her in a place where logically she would meet a lot of high-ranking politicians. If your plot requires that she know a lot about the workings of the FBI, and you don't want her to work for the Bureau itself, then she might be a journalist on the Washington beat, or a cop who regularly attends law-enforcement programs at the FBI training center in Virginia, or a caterer with a contract at the Hoover building. Be inventive.

GIVE HIM A JOB THAT YOU CAN WRITE ABOUT IN CREDIBLE DETAIL

As in all aspects of writing, the details make the difference. Your character is going to spend eight hours a day at this job—a third of his life. It's very real to him. Therefore, you must make it real to us. You can't do that if you don't know anything about it. *Personnel manager* may be no more than a vague label to you—but to a person who is one, it's a very specific set of tasks, headaches, triumphs, hurdles and goals. We need to share them. Not all of them, and not necessarily in exhaustive depth, but convincingly enough that we will believe this character really invests time and energy in what you say he does.

For instance, the reviews of Judy Blume's adult novel *Smart Women* almost universally pointed out that the teenage characters were much more successful than the adults. Blume, of course, has much more experience with creating youthful characters; she is one of the best-selling writers of young adult fiction in America. Nonetheless, I think the lack of realism in *Smart Women*'s mature protagonist related directly to that protagonist's job.

Margo Sampson is supposed to be an architect with a small Colorado firm, a position that demands a great deal of creative effort. Yet Margo is never shown thinking about her designs, sacrificing personal time to solve technical problems, handling job details, meeting with clients or encountering the frustrations inevitable to building anything. She has none of the professional highs, lows or absorption detailed in, for example, Tracy Kidder's wonderful nonfiction book about building, *House*. Instead, whenever Margo's job is mentioned, it's usually in connection with her love affairs: She had an affair with her boss; she keeps a list of her lovers in the top drawer of her desk; a design contract is determined by her boyfriend's ex-wife's jealousy.

But, you might ask, so what? This is a book about relationships, not about building. Why does it matter if Margo is not very convincing as an architect?

It matters because it makes *Margo* less convincing. In the real world, a job is many things to a person: means of support, proof of worth, daily challenge, path to social betterment, confirmation of worldview, source of exhaustion and pride and delight and frustration and, sometimes, incredible anger. Anything that real to your character must also be made real to us. Otherwise, this person lacks a major dimension. He seems less than fully there.

GETTING IT RIGHT

The easiest way to portray a job realistically is to give your character work you've done yourself. William Styron worked as a manuscript reader; so did his character Stingo in *Sophie's Choice*. P.D. James, mystery writer, was an administrator in the British justice system. John Steinbeck, like so many of his characters, had experience as a day laborer. Robin Cook, author of medical thrillers, is a doctor. Scott Turow, like Rusty in *Presumed Innocent* and Sandy in *The Burden of Proof*, is a lawyer. Employing your character where you yourself have worked means you know the territory. You can—and should—include details that deepen verisimilitude: the field's individual jargon, the duties, stress points, standard procedures, hazards, equipment, perks, career paths, pecking order, even insider jokes. In addition to deepening credibility, such details are often interesting to readers who have never worked in that job.

But your character *can* work in fields you have not. If you don't know what your protagonist's job feels like from the inside, find out. Talk to people in that line of work. Most people are flattered to be asked about their professions, and a good talker can tell you more personal details than any published source. Ask for the frustrations, glitches, problems.

For jobs that are at least partially on public display, observe carefully. How does the waitress address her boss? What tools does the locksmith use while changing your locks? What obstacles beset the taxi driver? How do the construction workers building the high-rise across from your office seem to structure their day?

Read trade periodicals, magazine interviews, memoirs. You can learn a lot from the more personal aspects of these sources. Study the "Letters" column. Read biographies for interesting views of jobs that celebrities held *before* they became famous. Playwright Moss Hart's autobiography *Act One*, for instance, contains unparalleled descriptions of the horrors and rewards and routines of being a summer-camp director.

This is your chance. If you always wanted to know what it would be like to be a costumer in a wax museum, sewing for effigies of Lizzie Borden and Lord Nelson and Elvis Presley, give that job to a character. Then you'll have a reason for researching costuming. How hard is it to dress wax? How authentic does the underwear have to be? Are the wax dummies anatomically correct? How do you dust a wax Count Dracula? The research books will even be tax deductible.

THE RIGHT JOB WILL SUGGEST MANY PLOT POSSIBILITIES

Once your character is gainfully employed, you have a strong tool for powering your plot in whatever direction you wish it to go.

How does this work? Suppose that the protagonist of your mystery novel is not a detective but a small-town vet. She visits a lot of farms, and a lot of smaller animals come to her clinic; she comes to know nearly everyone in town. She has scientific training. She gets called out on emergencies in the middle of the night. All these circumstances lend themselves to seeing things she shouldn't, to discovering facts that others want hidden, to making deductions from animal-related clues that others might miss. Look hard at the specifics of her job, and they will suggest all kinds of plot developments.

Or take another exotic example: that wax museum costumer (I'm fond of this job). What does a costumer do? Research into authentic period costumes, including acquiring actual old buttons, fabric, shawls, dresses. This could send her poking around attics, ware-houses, estate sales. Perhaps she's a real wheeler-dealer who tries to always get there early to make a presale deal with whomever it takes to sell her those buttons once worn by Princess Charlotte, or that Revolutionary War uniform from somebody's great-great-great-great-great grandfather. But what else does she find while poking around? And who knows she's doing it?

Many interesting possibilities!

Even if your character works in a conventional office, his job can provide plot developments. Ted Kramer, for instance, the protagonist of Avery Corman's *Kramer Versus Kramer*, sells advertising space in magazines. The novel isn't about his job; it's about divorce and parent-hood. Still, Corman makes good use of the volatility of advertising to add tension to Ted's situation. The sole support of his young son Billy, Ted loses his job during a company merger. He searches hard and finds another. During the custody hearing he's laid off a second time, greatly imperiling his case. Corman shows us Ted's heroic efforts to find another job within twenty-four hours.

In addition, how much Ted earns directly affects such plot incidents as hiring a housekeeper to take care of Billy, affording lawyers, even dating the second time around.

Do *your* character's job duties, industry conditions, work stresses or salary level suggest any incidents for your novel? If not, perhaps the character needs a career change.

SUMMARY: BE A FULL-SERVICE EMPLOYMENT AGENCY
- Find your character a job that characterizes his personality, class and talents.
- Further characterize him by his attitude toward his work.
- Choose jobs you know a lot about—or can learn about.
- Include enough realistic details about the job to make it seem as real as your protagonist does.
- Use the character's job to suggest plot complications and/or resolutions.

chapter five

SAY WHAT?
Characterizing Through Dialogue

In Karen Joy Fowler's wonderful novel *Sarah Canary*, the protagonist never speaks. Not a word. Not for 290 pages. And Fowler succeeds in characterizing her anyway.

Most of us, fortunately, do not have to labor under such a burden. We have a powerful tool to let readers know who our characters are. We have dialogue. "How forcible are right words!" says Job (6:25), and so they are.

However, not all dialogue is created equal. Mediocre dialogue can do more harm than good: by boring your reader, by misleading him, by offending him or by convincing him that none of these characters has a single spark of genuine life. (If you write really terrible dialogue, he may think the same thing about the author.)

So how do you write good dialogue? And after you have, how do you give it to the reader: in large unbroken chunks, or intercut with descriptions of gestures, voices, surroundings? And what about dialect—does it help or hurt?

Dialogue is a complex subject. This isn't surprising when you consider how many areas of the human brain are activated by speech: frontal lobe, temporal parietal region, hippocampus, vagus nerve and, sometimes, the deep emotional centers in the limbic. Such complexity means that no rules will hold true 100 percent of the time. Still, guidelines exist. Good dialogue characterizes, sounds natural and flows well. Simple guidelines—until you start looking closely at each one.

MARK MY WORDS: LETTING CHARACTERS REVEAL THEMSELVES

The basics first. Good dialogue is unsurpassed at telling us who your character is, both intellectually and emotionally. Which of the following excerpts give you a better picture of Thomas Wells?

> Thomas Wells was a bitter man, an angry man, a bigot. He disliked anyone different from himself, and said so often. Nor did he care who heard him.

> "Whole lot of 'em ought to be sent back where they come from," Wells said loudly in the Grain 'n Feed. "Jews, Spics, niggers—just send 'em all back! Dirty bastards!" Slowly, Saul Goldstein turned his head toward Wells.

The second version presents Wells more strongly, because it's more direct. Instead of the author labeling Wells a bigot, the character's words pin the label on himself.

Here is Muriel Spark's marvelous character, school teacher Jean Brodie (*The Prime of Miss Jean Brodie*), addressing her eleven-year-old pupils and revealing more about herself than she has any idea of:

> "I have spent most of my holidays in Italy once more, and a week in London, and I have brought back a great many pictures which we can pin on the wall. Here is a Cimabue. Here is a larger formation of Mussolini's fascisti, it is a better view of them than last year's picture. They are doing splendid things as I shall tell you later. I went with my friends for an audience with the Pope. My friends kissed his ring but I thought it proper only to bend over it. I wore

a long black gown with a lace mantilla and looked magnificent. In London my friends who are well-to-do—their small girl has two nurses, or nannies as they say in England— took me to visit A.A. Milne. In the hall was hung a reproduction of Boticelli's *Primavera*, which means the birth of Spring. I wore my silk dress with the large red poppies which is just right for my coloring. . . ."

Name-dropper, elitist, self-absorbed, more than a little silly . . . Jean Brodie's character is clearly revealed through her dialogue.

But, you may say, these two examples aren't typical. Thomas Wells and Jean Brodie are both extreme people, talking with unusual lack of inhibition. *My* characters are more ordinary, talking about more ordinary things. Can their dialogue still reveal individual personality?

Yes. It's true that in real life, much routine communication is generic: People in the same culture use essentially the same words to greet acquaintances, purchase a shirt, talk to their children ("What did you do in school today?" "Nothing."). In fiction, however, even routine dialogue can be used to differentiate and individualize characters.

Here are three different characters offering food to guests:

> "It's not *only* pot roast," Ezra said. . . . "There's something more. I mean, pot roast is really not the right name, it's more like . . . what you long for when you're sad and everyone's been wearing you down. See, there's this cook, this real country cook, and pot roast is the least of what she does. There's also pan-fried potatoes, black-eyed peas, beaten biscuits genuinely beaten on a stump with the back of an ax—"
>
> —EZRA TULL, IN ANNE TYLER'S *DINNER AT THE HOMESICK RESTAURANT*

> "I've brought you something to eat," said a voice; "oppen t'door!"
>
> Complying eagerly, I beheld Hareton, laden with food enough to last me all day.
>
> "Take it," he added, thrusting the tray into my hand.
>
> "Stay one minute," I began.
>
> "Nay," cried he, and retired, regardless of any prayers I

could pour forth to detain him.
—Hareton Earnshaw, in Emily Brontë's *Wuthering Heights*

Katie came in with the tray. "This may not be as refined as you're used to," she apologized, "but it's what we have in the house."
—Katie Nolan, in Betty Smith's *A Tree Grows in Brooklyn*

There's little chance of confusing any of these speakers with the others. Ezra's nurturing, Hareton's uneducated hostility and Katie's painful awareness of her own poverty come through in even these snippets of routine social interaction.

You don't, of course, want to overdo this. Even the most dramatic and eccentric character occasionally just says, "What time is it?" or "Pass the salt." But, on the other hand, if whole sections of your protagonist's dialogue could be switched with whole sections of another main character's dialogue, you haven't done an effective job of using speech to individualize them. Go back and rewrite. Give each a diction, a rhythm, a slant on the world (the essence of characterization) of his or her own.

An aside here: Dialogue is the one place in fiction where clichés can work well. If your character's thoughts and ideas *are* hackneyed and undigested, clichéd speech will convey that. In that sense, dialogue is a horse of a different color. If your character never has an original thought in her pretty head, let her spout clichés till hell freezes over. Just be aware that she may sound dumb as a fence post.

I DON'T LIKE YOUR TONE: MAKING DIALOGUE CARRY EVEN MORE WEIGHT

By one expert estimate, 70 percent of communication is nonverbal. If Harry says to Sue, "Can I see you tonight?" almost three-quarters of his meaning will be conveyed by the tone of his voice, his inflections, his facial expression, his hand gestures, his body language, the degree of his attention.

Perhaps he says, "Can I see you tonight?" in a weary tone of voice, while watching another woman cross the street, with the corners of his mouth turned down. Or perhaps he says it intently, his eyes on Sue's face, his whole body yearning forward. Each sentence will convey entirely different meanings to Sue, despite identical words.

In fiction, dialogue doesn't have the powerful support of these nonverbal clues. You can, of course, describe some of them: Harry's gestures, Sue's tone of voice. And you should. But you may also need to increase the emotional level of the words themselves, to compensate for the loss of nonverbal communication.

For instance, suppose a character named Stan has just learned of another character's death. If you were a playwright, you could write Stan's line as "Tom was a good man." The actor would supply the emotion with which the line should be said: resignation, irony, anger. But we fiction writers don't have John Malkovich or Meryl Streep to lend color to our prose. We have to do it ourselves. Therefore, you might heighten Stan's dialogue to "Tom was a good man. Damn it, he was such a good man!" The extra words, the mild profanity, the exclamation point—all make clear that Stan's emotion is anger that this good man is dead.

You might also use both heightened dialogue *and* description of nonverbal cues:

> "Tom was a good man," Stan said softly. He fumbled with a cigarette, lit it, dropped it on the carpet. And then, "Damn it, he was such a good man!" He looked out the window, dry-eyed, and the rug smoldered at his feet.

Here, dialogue that might seem theatrical in real life combines with distraught action to add layers of emotion to the little speech.

YOU WEREN'T LIKE THAT YESTERDAY: CONSISTENCY IN DIALOGUE

This is a tricky subject. Yes, you want your character to speak consistently from one page to the next. A teenage girl who says, "So I go, 'He didn't tell me that!' I was, like, totally grossed out," is not the same teenage girl who says, "I respond to the alienation in the novels of Camus." If you try to make her the same girl, we probably won't believe it.

On the other hand, everyone has more than one mode of speech. You undoubtedly use different language and sentence structures to your best friend, your six-year-old niece and the cop who has just stopped you for speeding. Good dialogue should capture this difference—while *still* sounding like the same person.

An example. Two characters are having an amiable discussion about where to have lunch. They decide, walk down the street to the restaurant, and one ducks briefly inside the post office to buy stamps. The other, waiting outside, is suddenly lunged at by a mugger who kicks him in the kneecap and grabs his wallet. The character falls to the ground, scraping his left hand and right palm. He no longer sounds amiable. In fact, he yells something unprintable in this book.

Has the dialogue become inconsistent? It doesn't match the previous diction or sentence structure. But it does match the new circumstances. Furthermore, it's still recognizable as something that a basically amiable person would say, in that it doesn't employ racial epithets, or go on for pages of invective, or lapse into Victorian epithets or outdated slang or threats of retaliation—none of which would have been in keeping with what we'd already been shown of the character.

In short, *consistency* is another one of those partly-true, partly-not statements about writing. Make your dialogue consistent—but not so unvarying that it ignores specific circumstances.

YOU'RE FROM THE SOUTH, AREN'T YOU: THE DANGERS AND DELIGHTS OF DIALECT

This aspect of fiction has both literary and political connotations. Consider the following uses of dialect:

- You 'ave it, guv'nor!
- Sho' will, massa, suh!
- At your service, old chap!
- Faith and begorra, but yer right, me fine lad!
- That's-a the way, paisano!
- Rike you rike it, A-san!
- Sa vah kum sa vah, sir!

None of those dialects are convincing, all of them are hackneyed, a few of them are offensive, and the last one is incomprehensible: a good catalogue of the pitfalls of using dialect.

So does that mean a writer should avoid dialect completely?

No. Just write it carefully. The goal is to capture the *feel* of nonstandard English by judicious variations of diction, word order, spelling and sentence rhythm, and by moderate use of common phrases. This works better than wholesale and probably stereotypical distortion of language. Here's a good example, from Eudora Welty's "Old Mr. Marblehall":

> "I declare I told Mr. Bird to go on to bed, and look at him! I don't understand him! . . . After I get Mr. Bird to bed, what does he do then? He lies there stretched out with his clothes on and don't have one word to say! Know what he does? . . . He might just as well not have a family."

Can you hear the regional flavor, definite but not overdone? The guideline here is that a little dialect goes a long way. It should suggest regional speech, not bludgeon us with it.

Dialect has another use, as well. Simple or very young characters may have only one mode of speech, the one with which they grew up. Older or more sophisticated people, however, frequently retain the ability to speak in their native dialect but also acquire the "standard" American network-news-anchor speech. Such a person can choose which speech he wishes to use when—and those choices alone may say something about him.

He may, for instance, deliberately pile on exaggerations of his own dialect to confuse, embarrass or otherwise gain psychological advantage over his listeners. Here, for instance, is Bruce Sterling's Grenadian character Winston Stubbs, from the novel *Islands in the Net*. Stubbs is perfectly capable of standard business English, and he uses it when he wishes. In the following speech, however, he's making sure that his listeners, Laura and David Webster, know that Stubbs's culture and beliefs are radically different from those of everybody else at an international banking conference:

> Laura had become seriously worried. She greeted them in the front lobby. "So glad to see you. Was there any trouble?"
>
> "Nuh," said Winston Stubbs, exposing his dentures in a sunny smile. "I-and-I were downtown, seen. Up-the-island. . . . We could use a public relations," Stubbs said, grinning crookedly at Laura. "I-and-I's reputation could use an upgrade. Pressure come down on I-and-I. From Babylon Luddites."

Even if you know that in island patois *I-and-I* means *we* and that *seen* is the equivalent of *you see*, this dialect feels foreign and striking. Laura and David are put on notice that Stubbs and his bank operate by different rules—which is just what Stubbs intends. He exploits his own awareness of his own dialect for his own purposes.

Everything that applies to dialect, incidentally, also applies to accents. "Those are your papers of identification, isn't it?" is preferable to the fake French of "Zat ees yourrr papeeyas of . . . how you say it? Bah! . . . *l'identification, n'est-ce pas?*" Only the staunchest reader will stick with you through pages of that stuff.

SHE JUST GOES ON AND ON: HOW MUCH DIALOGUE DO YOU NEED TO CHARACTERIZE SOMEONE?

It depends. Whom are you characterizing?

You can reveal character not only through what a person says, but through how much they say. Does your protagonist hoard words as if they were gold pieces? Does she have verbal diarrhea? Or is she somewhere in between?

The taciturn character can come across as "the strong silent type," or as uninterested in communicating with other people, or as in a very bad mood. Let us know which is correct through the content of the dialogue. In other words, quality and quantity should work together to characterize. Is this guy Gary Cooper, or is he James L. Page in John Gardner's *October Light*, who "was never a great talker—not like *her*, she'd lecture your arm off" (*her* is James's sister).

Similarly, volatility can indicate nervousness, self-centeredness or just high spirits. Is your great talker like Miss Bates, Jane Austen's spinster lady in *Emma*, who can rattle on for entire content-free pages, out of sheer pleasure in having company? Or is she more like Anne Tyler's Muriel (*The Accidental Tourist*) who also overwhelms her listeners with a flood of talk, but because she's so desperate to make human connections? Or is your talker like W. Somerset Maugham's Hayward (*Of Human Bondage*), who gives his opinions on and *on* because in his heart he believes he's the only one who possesses any valid opinions?

Let us know.

THE LAST WORD, ALMOST

Writing dialogue is a balancing act. Dialogue that characterizes is artificially informative—but not implausibly so. It indicates background—unless the character is trying not to do so. It's consistently interesting—except for the occasional brief break to discuss mundane topics that establish verisimilitude. It's emotional and individual—but not so much of either that it becomes parody. How do you learn this balancing act? The same way you learn everything else about writing—through reading authors you admire, and through practice. Write a lot of dialogue. Read it aloud. See how it sounds to you and to other people whose ear you trust. Rewrite it. Write some more.

And as if it weren't enough to concentrate on the content of a character's speech, you also need to think about its presentation. More on that in the next chapter. Meanwhile, the last word on using dialogue to characterize comes from a master of the art, Mark Twain:

> When the personages of a tale deal in conversation, the talk shall sound like human talk, and be talk such as human beings would be likely to talk in the circumstances, and have a discoverable purpose, and a show of relevancy, and remain in the neighborhood of the subject at hand, and be interesting to the reader, and help out the tale, and stop when the people cannot think of anything more to say.

SUMMARY: USING DIALOGUE TO CHARACTERIZE

- Rather than telling us what your characters are like, let them reveal themselves through what they say about their own tastes, hopes, dreams, prejudices, goals and worldviews, and their view of the other characters in the novel.
- Supplement dialogue with punctuation and narrative to fill in nonverbal clues.
- Make your characters speak consistently—but don't be rigid about it. Everyone alters his speech for different audiences and circumstances.
- Use dialect and accents with a light hand.
- Remember that how much your character speaks works along with the content of his speech to create a definite impression in readers' minds.

chapter six

THE ARTFUL DECEPTION
Making Dialogue Read Naturally
(Even Though It's Not Natural)

Good dialogue, everyone agrees, seems natural. Note the verb: It *seems* natural. But, in fact, it's not.

Consider great beauty. The Parthenon, perhaps. Or Sophia Loren. Or Babe Ruth hitting a high sweet curving home run. You know best what you consider heart-stirringly and memorably beautiful. Whatever it is, it probably looks completely natural: perfectly proportioned, radiantly curved, a gift of nature (that's the Parthenon I'm talking about, not Loren). And, almost certainly, it is not.

In art, the completely natural seldom works. Instead nature is refined, trained, pruned, heightened, unspontaneously considered and rehearsed. The perfect building, the liquid aria, the gorgeous football play—these are carefully composed. Choices are made, adjustments are constant, training counts. The results may look natural, but they are in fact artificial, which is itself a term derived from *art*.

Dialogue is like that, too. Writing dialogue that sounds natural is the result of artifice. Even though we talk all day, good dialogue is more than talk written down. In fact, it differs from real speech in several important ways.

TIGHT AND CLEAN:
GOOD DIALOGUE IS ARTIFICIALLY CONCISE

In natural speech, nearly all people repeat themselves, interrupt themselves, start over midway, stutter, use an inexact word and then spend four sentences explaining what they really meant. But when you reproduce all this on the page, the character will sound (depending on the content) boring, scatterbrained or under great stress.

If you want that effect, fine. (To see it done to perfection, read any speech by Miss Bates in Jane Austen's novel *Emma*.) But if your character is supposed to sound like a person of substance who is not in emotional crisis, you will have to edit his speech to a concision most people can't achieve in unrehearsed spoken communication (which is, after all, usually a first draft).

Here, for instance, is an actual phone call between friends, both writers. This is an unedited transcript of the recording:

FRIEND: Nancy? Have you got a second? I just got a letter from Rick [her agent] about—where is it, I had it right here, where *is* that . . . here it is. I just got this letter from him about electronic rights. [Publishing Company Z] is interested—he says they've "expressed interest"—in electronic rights to my first two novels. I'm not sure.

NANCY: Not sure they're really interested?

FRIEND: No, I'm not sure . . . I don't really know too much about electronic rights, I wasn't paying attention when it was being discussed so much, when everybody was talking about it . . .

NANCY: Last year? No, that big flap was—

FRIEND: I don't remember. But anyway, Rick says they're interested, and I'm not sure what's involved or—but, oh, I'm sorry, I forgot to ask! How did it go yesterday?

NANCY: A disaster.

FRIEND: Oh, I'm sorry. Again?

NANCY: The electronic rights thing—

FRIEND: I just should have been paying more attention when that big flap was going on.

If you can read this stuff with interest, you should consider going into phone tapping. This dialogue is repetitious, long-winded, and elliptical. It doesn't tell anything of interest. (*What* disaster happened again yesterday?) It doesn't make information clear. (What *was* the big flap about electronic rights?) Worse, it gives the impression that both people are twits, unable to organize their thoughts or complete a coherent sentence. This is not true. In fact, in real life, the phone conversation was completely satisfactory: The friends settled the issue of electronic rights to one's novels; they both understood what yesterday's disaster was; the whole conversation took only a few minutes. It's only *on the page* that the dialogue lacks concision.

So how should this dialogue appear on the page, if it were part of a story about two writers? Perhaps like this:

FRIEND: Nancy? I just heard from my agent. Company Z is interested in electronic rights for my first two novels. I don't actually know much about electronic rights. Should I be interested?

NANCY: You should be if you're interested in the future. That's where it lies. Have you heard about the Readerman that Sony is developing? It will be like a Walkman, but for books on disk.

FRIEND: That does sound interesting. Better—it sounds profitable. I'll tell Rick to talk more with them. And oh, by the way, how was the latest go-round with the insurance company?

NANCY: A disaster. But believe me, you don't want to hear about it.

FRIEND: (laughs) Sure I do. But maybe another time.

Of course, if this were part of a story, both the friend's electronic rights and Nancy's fight with the insurance company would have to be part of the plot. Maybe the insurance is life insurance on someone who turns up mysteriously dead, and the electronic clues ... all right, all right, we won't get carried away here. But you see the point.

Edited dialogue is not "natural." Instead, it is more informative, concise and detailed than natural speech. People may speak in near epigrams ("If you're interested in the future, you're interested in electronic rights"). Characters get to sound the way you wished you'd sounded when you couldn't think of the right thing to say until the next morning.

However, even a competent character may sound repetitious and disorganized when under great stress. Save the "natural" dialogue for those moments.

BUT GOOD DIALOGUE IS NOT *TOO* ARTIFICIAL

However, neither do you want to go to the other extreme: dialogue so edited and revised that the reader rejects it as implausible. Following are several categories of overly artificial dialogue.

Too Concise

You *can* overdo a good thing. If your character always speaks in precise, perfect epigrams, he is either Shakespeare reincarnated or Joe Friday from *Dragnet*. Everybody else's speech should include a few extra phrases, words not strictly necessary on topics not very consequential, to keep spoken dialogue from sounding like Western Union.

Here, for instance, are FBI agent Robert Hart and Department of Justice investigator Elizabeth Waring, in Thomas Perry's award-winning novel *The Butcher's Boy*. The two have just arrived in Denver because a United States senator has been killed.

> "I suppose all we can do tonight is wait for the forensics people to work their way through the other rooms, then."
>
> "That and wait for our replacements to arrive," said Hart. "As of an hour ago we're no longer here just to establish presence."
>
> "So they'll send in the first team?" said Elizabeth. "We haven't done so badly, considering we've hardly had time to begin."
>
> "No, we haven't," said Hart. "But just the same, I'm not going to do much unpacking."
>
> "Speaking of that, has anybody told you where we're supposed to be staying?"

This is not epigrammatic dialogue. There are phrases with little information content ("I suppose," "Speaking of that"). There are phrases with more words than strictly necessary ("That and wait for our replacements to arrive" could be shortened to "And wait for our replacements"). The subject matter (which hotel?) is unimportant to the plot. But by including some of this—by being less concise than he could be—Perry has made his investigators seem more like real people.

Too Stilted

The native-born character who never uses contractions, the uneducated man whose diction is all multisyllable Latinate words, the woman who sounds as if she's addressing a joint session of Congress rather than her bridge club—these characters' dialogue is too artificial. The woman at the bridge club, for instance, should not have her dialogue edited to "I do not think, even when taking all factors into account, that Jim's entrepreneurial venture is viable at this time." Instead, have her say, "Well, in *my* opinion, Jim's new business just won't work." Then another character can ask, "Why?" and you're off and running.

Too Informative

This is called the "As You Know, Bob" Syndrome. The author attempts to make dialogue informative and detailed so that he can slip information to the reader. But this must be done with a very light hand, because people do not commonly tell each other things they both already know. If you aren't careful, you get dialogue like this:

> "As you know, Bob, after Mom died we were very poor."
> "Yes, Martin. I had to leave school and take a job at the mall. And you had a paper route and grew rutabagas to sell at the farmer's market."
> "And then after Marie got in trouble with the law, nobody would hire us, so we moved away and didn't return to this town for ten years."

At this point, your reader won't return, either. Find another way to convey background information besides artificially sticking it into dialogue.

But . . . just to complete the picture, I should add that there are some times—a very few some times—when "As You Know, Bob" dialogue is indeed effective. It all depends on the emotional tone of the characters' exchange. People who are angry, patronizing, sarcastic or self-absorbed often do tell things to others of which both are already perfectly aware, although the reader may not be. Here is Tess Barnwell, from May Frampton's story "White Wine," furious at her husband:

> "You ask me to buy pot roast. Fine; I buy pot roast. Three days later you ask for German vinegar gravy on the pot roast. Fine; I buy all the ingredients for German vinegar gravy. Then you ask if we can have the pot roast and German vinegar gravy on Thursday night. Fine; I leave work early, rush home, and make the roast with German vinegar gravy. And then you're two hours late and don't even call! Ethan, what are you trying to do to me?"

Whatever Ethan may be trying to do, what the author is trying to do is have one character fling at another a long list of already-known grievances. And Frampton succeeds.

A PLEASURE TO READ: GOOD DIALOGUE FLOWS WELL

When you have a good exchange of dialogue going between characters—a nice rat-a-tat-tat of give-and-take—should you interrupt it with sentences of description? If you do, won't you break the flow? If you don't, will your novel start to seem as if it should have just been a play?

Again, there is (surprise!) no simple answer to this. There are options, choices, stylistic considerations. Some writers naturally use a lot of uninterrupted dialogue (Raymond Carver, Irwin Shaw, Anne Tyler). Others' style runs more to dialogue interwoven with large blocks of narrative (Toni Morrison, Eudora Welty). You shouldn't alter your natural voice, even if you could. Rather, become aware of the options *within* your preferred style.

So what are they?

With infinite variations, you have three basic choices: (1) mostly uninterrupted dialogue; (2) dialogue slowed down but not really stopped by bits of narrative; and (3) dialogue brought to a dead halt for judiciously placed chunks of narrative.

LET 'ER RIP: THE VIRTUES OF UNINTERRUPTED DIALOGUE

The following passage, from Irwin Shaw's *Bread Upon the Waters*, illustrates the two pluses of dialogue that is mostly uninterrupted: fast pace and readability. Almost no narrative details slow down the rapid-fire exchange of comments between protagonist Allen Strand and his eighteen-year-old son Jimmy. This is especially important in this scene because nothing much is happening. Shaw is building background for the story to come, setting up his characters. There is little tension, and so a sluggish pace or fragmented presentation might very well lose reader interest. Strand and his son are having breakfast together:

> "You look positively gaunt. People will think we never feed you. Have you eaten anything today?"
>
> "I only just got up a couple of hours ago. I'll do justice to Mom's dinner."
>
> "What time did you get in this morning?"
>
> Jimmy shrugged. "What difference does it make? Four, five. Who keeps track?"
>
> "Sometimes, Jimmy," Strand said, a touch of irony in his voice, "you must tell your old man what you do until five o'clock in the morning."
>
> "I'm searching for the new sound," Jimmy said. "I play or I listen to music."
>
> "I understand they stop the music at Carnegie Hall well before five o'clock in the morning."
>
> Jimmy laughed, stretched.... "Carnegie Hall isn't where it's at this year. Haven't you heard?"
>
> "You have purple rings under your eyes down to your shoulders."
>
> "The girls love it."

And so on, for another two pages. Swift and easily read. When that's what you want, let the dialogue flow without distraction.

BEST OF BOTH WORLDS: DIALOGUE BALANCED WITH NARRATIVE

Your second option is to intersperse narrative throughout the dialogue. If you do this well, you can keep the pace almost as fast as uninterrupted dialogue, *plus* add bits of narrative that visualize the characters and action. Two gains for the price of one. *Do this well* means choose dialogue and narrative that reinforce each other, not compete with each other.

Reinforce each other doesn't mean that dialogue and narrative both say the same thing ("Damn you!" he shouted angrily.) Rather, both add new information, but both kinds of information carry equal weight in moving the story forward. Here are Quill and John, from Claudia Bishop's mystery novel *A Taste for Murder*, breaking into a suspicious warehouse:

> Moonlight leaked through the open ventilation shafts in the roof, picking out the cab of a semi truck and four Thermo King refrigeration units. John took her hand, and they made their way carefully across the floor.
>
> "If anyone comes in," John said very quietly, "roll under the cab and stay there."
>
> Quill nodded. "These things are locked, aren't they? How are you going to get in?"
>
> "There's a maintenance door under the roof. Give me a leg up."
>
> Quill crouched down and cupped her hands together. John put his hands on her shoulders, stepped into her cupped hands, and sprang up. Quill staggered back; he was unexpectedly heavy.
>
> She waited, searching the darkness. It was quiet. Too quiet. Quill bit back hysterical giggles. Time stretched on. Suddenly, a dark shape appeared at the back of the unit. Adrenaline surged through Quill like a lightning strike.
>
> "Safety door," said John. "You can open the units from the inside once you get in."
>
> "God!" said Quill. "Did you find anything?"
>
> A low growl cut the air. Quill's breath stopped. John grabbed her hand. The growl rose, fell, and turned into a snarl.
>
> "The dog's back," said Quill. "Oh, hell!"
>
> John thrust her behind him. Quill could smell the rank, matted odor of an animal neglected. John flattened himself against the metal unit.

Notice how here, unlike in the Shaw scene, the dialogue includes only two or three exchanges between characters before being interrupted by an equally long stretch of action. Yet the reader's attention isn't fragmented; action and dialogue each add new information, and together they make a whole.

However, the reader's attention *will* be fragmented if you interrupt the dialogue too much. Consider this disastrous passage:

> Vivian said to her husband, "I'm just not sure." She set the plate of fried eggs in front of Dave and frowned. "There are so many problems with Mother coming to live with us." Vivian put a hand on her hip. "For one, you'd have to give up your den." She began to pace distractedly. "And I don't know how the girls would react to Mother's being here." She paused. "Or her to them."

This is fatiguing to read; we are constantly bounced between what Vivian is saying and what she's doing. We want to say to the author, "Oh, for heaven's sake, just let her talk!" This writer would do better to choose one or two worried gestures for Vivian and bunch them all either before or after her dialogue.

STOP THE PRESSES: DICTUS VERY INTERRUPTUS

Why would an author want to interrupt a conversation for long paragraph(s) of narrative, description or thoughts? Won't that completely distract the reader from what the characters are saying? And won't it also diffuse any tension in the dialogue?

It can, if used carelessly. But if used well, a long interruption to a conversation can actually *increase* tension. The trick is in placement. Coming just before the last exchange, or last few exchanges, the long interruption can have the same effect as that long pause at the Academy Awards after "The envelope, please." All the nominees are holding their breath, knowing that something important is coming. The fumble with the envelope, the silence while the presenter scans the results (the nominees are still holding their breaths), the smile as the presenter says, "And the Oscar goes to. . . ." That's the effect you're after.

Thomas Gavin gets it in his 1994 novel *Breathing Water*. Wilhelm, a reporter, is interviewing by phone an old woman whose long-ago-abducted grandson has been restored to her by a stranger named Dusseau. Above Wilhelm's desk is a picture of Toad of Toad Hall, from Kenneth Grahame's *The Wind in the Willows*:

"Do you trust him?" Wilhelm asked.

"The boy is my grandson."

"I mean Dusseau. Do you trust him?"

After the slightest pause Mrs. Kane said, "He's behaved like a perfect gentleman under my roof. . . ."

"Has he asked you for money yet?"

Mrs. Kane said nothing.

"I'm not trying to get a story out of you, Mrs. Kane. It just—when a body's got a strong reason to want to believe something, he doesn't always look at it too close. I'm asking the kinds of questions that a—friend might ask. Somebody with your interests at heart. You've let a stranger into your house. I'm only asking what you know about him."

On the other end of the line Wilhelm heard irregular breathing, like somebody with bad dreams turning in her sleep. "All I know, Mr. Wilhelm," said Mrs. Kane, "is that he brought my Powell back to me. That's all I need to know."

Wilhelm looked at Toad, thought of Toad's mincing trot as he came out from under the shadows of the prison archway, thought of Toad's manic glee at having once again outsmarted the stuffy Victorian forces of order. He thought of all the sorrow the real Toads of the world caused, and the sorrow he himself had caused the wife who left him in his own jolly Toadlike recklessness, and knew it made no difference that your passion was for justice rather than motorcars, the result in the life of a Toad's family was sorrow. He saw Dusseau, the drifter with *Driftwind* painted on his gypsy wagon, as a free-spirited Toad of Toad Hall, a hypnotic charmer who had charmed Mrs. Kane into a faith she was afraid to question. "Do you suppose, Mrs. Kane," he said, "that there's any chance—any remote possibility— that the reason this Dusseau happened to know what little town to drift through so the boy could recognize you is that he's the one who snatched the boy in the first place?"

This is almost all dialogue, until the last paragraph, when Gavin breaks the exchange with a long (comparatively) section of Wilhelm's thoughts, in which description and regret and memory mingle. The effect is to create high contrast, which makes all the punchier the return to dialogue in Wilhelm's last, emotionally significant question. Interrupted dialogue has been used to increase drama—and so increase tension.

To use this technique, choose a section of dialogue that culminates in an important speech; there's no point in using structure-induced drama for a discussion about cooking pork chops. Keep the dialogue interruptions minimal until the long narrative block right before the pivotal speech. Also, place both speech and interruption near the end of the scene (otherwise, whatever follows will seem anticlimactic).

PACING, DRAMA AND CHARACTER

What does all this have to do with creating good characters? Quite a lot, actually. A "good" character is not necessarily one we want to ask to dinner at our home; a good character is one we want to read about. Readable dialogue—natural-sounding, concise, well-paced—frees the reader to concentrate on the content of the speech. It's like setting a book in clear type, rather than in crabbed and frustrating handwriting (such as mine). What counts in creating characterization may be the content of the dialogue, but its presentation can determine whether or not the content is ever perused at all.

So pull out one of your scenes heavy on dialogue and experiment with it. First, remove all possible interruptions to the characters' exchanges. Does the characterization stand out more sharply? Is the scene improved?

Next, add to the stripped-down dialogue only those sentences that deepen visualization and/or understanding of the immediate emotional atmosphere: gestures, bits of description, tones of voice. How does the scene read now? Better or worse? What's been gained, what lost?

Finally, go back and take another look at the stripped-down version. Can you heighten its impact by adding one long chunk of emotional narrative, which might be character thoughts, memories, uncertainty, anger, etc.? Where should it go?

"Don't interrupt," your mother taught you. But your mother wasn't a writer. In your fiction, interrupt your people—or don't—according to whether it helps us better experience whatever *they're* experiencing. That's the best characterization method of all.

SUMMARY: THE WAY YOUR CHARACTER SPEAKS HIS IDEAS

- Unless the character is a real rambler, keep dialogue artificially concise—but not so concise that we feel we're listening to a slogan writer.
- Avoid stilted, wooden, formal dialogue—unless spoken by a stilted, wooden, formal character.
- Don't make use of "As You Know, Bob" dialogue. Find another way to convey background information.
- After you've written a scene with much dialogue, consider whether it would benefit from fewer bits of narrative interspersed among the speeches—or from more. If more, should it be in small chunks or one long, dramatic interruption? If the latter, where should it be placed for best effect?

chapter seven

WHEN LESS IS MORE
Pruning Character Descriptors to a Manageable Number

Appearance, possessions, nicknames, occupation, background, mannerisms, speech patterns—by now it may seem that you know too much about your character's externals, too many details. How will you fit them all into the novel and still have room for *action*?

Obviously, you won't. You will have to choose which to include, which to leave out. But leaving out even fascinating details needn't weaken your book. In fact, it can strengthen it.

To see how, consider a different art: cooking. You're baking a cake, and halfway through you discover you lack some ingredient. What will happen if you leave it out? You try it, and the cake turns out to be—

A flop.

Or: better than the original—less sweet, lighter, more satisfying.

Or: just about the same as if you'd put the ingredient in.

But you'll never know unless you experiment. And as it is with cakes, so it is with fiction. Sometimes leaving out ingredients usually considered necessary results in a purer, more focused, more original story. Sometimes it results in a flop. And sometimes all you get is the same story, slightly shorter.

Let's get specific. In previous chapters, we've considered several different ways to characterize your protagonist. Which might you experiment with leaving out, and what might happen if you do?

LEAVING OUT DESCRIPTION

The master of omitting description, of course, is Raymond Carver. His spare short stories are almost all dialogue, broken by stretches of the character's internal ruminations. Little of the external world is described. Here, for instance, is the opening to "Night School":

> My marriage had just fallen apart. I couldn't find a job. I had another girl. But she wasn't in town. So I was at a bar having a glass of beer, and two women were sitting a few stools down, and one of them began to talk to me.
> "You have a car?"
> "I do, but it's not here," I said.

Throughout the rest of the story, we will never get a description of the narrator, the bar, the car or the women (except for "They were both about forty, maybe older"). Why not? All three people are central to the plot. And wouldn't it aid characterization to describe the kind of bar the protagonist prefers (plush or sleazy?), the car he drives (Ferrari or Ford Escort?) and/or the kind of women he allows to pick him up? Yes, it would. But Carver gives up these chances for characterization in order to gain something else.

Read the opening again. Do you sense how the absence of the external world makes the story seem closed in, limited, suffocating? That's the way the world seems to the protagonist (this is often true of Carver stories). There are few physical details because these people's physical worlds are limited and uninteresting, even to them. Only words and thoughts have genuine force. By leaving out description, Carver underscores his characters' reality.

Should you try this in your work? Not if the surroundings are important to the protagonist, or demonstrate her individuality, or are exotic enough to the reader that he needs your help in visualizing them correctly. A historical novel, for instance, needs a wealth of physical detail, or it will feel too much like the present. A story about the fashion industry needs visual descriptions. So does one about baseball—the topic itself is physical.

If, however, you have a detached or alienated character and want an ambience to match, go through and delete nearly all the description. Is the story improved? If not, you can always put it back in.

LEAVING OUT DIALOGUE

The opposite approach is to concentrate on description (as well as on exposition and characters' thoughts) and to use dialogue sparingly. Pulitzer Prize winner John Cheever often does this. When he does include dialogue, it's often reported indirectly rather than reproduced word for word, as in the opening to "O Youth and Beauty!":

> At the tag end of nearly every long, large Saturday-night party in the suburb of Shady Hill, when almost everybody who was going to play golf or tennis in the morning had gone home hours ago and the ten or twelve people remaining seemed powerless to bring the evening to an end although the gin and whiskey were running low, and here and there a woman who was sitting out her husband would have begun to drink milk; when everybody had lost track of time and the baby-sitters who were waiting at home for these diehards would have long since stretched out on the sofa and fallen into a deep sleep, to dream about cooking-contest prizes, ocean voyages, and romance; when the bellicose drunk, the crapshooter, the pianist, and the woman faced with the expiration of her hopes had all expired themselves; when every proposal—to go to the Farquarsons' for breakfast, to go swimming, to go and wake up the Townsends, to go here and there—died as soon as it was made, then Trace Bearden would begin to chide Cash Bentley about his age and thinning hair.

We will never hear exactly what Trace says to Cash—and very little of what anyone says to anyone else in this story. What does Cheever gain from this?

Just the opposite of Carver's gain. In Cheever's story, the setting is everything—so much so that in real life people refer to a certain kind of New England upper-middle-class suburb as *Cheever country*. This distinctive milieu has shaped all his characters' attitudes, actions and feelings. Cheever conveys this not only by the richly detailed descriptions of social mores, but also by minimizing the dialogue. Dialogue is individual, and Cheever's characters very often are not. They're creatures of their place and time, even somewhat interchangeable. Giving them little dialogue subtly conveys this to the reader. It also reduces the story's immediacy—which in turn reinforces the sense of the author as an anthropologist detailing the strange tribal rituals of a distinctive culture.

Minimizing dialogue is tricky; most readers like to "hear" characters' own words. If you try this, compensate with three things:

- a setting compelling and individual enough to warrant all the attention you give it, and which you know in thorough detail
- a strong enough prose style to make lots of description interesting to read
- enough action to keep all that description from making the story too static

If you have those strengths, give minimalist fiction a try.

LEAVING OUT OTHER, CAREFULLY SELECTED DETAILS

Omitting a detail works like a hole in a photograph: The eye immediately focuses on the tiny bit that is missing. Why is that little piece cut out, rather than any other little piece? The effect is, paradoxically, to give heightened importance to what is not there.

One example: deliberately omitting the use of characters' names. William Carlos Williams does this in his classic short story "The Use of Force," in which a country doctor fights with a child to make her open her mouth so he can test her for diphtheria. Even after the doctor learns the little girl's name (Mathilda), he continues to think of her exclusively as "the child." This makes her seem less like an individual than like a representation of childhood itself—which is appropriate, because Williams's story is about the appalling bonds of love-struggle-sexuality between children and adults.

You must, however, present the omission of a critical name in such a way that we know it's deliberate, not merely carelessness. Williams accomplishes this by an overrepetition of "the child," until it becomes almost a mantra—or a battle cry.

Similarly, any other ordinary detail you conspicuously leave out of your story—genders, ages—will be emphasized. Judith Merril does this in her classic science fiction story "Survival Ship," about a space ship landing on a new planet. Merril leaves out gender. Not until the last paragraph do you realize that the ship's captain and officers are female and the entire crew male. Instantly you must rethink all your assumptions about the story—and about the world behind it. Of course, this is the author's aim. She achieves it by omission.

THE BEST WAY TO OMIT DETAILS

We touched on this idea in chapter one, but it bears repeating: The very best way to leave things out is by the artful choosing of what goes in. Suppose you know sixty-three details about your character, all of which *could* go into a given paragraph of description. The success of the paragraph depends not only on choosing a manageable number of them (Gustave Flaubert recommended three), but also the *right* ones. Artful choice thus dictates what gets left out.

For instance, consider this description from Paul Theroux's most recent novel, *My Other Life*:

> I sat in the shade of the verandah, watching the hot street and the white sky, the earth like pale powder, and everything still except the insects. I walked into the sun and immediately felt the weight of it on the top of my head. I stood alone in the middle of the street on the small black island of my shadow, and thought: I am where I want to be.

This is as good as it gets. You can see the scene, feel it, experience it. What makes such a passage work? Economy, originality, flow—all the things we think of as "good writing." But, mostly, something else: *Each phrase adds value.*

That may sound like a curiously businesslike statement to apply to fiction, but look again at the paragraph. Every image adds new information to the picture we're forming in our minds. The first eight words orient us. The next eight show us what the character himself sees, economically conveying both a visual picture (street and white sky) and a feel (hot). The next five words deepen the image by adding a metaphor ("like pale powder") that brings in a host of unstated connotations: Powder is dry, light, easily disturbed, a cover for what lies underneath. The next six words add a different sense: sound. The next sentence goes back to the issue of heat, emphasizing it with an original and extreme metaphor—*think* of the burning weight of the entire sun on your head!

More new information is packed into the last sentence: that the character is alone. That he stands on his shadow as on a "small black island," further emphasizing his aloneness and extending it into a realm beyond the simply visual ("No man is an island," etc.). And finally, in contrast to the heat and loneliness, which we might have interpreted as negatives, come the last seven words ("I am where I want to be.") Those seven words simultaneously let us into the character's inner life *and* reverse all our emotional expectations by showing us, in a simple and nonpretentious way, that he is happy.

As a result, Theroux's description:

- is personal, conveying the character's view of the scene, not the author's
- does not unduly slow down the pace, because it has meaning for the character; we thus receive it as more than just static pictures
- appeals to more than one sense (sight, sound, temperature)
- seems fresh, because the two metaphors are not hackneyed (especially the second one)

And all that in seventy-one words! Theroux left out everything nonessential—and that's the definition of good description.

But how do you define *essential*? Genre can be one guide. Readers come to books and stories—any books and stories—with preconceptions. Actually, they're more than that: They're pre-choices. A reader who picks up the *New Yorker* has chosen it precisely because he wants a certain kind of fictional experience. The same is true for those who plunk down $25.95 for a new thriller, romance, adventure, science fiction, "literary" or mystery hardcover. Part of this choice is how much description they expect—and of what.

A romance novel, for example, may include quite lengthy descriptions of clothes (read Judith Krantz), people's appearances and perhaps room interiors. Romance readers enjoy this. A fan of Tom Clancy, on the other hand, does not want to wade through page-length descriptions of someone's outfit. He *does* want page-length descriptions of the weaponry on a nuclear submarine.

Sometimes even the subgenre makes a difference. Usually readers of police-procedural mysteries neither expect nor want lengthy description (think of Ed McBain's Eighty-Seventh Precinct novels). On the other hand, mystery writers as diverse as Simon Brett and Miriam Grace Monfredo include lots of description. Neither writes police procedurals; Brett's "Charles Paris" mysteries are theater-based "cozies" and Monfredo's books are historical mysteries.

Do consider genre when you consider what to leave out. This applies to both what you describe and how long you describe it.

LEAVING OUT EXPLICIT MOTIVATIONS

Omitting explicit motivations works for many different genres, if done right. It does *not* mean leaving out motivation itself. Your characters must have plausible, consistent reasons for their actions. Usually these reasons are expressed one of three ways:

- through dialogue ("I'm not going to the wedding because I can't stand the thought of my father marrying that woman," Sue said.)
- through thoughts (She wouldn't go. It would just be too horrible. How could her father marry such a tart?)
- through exposition (The last thing Sue wanted to be doing on this lovely May morning was attending her father's wedding to a girl twenty-two years younger than he. But she didn't feel she had a choice.)

It can, however, be quite effective to skip all of these and simply let the character's actions stand by themselves, unexplained. Margaret Drabble does this in her novel *Jerusalem the Golden*. Clara has just met Clelia at a poetry reading and has had an argument with her in the ladies' room. Immediately afterward, Clelia speaks:

> "Look," she added, "if you give me your address when we get back there, I'll give you a ring, and you must come and see me and I'll tell you about it."
>
> And when they got back to the bar, Clara did indeed inscribe her name and address and common room tele-

phone number upon a page of Clelia's unbelievably occu-
pied diary. . . . And as she went home that night, she knew
that she was sure that Clelia would at some point ring her.

But *why* is Clara so sure? *What* has made Clelia ask for her number
when they've been squabbling? Author Drabble doesn't say, forcing
the reader to figure out the answers for himself. The result is to focus
his thinking on what the characters are really like . . . which also
focuses him more intently on the book itself.

One note: This works better with some kinds of fiction than with
others. Some commercial fiction, in all genres, subtly promises its
readers that they will receive large doses of emotion or action, not
thought puzzles. In such stories, you might do better to make motivations overtly clear.

How do you know whether any fictional element is better included
or left out? There's no right answer; it's a judgment call. Or—write it
both ways, and ask some trusty readers which works best. They might
just agree with Robert Browning that "less is more."

SUMMARY: WHAT YOU DON'T SAY

- You can't put in everything you know about your characters.
  Choose artfully.
- Leaving out description results in characters subtly unconnected
  to their surroundings.
- Leaving out dialogue puts emphasis on setting.
- Leaving out details *may* throw whatever is omitted into sharp
  relief.
- Leaving out explicit motivation forces the reader to supply it for
  himself.
- Genre should influence what you choose to include or leave out.

chapter eight

DON'T I KNOW YOU?
Basing Characters on Real People

Many, many writers are tempted to create characters by basing the externals on real people: Cousin John's appearance, a neighbor's weird gestures, a friend's background and speech patterns. After all, the models are indubitably real, so shouldn't that bolster the believability of their fictional counterparts? Wouldn't drawing on a real person's appearance, mannerisms, speech, tastes and observable behavior give you a boost up on characterization?

Maybe yes, maybe no.

It depends on who and what you copy, and how slavishly. Using a real person as a model can gain you a solid starting point for a fictional character. It can also gain you a watered-down and underimagined character—or a law suit.

So if your Aunt Minnie is a fascinating kleptomaniac (her collection of stolen doorknobs from places where Woodrow Wilson slept; her purloined cat collars), there are both legal and personal questions to consider before you put her in a story. Can her husband Uncle Dan, the quick-tempered lawyer, sue you for libel? Will your mother, Aunt Minnie's sister, ever forgive you? If you change Aunt Minnie's name, do you have to inform your editor that she's based on a real person? If you decide that Aunt Minnie steals something from Madonna, and you want to put Madonna in the story, too, can you do that without permission?

Laws, of course, change constantly. (Abraham Lincoln once wrote, "A nation may be said to consist of its territories, its people, and its laws. The territory is the only part which is of certain durability.") What I write now could be outdated next year, or not be applicable in your particular case. Specifics depend on who you copy, how you write about him and where you live. Nonetheless, let's examine some general guidelines, both legal and literary, for making use of the intriguing Aunt Minnie.

PRECEDENTS AND CONSEQUENCES: SOME FAMOUS CHARACTERS BASED ON REAL PEOPLE

Basing fictional characters on real people has a long and distinguished history. In *David Copperfield*, Charles Dickens based Mr. Micawber on his own feckless father, John Dickens. Scarlett O'Hara's life story drew on that of Margaret Mitchell's grandmother, Annie Fitzgerald Stephens, who survived the burning of Atlanta and went on to rebuild the family farm. In *Dodsworth*, Sinclair Lewis based his exploitive and selfish character Fran Dodsworth on his first wife—an interesting form of post-marital revenge also employed by Lady Caroline Lamb in *Glenarvon* and by Nora Ephron in *Heartburn*. A trio of famous dreamers—Jay Gatsby, Don Quixote and Alice in Wonderland—likewise all began as people their authors knew.

When such models recognized their fictional counterparts, there was a variety of consequences. Irascible critic Alexander Woollcott saw himself as the irascible protagonist in George S. Kaufman and Moss Hart's play *The Man Who Came to Dinner*. Woollcott was so delighted that he toured with the play. On the other hand, Truman Capote's jet-set friends were so undelighted to recognize themselves in "La Côte Basque" that some of them never spoke to Capote again.

Consequences can be legal as well as social. An important libel case in California, *Bindrim v. Mitchell* (1979), resulted from novelist Gwen Davis Mitchell portraying in her novel *Touching* a character who conducted nude therapy sessions. She was sued by Dr. Paul Bindrim, a therapist who did just that. Even though Mitchell's fictional protagonist differed in several important ways from Bindrim, Mitchell lost the case. Bindrim was awarded a substantial settlement.

THINK FIRST, WRITE LATER: SIX MODEL QUESTIONS

Acts have consequences, and writing is an act. But you can at least minimize the personal and legal risks by forethought (we'll consider the literary risks in a moment). Ask yourself the following six questions before you borrow Aunt Minnie.

Is What I'm Writing Actually Libelous?

Libel laws vary from state to state; there is no federal law. However, various federal court cases have built up a body of defamation law through interpreting the freedoms of speech and of the press. State courts are bound by United States Supreme Court pronouncements, but in the constantly changing area of libel, this can still create differences among the states in deciding what is libelous and what is not. You can look up individual state statutes in the library.

The strictest interpretations may find you libelous if the real-life model for your character can prove:

- your character was recognizable as the model by members of the reading public, *and*
- the character was portrayed negatively, *and*
- as a result the model was injured professionally, emotionally or financially

These are the grounds on which therapist Bindrim won his case against novelist Mitchell in California. However, other states have ruled differently on similar cases.

You probably can't be successfully sued if:

- you disguise Aunt Minnie so completely that not even all her family agrees that your character is her
- you stick to the publicly documented, unembellished truth (If Aunt Minnie's conviction(s) for theft are a matter of public record,

and if you don't add any made-up, unflattering elements to her portrait, you're probably on legally safe ground.)

- you say only positive things about the character (If your protagonist is based on your friend Karl, and you portray Karl as an absolute prince, he cannot claim your portrayal defamed him.)

Is Aunt Minnie a Public Figure?
The courts have allowed considerably more leeway to authors writing about public figures than to those writing about private citizens. Don DeLillo's novel *Libra*, for instance, gave Richard Nixon an extremely unflattering character. But even if Aunt Minnie qualifies as a private citizen, she still has to prove malice on your part in order to successfully sue. She has to prove that you published private, damaging facts that are identifiably about her.

Is Aunt Minnie Dead?
Most states—but, again, not all—hold that a dead person can't be libeled. Maybe Aunt Minnie's story will gain in richness and power if you mull it over for another decade.

If I *Am* Sued, Who Will Bear the Legal Expenses?
Almost always, you will.

Most novel contracts contain lengthy paragraphs in which you agree that you haven't libeled anyone, or if you have, it's your financial problem. It's also important in this context to remember that anyone can initiate a lawsuit for libel, no matter how unfounded. The case may well be thrown out of court, but by the time it is, you may have already incurred some legal expenses.

Whose Feelings Will Be Hurt by This Book, and How Much?
Here we leave the realm of legal consequences and enter into social ones. Obviously, this is a personal question. Some writers base characters on real models and trust that the model will understand, not care or never see the story. (I know several authors who do not want their landlord, mother or ex-lover to ever read specific works. The writers are not sure what they'll say if the respective models ever do get hold of the books.)

Other writers take the stance that both life and art involve pain, and to write honestly is worth whatever conflicts this causes, including estrangement from friends and relatives. (J.P. Donleavy went so far as to say that unless at least three people sue you after the publication of your first novel, you haven't been honest enough.) Still others work hard to make sure that their models are unrecognizable in the final draft, protecting themselves from lawsuits *and* Aunt Minnie from embarrassment.

How Much Can I Disguise Aunt Minnie— and How Much Disguise Is Enough?

There are no hard and fast rules about how much you need to change a character to protect yourself from successful legal action. However, merely changing the name is not sufficient. Changing a character's sex, locale, profession and family connections may or may not be sufficient: Is the character still recognizable? To whom? Would a jury think so? You can't be sure. Thus, the more you change, the legally safer you'll be. On the other hand, if you make Aunt Minnie not a kleptomaniac but an arsonist, make her husband not a lawyer but a dairy farmer, and her fate not to end as an antiques dealer but in a rest home, is this still the story you wanted to tell? Your goal was to disguise the model, not obliterate her.

MORE THAN A FAKE MUSTACHE: HOW TO DISGUISE CHARACTERS

Preliminary concerns are to change the model's name, appearance, hometown, etc. This is easy to do. It's also minor, compared to restructuring the model's unique personality.

Fortunately, that sort of basic restructuring may actually *strengthen* your story. This is because real live people contain masses of contradictions, unprocessed experiences, confused motivations and simultaneous emotions. In the space of five minutes, a human being can experience many memories, impulses (some acted on, some not), feelings, goads of conscience, insecurities, wishes, frustrations, old angers—even if outwardly all she's doing is standing by the stove frying bacon. If you could somehow get *all* of this into your novel, it would be exactly like real life.

But fiction is not real life. Fiction, as we saw in the chapter on dialogue, is the act of compressing real life in order to express something meaningful about it. To do that, those elements that contribute to the meaning are highlighted; those that are irrelevant are edited out.

In your novel about Aunt Minnie, for instance, you might emphasize her competitiveness (she wants what her friends have, even if she has to steal it), but downplay her love of gardening and her bad temper. You will have simplified Aunt Minnie for the sake of the story. You will also have taken the first step in the process of disguising her: subtracting some traits. Choose the ones that don't contribute to your overall plot. This will give greater prominence to those traits that do contribute. (Note: We've now moved from a character's external traits to her internal ones: What Makes Minnie Run. That's why this chapter is the last one in part one. It's a bridge to part two, where we'll consider your character's psychological innards.)

The next step is to *add* personality elements that will strengthen the story's meaning. Perhaps the real Aunt Minnie is a gregarious person. She has many friends, one current and two ex-husbands and six kids. However, kleptomania feels lonely to *you*. The more you think about it, the more you sense a connection between social isolation and the need to make pathetic connections through pointless theft. So you make your fictional Aunt Minnie friendless, with a workaholic husband who ignores her and one grown son wrapped up in his own life. That change, in turn, suggests others. Minnie steals different kinds of things than your real aunt does, because she's meeting different needs. She steals from different sorts of places, in different ways. She displays her booty differently.

The fictional Minnie thus becomes a different person from the original. Some traits are highlighted, some deleted, some added. Her "disguise," it should be noted, is not at all superficial, not the equivalent of a fake mustache and dark wig. The disguise consists of genuine changes, growing out of the needs of the story itself as it evolved in your mind. F. Scott Fitzgerald said that Jay Gatsby started as a man Fitzgerald knew, "but then became himself."

So can Aunt Minnie.

ANOTHER WAY TO DISGUISE CHARACTERS

An alternate approach is to combine two or more real-life models. Many writers do this. Literary historian William Amos has this to say about Anthony Trollope's famous fictional prime minister and hero of a book series, Plantagenet Palliser:

> For his patriotic tenacity, honesty, and modesty, Palliser is supposedly modeled upon Lord Palmerston. His candor and lack of social graces are believed to come from Lord John Russell, a poor mixer and of a retiring nature. Something of this stiffness of demeanor is also probably derived from Edward Henry Stanley, Fifteenth Earl of Derby. Trollope was a member of the committee of Royal Literary Fund, over which Stanley presided. The Earl considered him to be incorrigibly middle class.

Maybe Aunt Minnie could be both disguised as a person and strengthened as a character by combining her with your next-door neighbor, a woman over whom loneliness hangs like mist. You might use the neighbor's timid manner and speech patterns, Minnie's stealing and your dentist's unexpectedly biting jokes. Does that work?

A variation of this approach is to combine characteristics of the model with aspects of your own personality. Nearly all writers, to some degree, depend on their inner lives to fuel their fiction. You have probably never, for instance, committed a murder. Yet you know what it's like to feel angry enough that you *want* to kill somebody, and from that emotion you create the thoughts of a murderer.

Similarly, when the fictional Minnie feels lonely, her loneliness will inevitably have the flavor of your own. Since this process is going to go on anyway, exploit it for purposes of disguise. Where can you graft aspects of yourself onto Minnie? Where might the plot be able to use them?

THE FINAL DECISION

Basing characters on real people can be a great starting point. However, it is only a starting point. For literary as well as legal reasons, you'll want to augment, modify and heighten the original. If you do a good enough job of this, it's possible that Aunt Minnie won't even recognize herself in the finished work. (Seventy-two different women claimed to be the model for one of Honoré de Balzac's heroines!)

It's also possible that she will recognize herself, and you'll have to deal with the consequences. Should you write the story anyway? That's up to you. Consider, however, that your decision may confer or withhold immortality on someone else. Would the world now recognize the names Tom Blankenship, Delphine Delamare or Dr. Joseph Dillon? Well, it recognizes their fictional counterparts. And so would you.*

SUMMARY: BASING CHARACTERS ON REAL PEOPLE

- To successfully sue for libel, a plaintiff must prove that your character is recognizably based on her, is a negative portrait and has injured her emotionally, socially or financially.
- You have more leeway in writing about a public figure or a dead person than about a living private citizen.
- Avoid legal action and strengthen your novel by disguising characters in substantial ways.
- Strengthen those traits that highlight the story's meaning, and delete those that do not. Let the character evolve in your mind.
- Consider combining aspects of the original model with aspects of another real person or of your own personality.

---

* Huckleberry Finn, Emma Bovary and Sherlock Holmes

part two

Creating Strong and Believable Characters: The Internals

chapter nine

SHE'S GOT AN ATTITUDE
Using Personal Thoughts
to Characterize

Four teenage boys are hanging around the mall. Their externals are alike: same baggy, colorful clothes. Same jewelry. Same carefully sloppy posture. Same slang, same intonations, same jokes and buzz-words. In their pockets are the same objects: bus tokens, a few dollars, a comb, high school ID card and music cassettes of bands that, to adult ears, also sound all alike. These objects hardly characterize.

And yet, these are four very different kids. In ten more years, the differences will be evident. One boy will be a teacher. One will be an expatriate, the social toast of Buenos Aires. One will play professional ball. And one will be in prison for murder. For now, however, these four seem alike on the outside, and you, their creator, are taxed with the job of letting us know just how individual they really are.

You do this, of course, by letting us *inside*. You show us the boys' thoughts, feelings, attitudes, fears, longings, neuroses, driving

83

compulsions. What goes on in their gray matter, where each of us is irrevocably different and irrevocably alone.

Let's start with overall attitude toward the world.

BRAIN WAVES: REACTIONS vs. PERIPHERALS

Doug Hoover's got an attitude. So does Gene Forrester, Frederick Henry, Adam Dalgliesh and Harold, the dog who lives with the Monroes. And it's a good thing these fictional characters *do* have pronounced attitudes—good for their literary creators, good for the stories they inhabit, good for readers.

Attitudes are only personal thoughts, feelings and opinions—the stuff that goes on in our brains when we're not talking aloud to someone else. Characters with attitudes are lively and interesting. This makes them both easier to write about and more absorbing to read. On the other hand, characters who have few thoughts, or whose thoughts can't be inferred even from the action, come across as automatons: limited, dull and sometimes unbelievable. When was the last time you met a person in real life without a thought in her head?

But, you may ask, if I show my characters thinking about everything they see, won't I slow my plot to a crawl? Won't I be stuck with large chunks of digression? Won't I be setting myself up for readers to mutter, "Oh, for God's sake, get *on* with the story already"?

Not necessarily. It depends on several things: What thoughts are you stopping the story to allow your character to express? How long is he allowed to ruminate on them? What function do these particular thoughts and attitudes serve in the plot? (There again is that inescapable interweaving of plot and character.) And how fresh and interesting are the attitudes in and of themselves?

There are two kinds of thoughts your character can express to himself (and us): thoughts about events that have just occurred, and peripheral thoughts that could actually be omitted without damaging the primary plot. Let's discuss the latter first.

USING PERIPHERAL THOUGHT
TO ILLUMINATE CHARACTER

The primary function of peripheral thoughts is to build characterization, to let us know what habitually occupies your protagonist's mind. "I think, therefore I am," Descartes said. He might also have said,

"What I think, I am." The man who goes to sleep every night with thoughts of mathematical problems in his head is not the same type of person as the man who courts sleep with thoughts about assassinating the president. This is why it's important to consider carefully what your character spends time (and page space) thinking *about*.

Maybe he really dislikes cabbage. If this is going to be a plot device you use later, then it's fine to use space for him to think anticabbage thoughts (maybe someone will be poisoned by a homegrown cabbage, which absolves your protagonist; he gets sick if he gets within smelling distance of the stuff). If not, then don't bother writing this in, because a hatred for cabbage simply doesn't tell us much about personality or character. Anybody can hate cabbage.

On the other hand, here's Doug Hoover, hero of Neal Barrett Jr.'s wacky novel *The Hereafter Gang*, thinking about motels:

> Doug had always been drawn to the security of motels. When you closed that door and set the heavy brass chain you left your troubles all behind. The room was like a treehouse, a cave on the bank of a creek. No one even knew you were there. You could do whatever you liked. Just anything at all. The church offered sanctuary in medieval times. Now it was Rodeways and Ramadas. They couldn't touch you in there.

The novel has very little to do with motels—its major scenes actually take place in heaven—but nonetheless, Doug's thoughts about motels are not gratuitous. They subtly confirm his character as we see it unfold: secretive ("No one even knew you were there"), escapist ("you left your troubles all behind"), childish ("like a treehouse, a cave on the bank of a creek") and deeply distrustful of human intimacy and responsibility ("They couldn't touch you in there"). Motels may not matter to the plot, but the motels in Doug's mind matter a lot to the story—because Barrett *makes* them matter through giving Doug a definite attitude about them. His thoughts mean something.

Even at the very beginning of a story, where every word has to count, it can be worthwhile to show us your character thinking about a seemingly irrelevant topic. Here is the opening paragraph of the children's classic *Bunnicula*, by Deborah and James Howe:

I shall never forget the first time I laid these now tired old eyes on our visitor. I had been left home by the family with the admonition to take care of the house until they returned. That's something they always say to me when they go out: "Take care of the house, Harold. You're the watchdog." I think it's their way of making up for not taking me with them. As if I *wanted* to go anyway. You can't lie down at the movies and still see the screen. And people think you're being impolite if you fall asleep and start to snore, or scratch yourself in public. No thank you, I'd rather be stretched out on my favorite rug in front of a nice, whistling radiator.

What Harold thinks about going to the movies is irrelevant to the story; neither he nor anybody else will go to another one. But his thoughts about movies set up his character: home-loving, conservative, a little lazy, not particularly imaginative. These are the same traits that will fuel his actions later in the story. And they make him a nice foil for Chester, the family cat, who has a manic disposition and a decided penchant for the melodramatic.

USING INNER THOUGHTS AS PLOT ELEMENTS

The other purpose of letting us see your character's actual thoughts is to directly affect plot. This happens when your character is reacting not to peripheral thoughts drifting through his head but to story events that have just occurred. Used in this way, thoughts can either drive plot or validate it.

A common way for inner thoughts to drive plot is to start with a character possessing that commonplace of the contemporary scene, an "attitude problem." Such characters are disaffected, out of synch with their world, surly, abrasive. They don't fit in. During the course of the story, the character either undergoes an attitude change (the "character learns better" plot) or else is confirmed in his belief that the world is such a rotten place that his original attitude was the correct one (the "look out for number one or die" plot). Either way, the thoughts in his head are key to our understanding the plot.

For instance, Gene, protagonist of John Knowles's novel *A Separate Peace*, has a definite attitude problem during his last year of private school: He's insecure, jealous of his best friend Phineas, frightened about World War II looming on his personal horizon. When Phineas says what he likes best about a tree on campus, Gene responds:

> "Is that what you like best?" I said sarcastically. I said a lot of things sarcastically that summer; that was my sarcastic summer, 1942.
> "Aey-uh," he said. This weird New England affirmative— maybe it is spelled "aie-huh"—always made me laugh, as Finny knew, so I had to laugh, which made me feel less sarcastic and less scared.

By the end of the novel, Gene's thoughts have changed completely: about Phineas, about the war and about being sarcastic. He has negotiated his separate peace. But if Knowles had not so clearly shown us Gene's beginning thoughts, the changes might have seemed arbitrary or—worse—incomprehensible. To solve an attitude problem, you have to show us clearly that one existed in the first place.

This is, incidentally, the basic plot for much contemporary young adult fiction: The youthful protagonist encounters a problem with dating, divorce, drinking, drugs, death or some other disaster, and then spends the length of the story undergoing an adjustment to how he thinks about these things. In the adult, antihope version, the youth discovers that his bad attitude actually fit his world all along. See, for instance, Harlan Ellison's chilling science fiction story, "A Boy and His Dog," in which Vic learns that murder is a completely appropriate way to preserve what's important to him.

Sometimes characters' thoughts are explicated at the *end* of the story, not the beginning. Ending with character thoughts serves as validation for the plot events that formed them: Yes, this is what it all means; you the reader interpreted it right. There is obvious danger in doing this. The reader may feel lectured, which he will resent. Also, the writer may look uncertain of his material, wrapping it up in a neat attitudinal summary posing as character insight, because he doesn't trust the plot events to have already made the meaning clear.

However, when the summarizing thoughts expressed by a character constitute a genuine change in him, earned with enough pain to make it seem natural that he would be dwelling on it, then ending with a direct view into the character's mind can be very effective. Here is Ernest Hemingway's Frederick Henry, in a famous passage near the end of *A Farewell to Arms*:

> If people bring so much courage to the world the world has to kill them to break them, so of course it kills them. The world breaks everyone and afterward many are strong at the broken places. But those that will not break it kills. It kills the very good and the very gentle and the very brave impartially. If you are none of these you can be sure it will kill you too but there will be no special hurry.

Without this direct expression of Henry's thoughts about what has happened to him, the novel would have been far less moving. Henry is not a man who usually reveals much directly; we need to be shown what these events mean to him. When Hemingway lets us share Henry's thoughts directly, we see just that.

It is also possible to play inner thoughts and outer action against each other, thereby creating tension. The woman who expresses misery at her own wedding, the soldier facing death with relief, the anorectic cook who shudders at the smell of bacon frying—all command our interest, but *only* if you make their thoughts explicit and clear.

HOW LONG CAN CHARACTERS JUST STAND AROUND AND THINK?

There's another important point to be made about paragraphs that stop the story action in order to express character's thoughts: Such passages have to be either fascinating or short.

Brevity is especially important for those sections of thought that characterize but don't contribute directly to plot. Look back at our first two examples. Doug gets one brief paragraph in a novel of 348 pages to air his attitude about motels. Harold, the movie-disdaining dog, gets four sentences. Few readers will object to these expository breaks; most won't even consciously notice them.

Sometimes, however, a character has much longer and more involved thoughts about some crucial subject (don't you?). These *will* stop the story dead, so you need to be sure you're gaining more than you're losing, which means that the thoughts expressed had better be pretty interesting to the reader in and of themselves. The catch here, of course, is the question: interesting to which reader?

P.D. James's editor, Rosemary Goad, has told the story of a long passage in which James's hero Adam Dalgliesh is viewing a stained-glass window and thinking about its details. Dalgliesh has strong attitudes about church architecture. Goad cut the passage from the novel, only to find it reproduced word for word in James's next book—and then in the next, and the next, until Goad finally let it stand. Dalgliesh finds stained glass fascinating; James finds his thoughts interesting; Goad did not. It came down to a judgment call, as will those passages in which *your* protagonist has lengthy ruminations on Japanese cuisine, golf technique or quilting. If you *do* decide to allow such extended sections of thoughts, the viewpoint had better be original, the prose sparkling and the details fresh.

Giving your character an attitude—or three, or five, or twenty—can be fun. It makes him that much more vivid in your own mind, which in turn makes him vivid on the page. And readers will respond.

However, as with dialogue, there is another half to this subject. You need to consider not only the content of your characters' thoughts, but the way they're expressed: the diction, sentence structure, even punctuation. All this in the next chapter.

SUMMARY: YOUR CHARACTERS' OPINIONS

- Your character should not be affectless; to be interesting, she should have attitudes about the events and objects in her world.
- Character's thoughts that are present in the story solely to characterize should usually be brief.
- Any long expressions of attitude should be worth stopping the story in order to air them. Are your character's editorial digressions original, quirky, thoughtful, important, well-written—in a word, *interesting*?
- Character's thoughts that are there to drive plot should be clearly shown at the beginning of the story, so we can see what will change from the start of the story to its end.
- Character's thoughts that are there to validate plot at the end of the story should be expressed naturally by the character (*not* the author) in personal terms. This usually means that the character ruminates about what he has learned, what cost he paid to learn it, or both.

chapter ten

LOST IN THOUGHT
Making Clear What, When and How Your Character Is Thinking

So now your protagonist is thinking, and your readers are privy to at least some of his thoughts. That makes everything about him much sharper and clearer.

Or does it?

Only if readers can tell clearly which *are* the character's thoughts, and which the opinions of the author. How to present characters' thoughts without confusion, especially in a third-person story, is a perennial hot topic in writing classes. Should the diction match the character's dialogue or the writer's narrative style? Do you need "he thought" every time somebody thinks about something? How else will the reader know whether the sentence is in the character's mind or is the author's statement? Do you put thoughts in quotation marks? In italics? In their own paragraph? Do you switch to first person for intimate thoughts? What about dialect in the privacy of a character's head?

It's enough to make a writer stick to first person forever.

But you don't have to use first person in order to handle characters' thoughts smoothly. Certain techniques can help you get a grip on the more slippery third person. In fact, you can even strengthen characterization by paying attention to the mechanics, distance, diction and style of your characters' thoughts.

Let's first dispose of the simplest concern: format.

MECHANICS: I CAN COUNT ON YOU

Here are five different ways to present the same character thought in a third-person story written in the past tense:

> John looked at the girl across the room. *She's beautiful*, he thought. *I want to meet her.* [Thoughts in present tense, first person, italicized, tagged with "he thought"]

> John looked at the girl across the room. *She's beautiful. I want to meet her.* [Thoughts in present tense, first person, italicized, untagged]

> John looked at the girl across the room. She's beautiful, he thought. I want to meet her. [Thoughts in present tense, first person, not italicized, tagged]

> John looked at the girl across the room. She was beautiful, he thought. He wanted to meet her. [Thoughts in past tense, third person, not italicized, tagged]

> John looked at the girl across the room. She was beautiful. He wanted to meet her. [Thoughts in past tense, third person, not italicized, untagged]

Each of these is the choice of various writers. The only real rule is a reasonable consistency. Whatever presentation you choose for characters' thoughts, use it consistently so that your reader, once she's caught on, doesn't have to make mental adjustments for mechanics. That will only distract her from more important things.

For the same reason, don't use quotation marks, single or double, around characters' thoughts. The reader will see the opening quotes and assume that what follows is dialogue. If she then finds a "he thought" tacked onto the end, she'll have to adjust her mental picture:

This guy is not talking out loud after all. That's distracting. And the next time she encounters quotes, she won't know if the character is talking aloud or just ruminating.

Once consistency is out of the way, do the five formats for presenting thoughts offer different advantages and disadvantages? Yes.

Using italics (which are always indicated in manuscript by underlining—but you already knew that) means switching both tense (from past to present) and person (from third to first). Let's see this in a slightly longer passage:

> Carla looked into John's face, which was bleary from four whiskey-and-waters before lunch. His pupils were unfocused. His smile—that smile she had once loved—looked equally unfocused, the foolish beaming of a man to whom all events are benevolent because no event is seen clearly. Dried egg crusted his beard. *I can't do this any more*, she thought. *It's impossible.*

This technique works for short thoughts. However, for anything longer than a sentence, or if used often during a story, it can seem intrusive. The reader may feel that the writer can't make up his mind whether he's writing in third person or first. In addition, because italics are also used for emphasis, instance after instance of italicized thoughts may feel like artificial inflation. Characters who think emphatically all the time are just as tiresome as people who shout all the time.

A smoother way to combine first-person thoughts with third-person narrative is to drop the italics but keep the "she thought" and the present tense. Thus, the above passage becomes:

> Carla looked into John's face, which was bleary from four whiskey-and-waters before lunch. His pupils were unfocused. His smile—that smile she had once loved—looked equally unfocused, the foolish beaming of a man to whom all events are benevolent because no event is seen clearly. Dried egg crusted his beard. I can't do this anymore, she thought. It's impossible.

If you're consistent about this, the reader will accept the sudden switch to first person—if the sections of first-person thought are fairly short.

But what if your character thinks a lot, and you have longer sections of thought to pass on to the reader? One option is to switch the thoughts from first person and present tense to third person and past tense, to match the past-tense narrative. Then the passage becomes:

> Carla looked into John's face, which was bleary from four whiskey-and-waters before lunch. His pupils were unfocused. His smile—that smile she had once loved—looked equally unfocused, the foolish beaming of a man to whom all events are benevolent because no event is seen clearly. Dried egg crusted his beard. She couldn't do this anymore, she thought. It was impossible.

This is a more seamless, less intrusive way to handle thoughts, because you switch neither person nor tense. It's true that the third-person thought will feel slightly less immediate—more reported to us than directly overheard by us—but the difference will be slight. And the gain in readability should offset that.

Finally, you have one more option, which I think is the best because it's the most streamlined. Keep thoughts in third person and past tense but drop the "she thought" entirely, thus:

> Carla looked into John's face, which was bleary from four whiskey-and-waters before lunch. His pupils were unfocused. His smile—that smile she had once loved—looked equally unfocused, the foolish beaming of a man to whom all events are benevolent because no event is seen clearly. Dried egg crusted his beard. She couldn't do this anymore. It was impossible.

But won't the reader wonder *who* thinks that Carla can't do this anymore: Carla herself, or the author? That depends on another important factor in handling thoughts: distance.

DISTANCE: UP CLOSE AND PERSONAL—OR NOT

The above technique will work when the third-person point of view (POV) is so close inside Carla's mind that the reader automatically assumes the last two sentences are Carla's thoughts. That happens when, throughout the whole story, everything we see and hear and experience has been through Carla's eyes, rather than reported to us from the outside by another pair of eyes (the author's). This is a crucial point, called *distance*.

Distance is the measure of how far away you, the author, are standing from your character as you tell the story. Are you observing completely from the outside, as if you were a camera recording what your character does, and (like a news anchorman) occasionally commenting on it, as well? This is a far distance from the character. Are you standing right beside the character, so that you see (and tell us) the same things the character sees, with occasional forays into the inside of your character's head to give us his direct thoughts? This is a middle distance. Or do you spend the entire story standing inside your character's head, so that everything we see is filtered through your character's perceptions? This is close distance, often just as close as first person.

Distance affects many things in fiction, among them the choice of format for characters' thoughts.

When you the author spend most of your prose describing from the outside how a character is feeling, then the reader might very well experience some confusion over thoughts given without any "she thought" tag. Is this more description from the author, or is this the character's perceptions? Both a distant third-person POV and a close one can be effective, but which one you set up at the beginning of your story will influence our reactions to untagged thoughts.

This is easiest to see through example. Here are two subtly different versions of the same passage:

> Amy walked home as fast as she could, her fingers numb with cold. She allowed herself a moment of self-pity, her usual failing. Other kids' parents often drove them places, she thought. Carol's mom, for instance, drove Carol to soccer practice every day. She wished her mother was like that.

> Amy walked home as fast as she could, her fingers numb with cold. *Other* kids' parents drove them places. That stuck-up Carol, for instance—Carol's mom drove her to soccer practice every day. Why couldn't Amy have a mother like that? It wasn't fair.

What's different here? In the first, more distant passage, we observe Amy from the outside. We are *told* that she feels self-pity; we are *told* that this is her usual failing (no teenager views herself dispassionately enough to make this judgment); we are *told* what Amy wishes. Given all this viewing from the outside, the "she thought" at the end of the third sentence is probably necessary to make sure that we understand we aren't also being told this information by the author, but that instead it represents Amy's actual thoughts.

In the second example, we know from the second sentence onward that, instead of being told about Amy's state of mind, we're being *shown* her thoughts directly. This is made clear by the italicizing of *other*, reproducing the way teenage girls emphasize certain words; by the use of *stuck-up*; by the question Amy asks herself; and by the whining "It wasn't fair." In this version, we don't need the label "she thought" because we're so close inside Amy's head that it's clear these are her thoughts, not the author's observations. And if you don't need the tag, drop it. It's just excess baggage.

Often, of course, this is a judgment call. And nobody is going to reject your story if a few extra "she thoughts" creep into otherwise lean prose. Still, you can cut many tags once you become aware that they're unnecessary to a close third-person POV (although they may be necessary to a more distant one). The list includes, but is not limited to:

- His thoughts drifted to . . .
- He wondered . . .
- He realized that . . .
- He remembered the time when . . .
- He contemplated the . . .
- He mused . . .

It's sharper and more economical to just let your character get on with the content of his thinking, wondering, realizing, remembering, contemplating or musing, rather than to announce that he's about to do these things. And, of course, I don't have to tell you not to write, "He thought to himself." Except for telepaths, there is no other possibility.

DICTION AND PERSONALITY: GETTING TO KNOW YOU

As we discussed in the last chapter, the content of characters' thoughts is tremendously important. *What* your character thinks about helps to create his personality for the reader. So does *how* he thinks: in what words, with what sentence structure, with what level of grammatical correctness.

Consider two characters, both in close third-person POV, both imagining themselves shooting a hated enemy:

> Guts. That's what he wanted to see. Grayson's guts, sprayed red and purple all over the wall. And Grayson writhing underneath. Still alive. A long time alive. Yeah.

> He would watch the entire brief performance, the one-act passion play, from over the barrel of the rifle. The gun would feel cool and smooth in his hands. He could feel it there now, could see the staging: the setup as Grayson turned toward him with a shocked face, the climax as the bullet slammed into Grayson's chest, the denouement as his old rival lay dying. Oh, yes, he would watch closely, and no other performance would ever have felt so rich, so nuanced, so completely satisfying.

These are very different men. Their thoughts are equally violent, but the first character comes across as more visceral, more direct, less sophisticated. That's due to the Anglo-Saxon diction, the short and choppy sentences (only one is grammatically complete), and the lack of outside references. This guy thinks in concrete, brutal images. By extension, we see him as concrete and brutal.

The second character's thoughts, in contrast, use more Latinate words, longer and grammatically complete sentences, and an entire metaphor lifted from theater. Both writers have adjusted their narrative style while in their characters' thoughts—and both have succeeded in strongly characterizing their fictional killers.

The result of this matching of diction, sentence structure and level of sophistication to a character's personality is twofold. First, a given character's dialogue and thoughts will end up sounding consistent with each other. And why not? The same person is having thoughts inside his head and speaking thoughts out loud.

Second, the closer the distance between author and character, the more alike thoughts and dialogue should sound. At the very closest third-person POV, the author's language disappears and the entire story is told in the character's language. Any distinction between the style of thoughts and the style of, say, description, disappears. In essence, the entire story is the character's thoughts (just as in first person), and the language subtly reflects that.

Here, for example, is a passage from Mary McCarthy's *The Group*. The POV character is Libby MacAusland. And even though this brief passage is a description of Libby's boss, the content and language are Libby's own:

> She often found him reading a magazine: *The New Masses*, she noticed, or another called *Anvil*, or still another with the peculiar name of *Partisan Review*, which she had tried to read in the Washington Square Bookshop. That's what gave her the idea of slipping words like "laborer" into her conversation, to remind him that she too was one of the downtrodden. Rumor had it that there were quite a few pinks in the publishing biz.

Who thinks that *Partisan Review* is a peculiar name? Not the author. *Pinks, biz, Rumor had it*—this is all Libby's language, a reflection of her desire to be hip and snappy without having a clue as to what her boss (or anyone else) is really all about. These words would not work in a more formal novel with a greater distance between author and characters: E.M. Forster's *A Passage to India*, for instance. McCarthy's language reflects and subtly reinforces the intimacy with which we've invaded Libby's mind.

THINKIN' REAL SMOOTH AND EASY: DIALECT IN THOUGHTS

You can even extend this technique to include reproducing regional or ethnic dialect in a character's thoughts, not just in her dialogue. This is from Susan Glaspell's story "A Jury of Her Peers," which was made into the often-produced play *Trifles*:

> Harry was Mrs. Hale's oldest boy. He wasn't with them now, for the very good reason that those potatoes never got to town yesterday and he was taking them this morning, so he hadn't been home when the sheriff stopped to say he wanted Mr. Hale to come over to the Wright place and tell the county attorney his story there, where he could point

it all out. With all Mrs. Hale's other emotions came the fear now that maybe Harry wasn't dressed warm enough—they hadn't any of them realized how that north wind did bite.

In that last sentence you can hear the distinctive phrasing of the rural Midwest. But, as with spoken dialogue, a little dialect goes a long way. Author Glaspell has used a light hand with her regional phrases ("hadn't any of them realized how that north wind did bite"). To use dialect in thought without being hackneyed or distracting, follow the guidelines for dialect in dialogue (see chapter five).

Your character thinks about certain things, in a certain way, because of who he is. Through thoughts whose diction and sentence structure reflect that identity, and through keeping the mechanics and POV distance consistent, you help us to understand this character's individual personality. How could we not? We're inside his head, where identity resides. He thinks, therefore he is . . . alive.

SUMMARY: CLARITY IN CHARACTER THOUGHTS

- Be consistent in whatever format you choose for presenting thoughts.
- Make your choice partly on the basis of how much distance you're keeping between author and character.
- Do write thoughts in the diction, sentence structure and level of sophistication that match the character's personality (which means that dialogue and thoughts will sound similar). The closer the distance, the more alike thoughts and dialogue should sound.
- Keep italicizing to a minimum, to avoid looking as if you think every character thought is worthy of great emphasis.
- Keep "he thought" tags only when you need them to avoid confusion.
- Use dialect with a light hand.

chapter eleven

THE PYGMALION TRAP
How to Not Let Your Assumptions Torpedo Characterization

Recently I saw a story from a young writing student. The story had three characters: a young man, his fairly young stepmother and his retired father. The first two characters were interesting and individual. The father, on whom the point of the story depended, did nothing but sit around and say little. We not only didn't see much of his externals (appearance, gestures, dialogue—all the good stuff we discussed in part one), we also didn't get much sense that anything was going on internally.

"The father isn't strong enough a character for his part in the story," I said. "What's he really like as a person?"

The student shrugged. "Oh, you know—he's retired. Nothing to do all day. So naturally he's depressed and bored. I just assumed you'd get that."

Well, no, I didn't. My student was making an assumption about his character—that all retired men are depressed and bored—and then a further assumption that I would share the first assumption. I didn't share it. I know too many retired men who are not depressed and bored (including my own father). As a result, I came to the story with a different set of assumptions, and what was on the page didn't communicate.

The young writer assumed way too much—about both his character *and* his reader.

This is not as simple a subject as it might at first seem. Assume that we need every single detail explained, and you will show us so much detail that we become bored and impatient.

Assume that we completely share your view of the character and you will leave out necessary details: the thoughts, gestures, attitudes that illuminate your character and bring him to life on the page.

Make the wrong assumptions about our reaction to the character, and you will supply the wrong details, leaving us thinking, "Huh? Why on earth did the character do *that?*"

Any of these can kill a story. On the other hand, the *right* assumptions let you include the right thoughts, attitudes and reactions to really bring your character alive for your readers. This is probably easiest to see through examples.

WHEN READER AND AUTHOR SHARE ASSUMPTIONS—OR DON'T

Suppose, for instance, you are writing a story in which the first scene is a mother wheeling her shopping cart out of the supermarket with a full load of groceries and her two-year-old in the child seat. A car pulls alongside and a man leaps out, knocks the mother to the ground, grabs the baby and screeches away. The mother's reaction is screaming hysteria. You stop the scene there.

You are assuming that we will understand why the mother is upset. And if the next scene is two cops discussing the fact that the mother can't supply the license plate number, we will assume the intervening action: someone called 911, the distraught mother was interviewed, she was too hysterical and terrified to think clearly enough to catch the plate number, etc. Your assumptions are:

- Mothers get very upset when their children are kidnapped.
- They turn to authority for help.
- Hysteria and terror can interfere with clear thinking.
- The reader will share the above three assumptions without your explaining them.

The last point is the most crucial. If you *don't* think readers will share the first three assumptions, you will put in scenes that dramatize her failure to note the license number, her phone call to the police, their arrival, their interrogation of her and any witnesses. If these scenes are doing something more than supplying us with characterization of the mother (supplying clues, for instance, or setting up the attitude of the police), they may work fine. But if the scenes' only point is to characterize the mother's distraught worry, you will be putting in far too many scenes *that slow the story down*. And the reason you will be putting them in is that you've made a false assumption about how much the reader assumes about character. You should realize that we will assume that a kidnapped child can lead to both hysteria and an appeal to the authorities. Knowing that gives you the option of showing the interrogation scene—or not.

Now consider an alternate scenario. Suppose the mother is not hysterical. Suppose she coolly notes the license plate number of the abductor's car, calmly calls the cops (no quaver in the voice, no pleas to hurry) and goes through their interrogation without so much as moving a facial muscle. This is not what most readers assume about the mothers of kidnapped children. As a result, you no longer have a choice about showing that scene. You must show it, and in enough detail for the readers to decide if the mother's calm is the result of shock, cold-bloodedness, complicity in the kidnapping, or pathology. We will need a lot more detail to create a believable character, because her behavior runs contrary to our assumptions about motherhood.

And if she doesn't call the cops at all, ever, we will need even more detail to make this feel real. An example: In her novel *Sula*, Toni Morrison takes an entire complex social background, with many scenes' worth of dramatization, to make clear why Sula and Nel don't report the freak, accidental drowning of a younger child.

But—and here's the crucial point—to realize how many scenes you must supply to make a character feel real, you as writer first must have a good sense of what the readers' assumptions are. Not your assumptions—*theirs.*

The mother of a kidnapped child is an easy example. Most people would assume that she would be upset and would call the cops. The case of the student writer's retired man is more subtle. The student held certain assumptions about old retired people, and he further assumed that his ideas were universally shared. As a result, he failed to create the character's depression and boredom *on the page* through specific details, dramatized scenes, pointed dialogue. If he had done so, I would have accepted his bored and depressed retiree. But the writer did not do the necessary work, and so the story failed. And it failed not from lack of skill, but from lack of insight about what needed to be depicted and what didn't.

In order to avoid making this mistake, you must examine your own assumptions about your characters to determine if they are pretty much universal (like distraught mothers of kidnapped babies) or specific to you as a person. This isn't easy (examining our map of personal reality never is). But such examination can determine how much detail you need to supply, and that in turn can make or break your characterization.

THE RULE OF SOME

Again, making assumptions about characters isn't necessarily bad. It can be very useful, allowing you to skip long scenes of the obvious and get on with the story. But the assumptions must be ones shared by editors and readers outside your particular group (age group, gender group, social background, occupation, political persuasion, religion, whatever). If you assume too much, you will (like that student) stint on the work of creating details that reveal character and motivation.

Do you share any of these assumptions (answer honestly!):

- A middle-aged woman sitting on a bus, frowning, with deep lines from nose to mouth and an abstracted gaze, is probably sour and bitter about life.
- A man who's been divorced three times must not be a very good husband.
- Old people don't notice each other sexually.

- Old people don't notice younger people sexually.
- Corporate executives are greedy, rapacious and unprincipled.
- A mother likes all of her grown children.
- A mother likes all of her young children.
- Fighter pilots are fearless, calm people.

In fact, every one of these assumptions falters on what author Gene Wolfe astutely calls "The Rule of Some": Some are, some aren't. Some conscientious mothers do not like all their children, young or grown (and may feel very guilty about it). There exist decent CEOs. There also exist sexually observant oldsters, fighter pilots terrified to fly who do it anyway and thrice-married men who are good husbands but bad choosers of wives. More important, these are not isolated phenomena. The numbers are substantial enough that many readers may depart from the assumptions around which you've constructed your fiction.

It's important to note that this is not a political question. You can believe that corporations, divorce or marriage are either good or bad. Go right ahead. What you must not do, if you want your fiction to convince us, is assume that we believe the same things and so you don't have to put on the page the details and motivations that convince us *your* character is a fully rounded individual.

How do you add those details? Let's look more fully at that middle-aged woman on the bus.

ONE BUS, MANY WOMEN

From the outside, what we notice about the woman is her age, the deep lines from nose to mouth and her frowning, abstracted gaze. But what do the lines mean? That she has scowled all her life and is, in fact, a sour and angry person? That she was not regular about the Oil of Olay? That that's the way her chromosomal lottery fell? (Those lines are called "nasolabial grooves," and they are partly genetic.) And what about that frown? Is it really disapproval . . . or preoccupation? The result of thinking hard? Or a temporary bad mood, only part of a complex and volatile personality?

In a novel, these questions may eventually be answered by the accretion of scenes. The woman frowns and looks sour on the bus and in the kitchen, but never at her job . . . eventually we form an accurate picture of her. But although sheer verbiage may eventually round out your character, it's also important that our first impression of her not be founded on misdirection. This means you want to provide an accurate introduction to your character, one we can build upon, not have to replace entirely. This in turn means you need to go beyond your assumptions about how we will see this woman, and *show* her to us.

Here are three of those middle-aged women on that bus:

> Hattie frowned, the lines deepening from nose to mouth, her gaze abstracted. She didn't trust those two boys two rows up on the left. Heads shaved in the back, what kind of mothers did they have letting them get out of the house like that? Punching each other and grinning. Just the kind that might grab her purse, or assault her, or worse. You couldn't be too careful nowadays. They were everywhere; if people could find a way to take advantage of you they would. Especially on the bus, which certainly wasn't the safe vehicle it had been when *she* was young. But, then, the whole country had just decayed, it was disgraceful.
>
> Mabel frowned, the lines deepening from nose to mouth, her gaze abstracted. She tried to concentrate. What *would* Ben and Sue like for the baby? Mabel wanted to give them just exactly the right gift, they'd been so good to her. A baby buggy? No, they probably had one. A really beautiful dress? But nowadays parents didn't seem to dress babies in frilly outfits that needed hand-washing and ironing. Young people were so much more sensible now. They knew the value of time. Sue did so much, with her job and the house and now that beautiful baby. . . . Oh, yes! Perfect! She'd get Sue a month's worth of a cleaning service! And maybe it would be a small repayment for all the kindness her niece had shown her.
>
> Jean frowned, the lines deepening from nose to mouth, her gaze abstracted. Damn, she hadn't gone over the copy for the McAllister account with Ben before she'd left the office. She'd meant to do that; Carl McAllister was too important a client to not supervise the work the agency did for him. Jean had just been distracted by bus schedules; she'd

certainly be glad when the Mercedes was out of the shop on Thursday. What were the chances of a cab strike the same week her car developed engine trouble? But those were the punches; you rolled with them. That was how she'd built the agency in the first place. Rolling with the punches. That and carefully supervising the talent in every last, crucial detail.

Very different women, aren't they? One way to deepen individuality is to show us a character's thoughts. But—again—first you must realize when this needs doing, and when (as with the distraught mother of the abducted child) you can safely assume that readers will fill in the character's thoughts accurately.

You can also, of course, particularize characters through their dialogue, their reactions to other people's actions, their choice of clothing and furniture and vacations and music—everything we discussed in part one. Just don't assume that characters' actions alone will characterize them; actions can spring from too many different motives and worldviews. Even worse, don't assume that a label (*retired man, CEO, Republican, adulterer*) conveys the same ideas to us that it does to you.

THE MOST DANGEROUS ASSUMPTION OF ALL

If the aforementioned assumptions can cripple your story, the next one can kill it entirely. This is the most counterproductive—and the most common—assumption that many new writers make: *A character just like me is automatically interesting to the reader.*

Now, this assumption may be true. You may be a fascinating person, either flamboyantly fascinating or subtly fascinating. The problem here is the "automatic" part. To create yourself on the page (or its analogue, a "character much like myself") is even *more* work than to create a totally different character. Beginning writers often think it will be easier to write about a character like themselves, especially if they use first person. After all, you know the character so well, don't you?

Yes. You know him too well. You make all kinds of assumptions about yourself, and because these assumptions are part of your own mind, they're hard to examine. It's therefore hard to see which details you must artfully create on the page in order for this character—whom you know so well!—to be equally vivid to the reader. Most of the time, it's actually easier to write a character much different from yourself. The distance allows you to more readily identify effective details.

This is why some writing teachers discourage students from using first-person point of view. I wouldn't go that far, but I understand the point. Third-person lends more distance than first. A character unlike yourself is more distant than one who is you. Distance lets you grasp the outline of the character as a whole and so fill in the details, both large- and small-scale.

If you *do* create characters like yourself, give special thought to the assumptions you're making about your type of person, your reactions, your motives, your beliefs. Are they really so universal as to need little dramatizing?

It's never easy to examine our own assumptions about the world (which is why psychotherapy exists). But do try to cultivate a feel for which of your assumptions about a character are likely to be shared by most readers, and which will need much supporting detail to render vividly. Knowing the difference can greatly affect your success with characterization.

SUMMARY: HOW YOUR READER READS YOUR CHARACTER

- Don't assume your readers will evaluate your characters the same way you do.
- Include sufficient details and dramatizations to make clear how we are supposed to view these people. Do not rely on labels.
- The greater your characters' personalities diverge from common assumptions, the more details and dramatization you must provide.
- Be especially careful to fully flesh out characters who are very much like yourself.

chapter twelve

AIRY DREAMS AND SOLID NEWS
How to Use Dreams and Newscasts to Enhance Characterization

It's amazing how many beginning writers have their characters dream during the course of a story or novel. A lesser, but still significant, number have characters watching TV news or listening to the radio. Are these scenes really useful to your fiction? They may get your character through the night, or through that hour between more concrete fictional events, but can they also add more substantial value? Or are they just hokey and contrived fillers?

The honest answer: It depends.

Both dreams and newscasts *can* be hokey padding. But they can also provide genuine character enhancement, in quite moving ways. Admittedly, neither dreams nor newscasts are among the major techniques for building characterization. But because they can be effective supplementary techniques, it's worthwhile to discuss how and when to add one or both to your fiction.

Dreams first. Some uses of dreams, unfortunately, are almost guaranteed to fail. By discussing these upfront, we'll prepare the ground for more positive suggestions. There are three pitfalls to avoid.

DREAM PITFALL NUMBER ONE: THE PLOT THAT HINGES ON A DREAM

The greatest mistake in using dreams in your fiction is to make the plot *require* the dream. Except in certain kinds of fantasy or science fiction, where dreams are part of either magic or alternate science, dreams should not be used as character motivation, climax or resolution.

By "character motivation," I mean the kind of story in which the character doesn't know a vital piece of knowledge until it's revealed to her in a dream: the location of her grandmother's locket, the meaning of a cryptic message or the revelation that her husband is having an affair. The problem with this device is that it looks contrived. The effect is not that the character is sensitive, but that the author is desperate. Not knowing how to move his plot forward, he leads into the next set of incidents by giving the character a dream she will have to act on.

Sometimes new writers defend this practice on Freudian grounds: "It's her subconscious that actually knows this information all along, only she can't admit it. She's in denial. Then it comes out in a dream, and so the character is forced to act on it."

This defense at first seems to make a certain amount of sense. Undoubtedly there are times for all of us when our subconscious knows more than we do, and that knowledge may well turn up in dreams. Real life is like that. The problem is that real life is not fiction. Real life, as a rule, is much messier and less organized than fiction, which seeks to impose a pattern on the world. So on those rare occasions when real life actually produces an event *more* patterned and neater than fiction, we marvel. "Truth really is stranger than fiction," we say, as the murderer turns out to be the long-lost cousin of the victim. We accept real-life coincidence because we have to. It *happened*. But in fiction we don't have to accept it, and if it seems too convenient, we won't. A dream that unfolds the next section of plot— or even worse, the climax of the plot—seems too easy, too much engineered by the author. Don't do it.

The very worst version of the dream-as-plot-device is such a cliché that I hardly need mention it (do I?). This is the dream forced into service as story resolution: "Then I woke up and it was all a dream." Readers hate this. They feel cheated. They believed the story was a story—that is, that it was actually happening to someone, even if that someone is fictional. To discover that the story wasn't happening even to an unreal person is a great blow. Don't inflict it.

DREAM PITFALL NUMBER TWO: THE OVERLONG DREAM

Because dreams are unreal, they call subtle attention to the unreality of the entire work. Sort of a second-layer unreality: the unfactual illusions of someone who is already an unfactual illusion. You can minimize this effect by keeping your characters' dreams short.

I cannot emphasize this enough. The brief retold dream becomes a story detail, one of many, that contributes to characterization. The long retold dream becomes a scene in itself and is almost always too fragile (an "airy nothing," in the Bard's words) to carry such importance.

So how short is short enough? That depends on what function the dream serves. Usually one lengthy paragraph is enough, but not always. We'll look at some examples in a minute, in the section on using dreams well.

DREAM PITFALL NUMBER THREE: THE FREUDIAN CLICHÉ

Finally, including a protagonist's dreams can actually *harm* characterization. Dreams become pitfalls when they are so overtly Freudian or Jungian that it appears the author has constructed them from a Handy-Dandy Psychology of the Unconscious Kit. Freudian psychology does indeed have an elaborate and significance-fraught lexicon of dream symbols. Some of these have entered the common culture: cigars as phallic symbols, flying as sexual metaphor. Similarly, many people talk easily about "Jungian archetypes," to the point where it may seem reasonable that the audience for literary fiction should be able to translate the symbols you've put into your character's dreams. And perhaps many readers will be able to do that.

However, this is a mixed blessing. One part of your reader's mind may well register, "Ah! A dream about being born! Well, that makes sense, this character is certainly struggling to begin a new life." But

109

another part of the same reader's mind is going, "So neat, so pat, so connect-the-dots." You can avoid this by keeping your character's dreams quirky, not Freudian-mechanical. Quirky, individual and short.

USING DREAMS WELL: DREAMS UNDER PRESSURE
The legitimate use of dreams in fiction is not to drive plot, but to illuminate character. There are a few different ways to do this.

The most straightforward is to simply recount the dream as the character has it. This works best when the character is under great internal pressure because of story events, and his dreaming is just one among many ways of dramatizing that pressure. If the pressure is building to a climax, the character's tension may be so great that more than one paragraph is justified for the dream. Here is Alice Hoffman's protagonist, Polly Farrell, from the novel *At Risk*. Polly's eleven-year-old daughter Amanda is dying of AIDS contracted from a blood transfusion. This has affected every area of Polly's life. Just before Amanda stops going to school, Polly dreams:

> Tonight she dreams that she has lost Amanda and cannot find her. She enters her dream through an alleyway made of stones. She can hear children crying, and the sound of shovels, methodically hitting against the earth. It's raining and the ground is slippery; as she runs, mud splashes up and coats her legs, turning them the color of blood.
>
> This is what she knows: Someone has taken her daughter. Someone has put up a fence ringed with spikes. Someone is screaming in the distance. There are other children here, with no one to care for them, but Polly has no time for them. She runs faster. Her heart is pounding. She reaches the shelter she's looking for, and when she goes inside all she can see is one bed after another. Rows and rows of iron beds made up with white sheets. This is the children's house. This is the place where they're given food and water every day, but there is still no one to hold them. As she walks through the shelter, children cry out to her, babies lift their arms, begging to be picked up. They all look the same to her, that is what's horrible. They look like

Amanda, but they're not. Polly knows she will recognize her own daughter; she must. There she is, in a small bed pushed up against a wall. Amanda can no longer speak, but Polly can tell she recognizes her. She wraps her in a sheet, and after they leave the shelter, after they step outside, the sheet trails in the mud and makes a hissing sound.

The alley she first entered by is the only way out, and, without seeing them, Polly knows there are guards. But all guards grow careless, they grow sleepy when their stomachs are full, when the screaming is in the distance and not right at their feet. So Polly crouches down low; it is dusk now, but that won't last forever. They will wait until dark. When no one is looking, when their backs are turned, Polly will hoist Amanda over her shoulder and make her way back to the alley. The only thing they really have to fear is a full moon, because in this dream even moonlight is dangerous.

The chapter ends there. It would be hard to imagine a more effective dramatization of Polly's fear, helplessness and pain.

A shorter dream, merely mentioned in passing, can nonetheless hint at complex emotions underneath. The narrator of Lynne Reid Banks's *The Backward Shadow* has come through complicated story events involving her single motherhood of David, now a toddler, plus failed romances, a new business and the mental illness of her best friend, housemate and business partner. Near the end of the book, when the protagonist has emerged from her trials stronger than before, a briefly cited dream forms only part of her moment of self-realization:

Dottie and I would be real partners now; I had served my apprenticeship and could work with her on an even footing. The business now mattered to me as much as to her, and I knew almost as much about it. There seemed no reason at all why we shouldn't make a real success of it between us. And as for our common personal problem—to wit, men—in that elevated moment of anticipated happiness, there was no room for doubts. My old conviction returned to me full force—once one achieves self-reliance, once one has overcome the need for men, that's when they come, usually in

droves. I laughed into my pillow, fell asleep, and dreamed
of David, grown tall and handsome, making love to me . . .
horrors! But I woke the next morning laughing because it
was so obvious and Freudian, and I felt so happy suddenly,
I felt that I, too, had been cured.

Is your protagonist at an emotional turning point in the story? Is she
under enough pressure to be dreaming about the situation? Can you
concoct for her a dream that is both clear enough in meaning so that
it dramatizes her emotional state, but not so clear it seems mechanical? If so, recount her dream as she has it.

USING DREAMS WELL: CHILDHOOD MEMORIES
Another way to use dreams is to have the character experience the
dream not at the time of the story, but years earlier. He then recalls
the dream when story events remind him of it. This makes the dream
seem less author-engineered than when his current dreams conveniently convey current information. Herman Wouk uses this technique to enhance a descriptive passage in *The Caine Mutiny*. Willie
Keith is at his preliminary hearing for court-martial for mutiny:

There were a few dreams of childhood which Willie could
never forget, one in particular, in which he had seen God
as an enormous jack-in-the-box popping up over the trees
on the lawn of his home and leaning over to stare down at
him. The scene in the anteroom of the Com Twelve legal
office had the same quality of unreal and painful vividness.
There were the green close walls; the bookcase full of fat
regular legal volumes bound in brown and red; the single
fluorescent light overhead, throwing a bluish glare; the ash-
tray full of butts beside him on the desk, sending up a
stale smell; the "board of investigation," a surly, thin little
captain, his voice dry and sneering, his face the face of a
nasty post-office clerk refusing a badly wrapped package.

Does your story contain description—or thoughts, or exposition—
that might be similarly made graphic by a remembered dream?

Similar to remembered dreams are recurrent dreams, those
dreams we have over and over again throughout our lives. Suppose,

for instance, your character, who is now forty-seven years old and a successful surgeon, has had the same dream ever since he was thirteen: He's on the third floor of his high school, the school bus is pulling away without him, and he can't get his locker open. Throughout the course of your novel, you might briefly show this dream recurring whenever this grown man feels particularly incapable and at the mercy of external events. Used this way, it can add to his characterization, showing us a vulnerable side to a usually decisive person.

USING DREAMS WELL: LISTEN TO *THIS* NIGHTMARE!

Sometimes remembered dreams can be used effectively in dialogue. One character can recite last night's dreams to a second character— and by including that second character's reactions, you characterize both of them.

There are two possibilities. One, the character reciting the dream is the POV character. Here, for example, POV character Pamela is relating a dream to her husband, Ben:

> "I dreamed again last night about Judy," Pamela said at breakfast. She spoke carefully, keeping her voice steady. Lately Ben had seemed to flinch at hearing Judy's name.
>
> "Oh?" he said. He picked up the *Post.*
>
> "She was standing in the cemetery again, beside her grave. We were all there, even the babies, and I was crying. Then Judy came up to me and tapped me on the shoulder and said, 'Pam, honey—don't cry. I'm here.' I said, 'But you're dead!' and Judy said, 'Yes, well, you can't have everything.' "
>
> "Ummm," Ben said. He turned to the Metro section.
>
> "The odd thing was that after she said that, I felt better," Pamela said. But that didn't really do the dream justice. How to convey to Ben the warm, wonderful tide of comfort the dream had given her? Comfort that felt—never mind if this was irrational—directly from Judy herself. You can't have everything—that was Judy, her own personal mix of cheerful irreverence and practical acceptance, and just hearing it had made Pamela so happy she'd wanted to go on crying, but now not from grief. How to let Ben know the

difference this dream—unlike the others—had made for Pamela?

She said, "Ben, when I woke up, I felt so . . . so . . ."

"I think, Pam," Ben said, rustling the newspaper, "that it's morbid to start each day with talking about Judy. We could have some other topic of conversation at breakfast, don't you think?"

The content of Pamela's dream, her thoughts about it, Ben's reactions—all characterize these two people. And if the plot includes the dissolution of this marriage, Pamela and Ben's sharing (or nonsharing) of this dream also furthers that dissolution.

The other use of dreams in dialogue occurs when the character reciting the dream is not the POV character. Here you lose the chance to contrast the spoken version of the dream with the dreamer's thoughts about it. But you gain the chance to give more intimate reactions of the listener, who is the POV character. In W. Somerset Maugham's *Of Human Bondage*, for example, Mildred daily recites all her dreams to Philip, who is bored to tears by them. We see quite concretely both that Mildred is a drag and that Philip has fallen out of love. Her dreams form part of his nightmare.

A SPECIAL CASE: USING DAYDREAMS

Not all dreams, of course, happen when we're asleep. Because daydreams are under conscious control, they dramatize different aspects of a character: conscious wishes, plans and fantasies. Many writers use daydreams in this way.

One who takes the technique farther is Marilyn French in *Her Mother's Daughter*. French shows us in great detail the daydream that Belle has about her photographer daughter Anastasia, who has been sent on a photography assignment to the Middle East. In Belle's imaginings, Anastasia is feted by kings, lionized for her talent, superbly dressed in satin gowns, "disdainful and unattainable." Juxtaposed to Belle's daydream is Anastasia's reality:

She is happy to be on the road again, doing, riding in the wind, drying up under the desert sun, collapsing exhausted in a dusty hotel or on a sleeping bag laid beneath palm trees, the smell of camel dung on the air, the camels' squeaks and grunts punctuating the silence, night as night never comes where she lives . . . smelling camel dung and desert flowers and thinking of her mother.

The daydream's divergence from the reality shows us a lot about Belle's expectations about her daughter—and the burden those expectations place upon Anastasia.

What kind of daydreams does your character have? Do they reveal anything sufficiently significant to justify including one in your text?

" . . . AND NOW THE NEWS": HOW DAN RATHER CAN ILLUMINATE YOUR CHARACTER

Just as the nature of a character's dreams shows us her hopes and fears, her reactions to the daily news can show us how she views the world she must actually inhabit. It doesn't matter whether this "news" comes to her via TV, radio, newspapers, letters, war drums, town crier or interstellar ansible. It doesn't even particularly matter what specifics the news contains. What matters is her *response*.

Why? Let's explore that question through a detailed example.

A family is sitting around the living room after dinner, waiting for *Seinfeld*. The family consists of Grandma Ann, her son Bill and his wife Janet, sixteen-year-old Todd, Todd's girlfriend Karen, thirteen-year-old Melissa and ten-year-old Jack. All these people belong to the same socioeconomic group and ethnic background. They all talk roughly the same, which is with middle-class American diction. They all like potato chips, jeans and going to the mall. Except for the obvious differences of age and gender, they all look pretty much alike (even the girlfriend).

While they're waiting for their sitcom, they watch the news. These are the stories:

- Two major local companies are merging, causing both stocks to jump.
- One teen shot another fatally, allegedly during an argument over a leather jacket.
- Jimmy Carter has left on a peacemaking mission in a war-torn third-world country.
- Scientists have announced a major breakthrough in cancer research, involving experimental gene therapy.

- A storm will move in over the weekend, with heavy rain.
- The Chicago Cubs lost to the Pittsburgh Pirates, six to nothing.

As they listen to all this, what goes through the mind of each person in that living room?

First of all—does it matter? Yes, it does, even though none of these news stories has the slightest connection to your plot. These seven people's reactions matter because what *you* observe as you conveniently read their minds tells you more about *them* than about the news or their environment.

A wise man once said, "We see the world not as it is, but as we are." To discover what a person is really like, decipher his *map of reality*. We all carry one around inside, and it dictates which parts of reality we focus on and how we react to that focus.

For instance, Grandma Ann zeroes in on the shooting. Her inner monologue goes something like this: *Taking a life over a leather jacket! I don't know what's happened to people. It was never like this when I was young. The world has just gone downhill ever since . . . still, what can you expect from those people. If they'd all get jobs they could afford to buy their own jackets instead of . . . and leather isn't even a good buy, not warm enough, young people have no sense. We knew better when I was young. What a world! I'm glad my kids are all grown but still they certainly have room for improvement look at Jack drinking another beer he's going to get fat if he isn't careful. . . .*

And so on. Ann has chosen—although without being conscious of choosing—to focus on the shooting story. She remembers only vaguely that the news mentioned Jimmy Carter or a corporate merger, and she's under the impression that the Chicago Cubs are a football team. The shooting story matches her pre-existing beliefs about the world, her map of reality, and that's what dictates her reactions.

Bill, on the other hand, notices the shooting only in passing: one more act of modern urban violence. He's thinking about the merger of Acme Corporation and Widget Industries, because he owns stock in both. Would this be a good time to sell? And if he did, what should he invest in next? He thinks about this throughout the shooting, Jimmy Carter and cancer research, and returns his full attention to the screen during the weather report only, because he's planning on mowing the lawn on Saturday.

Janet munches potato chips mildly throughout the first three stories, half-listening. But her eyes fill with unexpected tears during the cancer research story. Her mother died of cancer just three months ago. Why couldn't the scientists have discovered this new gene-therapy breakthrough earlier, when it might have done her mother some good? Some people just never get a break.

Todd and Karen don't really register any of the news. They don't own stocks, don't attend schools where violence is a big issue, aren't interested in politics and are decades away from dying. They're most interested in gazing at each other.

Young Melissa, however, is an idealist. She pays close attention to the story about Jimmy Carter. How wonderful to have the power to help end war! When she grows up, she wants to do something like that. She won't just waste her life, like her parents. She's going to make a difference in the world: be a peace envoy, or a great spiritual leader. Or maybe—the cancer research story is on now—she'll be an important scientist and discover ways to save the planet from pollution. Her grades in science are very good.

Jack reads a comic book throughout the news until the sports come on. The Pirates won! All right! Now he can collect his fifty-cent bet from that stupid Keith Smith at school tomorrow!

All these people watched the same news program. But you'd never know it. Each saw the news not in terms of what happened that day, but mostly in terms of *who he or she is*. This is what makes imagining your characters' reactions to news broadcasts so valuable. You learn so much about them.

Try an experiment. Sit down and watch a news show not through your own eyes, but through your character's. Ask yourself:

- Which news story would interest him the most? Why?
- Which stories would he ignore, or only register peripherally?
- For the stories he does react to, what emotions are evoked? How intensely?
- What does all this say about his map of reality?

Once you know the answers to these questions, you're ready for the next step: deciding how to use your new insights into your character. You may decide the insights should be used only to help you better understand the way he views the world. Alternatively, you may decide to incorporate a news-watching scene directly into your story.

PUTTING THE NEWS INTO YOUR FICTION

A word of caution here. Scenes in fiction, especially short fiction, should do two things: deepen character *and* advance the plot. If a reacting-to-the-news scene is going to do only the former, you are much better off without the scene. Just let it form what journalists refer to as *deep background.*

Sometimes, however, both plot *and* character can be advanced by including a session with the news. If so, it provides a good way to let the reader glimpse the protagonist's map of reality.

For instance, note what catches Harry "Rabbit" Angstrom's attention in John Updike's *Rabbit Is Rich*:

> The music stops, the news comes on. A young female voice reads it, with a twang like she knows she's wasting our time. Fuel, truckers. Three-Mile Island investigations continue. Date for Skylab Fall has been revised. Somoza in trouble too. Stay of execution of convicted Florida killer denied. Former leader of Great Britain's liberal party acquitted of charges of conspiring to murder his former homosexual lover. This annoys Rabbit, but his indignation at this pompous pansy's getting off scot-free dissolves in his curiosity about the next criminal case on the news, this of a Baltimore physician who was charged with murdering a Canada goose with a golf club.

There's Rabbit captured in a perfect cameo: passing over the weighty news, interested in the sexual, airing his prejudices and finally interested most in the trivially bizarre.

Don DeLillo's characters in *White Noise*, on the other hand, are captivated by the large scale:

> That night, a Friday, we gathered in front of the set, as was the custom and the rule, with take-out Chinese. There were floods, earthquakes, mud slides, erupting volcanoes. We'd never before been so attentive to our duty, our Friday assembly. Heinrich was not sullen, I was not bored. Steffie,

brought close to tears by a sitcom husband arguing with his wife, appeared totally absorbed in these documentary clips of calamity and death. Babette tried to switch to a comedy series about a group of racially-mixed kids who build their own communications satellite. She was startled by the force of our objections. We were otherwise silent, watching houses slide into the ocean, whole villages crackle and ignite in a mass of advancing lava. Every disaster made us wish for more, for something bigger, grander, more sweeping.

Nothing could better capture this family's unhealthy, growing obsession with—and inhumane relish for—death and tragedy.

Sometimes news-reacting can be used to characterize not just an individual but an entire group. Here, in *A Tree Grows in Brooklyn*, are Betty Smith's first-generation, working-class men reacting to news in 1916. They're talking in a saloon, overheard by protagonist Francie Nolan:

> It's a fact. They're gonna stop making liquor and in a few years the country will be dry.
> A man that works hard has a right to his beer.
> Tell that to the president and see how far you get. . . .
> G'wan! They'll never give wimmen the vote.
> Don't lay any bets on it.
> If that comes, my wife votes like I do, otherwise I'll break her neck.
> My old woman wouldn't go to the polls and mix in with a bunch of bums and rummies. . . .
> Airplanes! Just a crazy fad. Won't last long.

An economical way to convey how fast the world is changing on these people.

But what if you write genre fiction, with its specialized conventions? Can you still use this device? Yes.

Regency romances, to take just one example, are set before radio or TV. But news is eternal. Georgette Heyer makes good use of this to differentiate her two heroines, Fanny and Serena, in *Bath Tangle*. The point of view is Fanny's:

. . . and in another moment they were in the thick of the sort of conversation Fanny had hoped might be averted. Rotherham seemed to have recovered from all his ill-humor; he was regaling Serena with a salted anecdote. Names and nicknames were tossed to and fro; it was Rotherham now who had taken charge of the conversation, Fanny thought, and once again she was laboring to keep pace with it. There was something about the Duke of Devonshire dining at Carlton House, and sitting between the Chancellor and Lord Caithness: what was there in that to make Serena exclaim? Ponsonby too idle, Tierney too unwell, Lord George Cavendish too insolent for leadership: what leadership?

"I *thought* they had made no way this session!" Serena said.

Serena loves political news and has a sharp mind to understand it; timid and sweet Fanny is bored. The same device can be—and is—employed by writers of historical mysteries, medieval thrillers and even far-future science fiction.

BUT WON'T INCLUDING THE NEWS DATE MY STORY?

One final consideration: Including contemporary news events may or may not make your story seem dated. It all depends on how specific the news is. *Rabbit Is Rich* is clearly 1979; Skylab is falling, the fuel crisis is on, the President collapses in a marathon. Updike intends his novel to belong to a definite time and place. On the other hand, reread the passage from *White Noise*. The news is generic, thereby avoiding pinning the novel to any specific year and so dating it. The choice is yours.

SUMMARY: USING DREAMS AND NEWS IN FICTION

- Except in special cases of fantasy, do not have your characters' dreams affect plot. Instead, use their dreams to characterize their personalities and/or current crises.
- Keep dreams brief relative to other methods of characterization.
- Choose from among current dreams, recurrent dreams and child-hood dreams recalled, using each when most applicable.

- Consider having a character relate his dream to another, so that you can include either the dreamer's hidden thoughts or the listener's hidden reactions.
- You can deepen your own understanding of a character by imagining how he would react to the news of his day: *what* stories he pays attention to, *why*, *how* he reacts and *how strongly*.
- You can also put your character's reactions to news directly into the story, if it serves a purpose there.
- To keep your story untethered to any specific year, manufacture generic news events.

chapter thirteen

THE BAD GUYS
How to Make Your Villains As Readable As Your Heroes

John Milton had a villain problem. Generations of scholars have noted that Satan, the villain in *Paradise Lost*, easily upstages Christ, Adam and an entire phalanx of archangels. Satan is more forceful, complex and interesting. He also ends up with all the best lines ("Better to reign in hell than serve in heav'n") and most of the best plot developments.

However, Milton was an exception. Many writers who can characterize their heroes well have trouble making their villains equally interesting and readable. All too often the villain ends up one-dimensional, a stereotype of evil that doesn't convey the horror intended because he's so drearily familiar. Or the villain is such a caricature of perversion that the reader can't suspend her disbelief. Or the villain is so weird that the reader is tempted to laugh—and the novel isn't supposed to be humorous. Or the villain is so powerless and wimpy that the reader thinks, "*This* guy is a problem? What's wrong with our hero that he lets this so-called villain bother him for half a second?"

So how *do* you create believable, interesting and suitably menacing villains? The first step is to recognize that there is more than one category of villain. In fact, there are five. You must decide which type suits your plot, since villainy is another area where character and plot are virtually inseparable.

YES, WE HAVE NO REPROBATES

Of course, you don't actually *have* to have a villain in your story at all. Many novels flourish without any bad guys. The conflict in these books comes from the wrongheadedness, moral muddles, human confusion and incompatible goals of basically sympathetic characters. Men and women being what they are, these qualities are often enough to create complicated plots and strong suspense, without any outside menace at work.

One famous example is Leo Tolstoy's *Anna Karenina*. Neither Count Vronsky nor Anna, the sympathetically drawn adulterers, is a villain. Neither is Anna's husband, who may be stiff-necked and boring but is not wicked. The misery that Vronsky and Anna encounter springs from a combination of their own choices, the values of their society, and the limitations of human beings, such as an inability to sustain passion in the face of isolation and idleness. *Anna Karenina* is a tragedy, ending in the despairing suicide of the heroine, but there are no villains here.

This raises the question: What *is* a villain? Who qualifies? Although this is clearly a philosophical question, open to hours of debate, let's set a fairly simple definition. A villain is "a character who from motives of selfish gain knowingly seeks to injure, kill or loot another person."

Within this definition, you can choose from five approaches to villainy. Each demands different techniques for intertwining characterization and plot.

THE ACCIDENTAL VILLAIN:
"I NEVER MEANT IT TO END THIS WAY"

The classic approach to tragedy, defined by Aristotle, is the "fatal flaw." A character does not set out to do anything wrong. But he has a weakness he cannot control, and that weakness moves him farther and farther along the path to wickedness, until finally he crosses over and performs an act of genuine villainy. He may bitterly regret this act. It may or may not destroy him.

The classic example is Shakespeare's *Macbeth*, in which Macbeth begins by strolling home through a forest, minding his own business, innocent of evil plans. Three witches prophesy that he will become king, activating Macbeth's fatal flaw: ambition. From that point on, he becomes more and more sucked in by circumstances, including his wife's ambition. Finally he murders the rightful king, an act he regrets the second he's done it. But it's too late. Macbeth is now doomed, and all the rest of the murders that confirm his villainy spring from trying to hold onto the power he bought with his first sin.

This approach to characterizing evil is just as valid today as when Shakespeare used it four hundred years ago. A contemporary example is John Knowles's novel *A Separate Peace*, which we looked at briefly in chapter nine. Sixteen-year-old Gene Forrester never intends to harm his best friend, Phineas. He admires and loves Phineas. He's also jealous. The jealousy grows throughout incident after incident in which Phineas, less bright and insightful than Gene, nonetheless triumphs through sheer charm and athletic ability. Eventually, when the two boys are standing dangerously high in a tree in one of Phineas's crazy stunts, Gene can't stand it anymore: not Phineas's confidence nor his own constant fear. He wiggles the branch, just a little, without thinking it through. And Phineas falls, is crippled and eventually dies of complications from the fall. One tiny, unthinking act—and Gene becomes a villain, at least to himself.

He also learns from what he has done that all villainy springs from fear. The novel ends thus, after all the schoolboys have turned eighteen and been sent off to fight World War II:

> Only Phineas was never afraid, only Phineas never hated anyone. Other people experienced this fearful shock somewhere, this sighting of the enemy, and so began an obsessive line of defense, began to parry the menace they saw facing them by developing a particular frame of mind. . . . All of them, except Phineas, constructed at infinite cost to themselves these Maginot Lines against the enemy they thought they saw across the frontier, the enemy who never

attacked that way—if he ever attacked at all; if he was indeed the enemy.

How do you construct a successful *accidental villain*? Not accidentally. Rather, you must take considerable care:

• Set up the fatal flaw early in your story. Gene's rivalry with Phineas is hinted at in the very first scene in story time: "He weighed a hundred and fifty pounds, a galling ten pounds more than I did." "Why did I let Finny talk me into stupid things like this? Was he getting some kind of hold over me?" " . . . and then Finny trapped me again in his strongest trap, that is, I suddenly became his collaborator." You, too, need to present many repeated variants of the trait that will eventually cause your character to commit evil.

• Make the character *more* than just his fatal flaw. We would not believe Gene, or find his act of cruelty nearly as compelling, if he were nothing but Phineas's jealous rival. Instead, Gene is also Phineas's friend, and Knowles includes scene after scene of their good times together. Gene is good at his studies, shrewd in his observations of others and needy of adult approval. Make sure *your* accidental villain is fleshed out with sympathetic character traits that nonetheless don't conflict with his fatal flaw. Spend wordage on this. Often, to make this easier, the accidental villain is a POV character.

• Keep the villain's reaction to his own villainy self-consistent. If you've drawn an introspective character like Gene, it's reasonable to believe he will think a lot about what he's done. If you've drawn one who, like Macbeth, has always been loyal to his king, he shouldn't suddenly become a conscienceless renegade who does the rest of his killing without a qualm (and Macbeth does not).

• If, on the other hand, your accidental villain has blundered into evil through sheer stupidity, he must go on being stupid about what happens to him next. Each of these character traits should be part of what you set up while fleshing out the character *before* his act of villainy. Be consistent, and your villain will be plausible.

THE EXAMINED VILLAIN: PORTRAIT OF EVIL

In contrast to the accidental villain, the *examined villain* intends to sin. He plans the arson or rape or serial murders, sometimes very carefully. What the author intends is to create a portrait of who such a person is and why he acts as he does. This is the villain's book and he, not the hero, is the protagonist, and also usually the POV character. There may not even be a hero.

Diverse examples of this approach include William Makepeace Thackeray's *Barry Lyndon*, a first-person portrait of a villain who doesn't know he's one; Truman Capote's *In Cold Blood*, in which the victims are not nearly as important or interesting as the psychology of the killers; and Thomas Perry's Edgar-winning *The Butcher's Boy*, which examines the techniques and thought patterns of a freelance hit man.

The Butcher's Boy illustrates an interesting facet of the examined villain: If the portrait is thorough enough, we can come to feel sympathy for even the coldest-blooded of killers. It's hard at times not to root for Perry's nameless protagonist, even while he's indiscriminately murdering wiseguys, FBI agents and a blameless United States senator. Is this character the villain or the hero? The line blurs.

Whether you're examining a repulsive villain or a semisympathetic one, you need to do the following:

• Make the villain a POV character. Otherwise, it's very difficult to give us the thoughts, emotions and childhood background that let you examine him thoroughly. Show us how he became what he is.

• Add something to the stereotype. If your villain fits into a class that's been overused lately—Mafia hit men, serial rapists who hate women, deranged Vietnam vets, rogue CIA agents, white supremacists—you're going to have to work twice as hard to create the character. You need to add something new to the portrait—without making it implausible. The butcher's boy, for instance, is *not* secretly a sentimental man who loves children. But he does have some unexpected facets: the modest way he lives between jobs; his affection for Eddie, his dead mentor and foster father; his awareness of the price he pays for his profession:

> The girl had put him in a bad mood, reminded him of how impatient he was for this trip to end so he could go back to Tucson and relax. It wasn't easy to live for days at a time without so much as talking to anybody, and for weeks without saying more than, "What's the soup of the day?"

- Look for the traits and details that make your examined villain individual enough to stand prolonged examination. He should have texture, complexity, personal quirks—all the things that go into creating any other character, and that we've discussed so far in this book.

- Be accurate and realistic in all other details of your story. You are asking us to stay with you during an examination of a character that we probably can't identify with and that we may find morally repulsive. Make sure the rest of the story—setting, secondary characters, law-enforcement procedures—does not cause us plausibility problems. If we can accept everything else, we are more likely to also accept your villain protagonist.

- Provide the villain with self-justification. Even Hitler thought he was justified in genocide. The more twisted and evil your villain, the more important it is to show us how he justifies his actions to himself. Everybody has an internal story about why they're actually right in what they've done. Show us his, and in terms we can believe that he believes. Do this by having his self-justifications invade every area of characterization we've discussed so far: thoughts, dialogue, background, peripheral attitudes, even dreams.

THE SURPRISE VILLAIN: OH! *HE* DID IT!

The *surprise villain* is the character who is introduced to us sympathetically, and we don't see his actual evil until farther into the story. A standard device in mysteries, it also can be used to good effect in other types of fiction. Classic examples are Willoughby in Jane Austen's *Sense and Sensibility*, Steerforth in Dickens's *David Copperfield* and Rebecca in Daphne du Maurier's *Rebecca*. Let's look at Rebecca.

She never appears in the novel, having already drowned when the unnamed narrator marries Rebecca's widower, Maxim de Winter. But everyone is full of praise for the dead woman, and through the shy and awkward second wife we get a textured, nuanced portrait of Rebecca: charming, gracious, organized, competent, beautiful, spirited, adaptable. Everything the poor narrator is not. The novel is nearly over before the second wife—and we—learn that in actuality Rebecca was cold, wanton, selfish and cruel enough to trick her husband into killing her so that she didn't have to do it herself.

How does du Maurier pull off such a surprise villain—one that seems to emerge plausibly from the setup of an entirely different personality? And how can you do the same? Some considerations:

- Don't make the surprise villain a POV character. Not even for one scene. This is cheating, because we expect to have access to all of a POV character's important thoughts, and the fact that she's seducing her brother-in-law, say, is fairly important. You can't conceal it.
- Plant hints that all is not as it seems. These should not be blatant, but they must be there, so that the POV character can recall them after the revelation and thereby lend it credibility. Maxim de Winter, for instance, does not like the stone cottage by the bay: "If you had my memories you would not go there either." Also, Maxim never mentions Rebecca's name. Choose such hints carefully, plant them unobtrusively and use them later.
- Make sure the two sides of your surprise villain—the positive Before and negative After—are plausible together. Rebecca's positive traits—charm, taste, brains, beauty—are not incompatible with being selfish and manipulative. Other positive-negative combinations would be harder to make credible. A person who is represented as boorish and stupid, for example, probably can't be revealed as an international art thief—that criminal career takes too much education, finesse and adaptability. Similarly, if your placid, constantly knitting grandmother is to be plausibly revealed as a surprise serial killer, we had better be shown some degree of anger, self-deception or sheer craziness long before the revelation.

STANDARD VILLAINS I: THE OVER-THE-TOP WEIRDOS

Standard villains are standard only in the function they fulfill in the plot: They're the unrepentant, untextured bad guys who are deliberately making life tough for the good guys. They're classical antagonists, generators of conflict, the black hats hassling Dodge City. They come in two varieties.

The first type, which is increasingly popular, are over-the-top exaggerations. The blackest of evil, the deadliest of weapons, the coldest of hearts, the most colorful of personalities. The movies have a lot to do with this: the Joker and Penguin in *Batman*, the mad bomber of *Speed*, right up to Oliver Stone's Mickey and Mallory of *Natural Born Killers*. In print, we have similar hyped-up, exaggerated villains: Loren Estleman's Lake Erie terrorists in *Kill Zone*; all of Ian Fleming's weirdos, killing people with bizarre inventiveness; the Walking Man in Stephen King's *The Stand*; legions of invading aliens in much (although not all) escapist science fiction.

The appeal of the over-the-top villain is not realism but novelty. As such, many of the methods of characterization we've discussed so far simply don't apply. This brand of villain does *not* need background, complexity, individuality, unique thoughts. You aren't creating a real person here, but a colorful sideshow. If that's what you really want, then you must:

• stretch your imagination. Anything not absolutely fresh will fail. Give the villain larger-than-life beliefs ("I am the devil incarnate"), crimes, weapons, daring. Don't hold back. Think big.

• match the villain's evil to the hero's weaknesses. In Ed McBain's *Doll*, the villain, a sexy temptress who ties up the cop hero and injects him with heroin to turn him into an addict, plays directly to his weaknesses: a dislike of being confined, and a male response to female nakedness. (Note: Drugs are not fresh or larger-than-life menaces now—but *Doll* was written in the early 1960s.)

• surround your weirdos with factual details. Although plausibility isn't as much of a requirement in this kind of book as in many others, accuracy in details can still help hook readers into accepting the rest. Estleman's weapons, from assault weapons to depth charges, perform as in real life. The police procedures in *Doll* are accurate. King uses actual Las Vegas geography in *The Stand*.

• enjoy your villains. This kind of book is not gritty, painful realism. If you don't have fun with it, neither will your reader.

STANDARD VILLAINS II: THE MUNDANE EVIL ALL AROUND US

The second class of villains who fulfill a standard plot function are actually the hardest of all to write. They are the mundane, no-larger-than-life antagonists who are evil out of stupidity or weakness or selfishness. They ruin (or at least, try to ruin) others' lives without being colorful, without being original, without repenting, without surprising us. They're criminals as most criminals are in reality—even though fiction is charged with creating more heightened emotion, and more coherent patterns, than does real life. No wonder they're hard to write.

Yet brilliant examples of the mundane villain abound. Captain Queeg, petty and tyrannical, in Herman Wouk's *The Caine Mutiny*. Bob Ewell in Harper Lee's *To Kill a Mockingbird*: "a low-down skunk with enough liquor in him to make him brave enough to kill children." Dennis Nedry in Michael Crichton's *Jurassic Park*, selling out his employers and exposing a parkful of researchers to unfenced cloned dinosaurs. Gary Cooper White, criminal drifter, who brutally murders Theresa Dunn because she won't let him stay the night, in Judith Rossner's *Looking for Mr. Goodbar*.

To create such villains, you must apply all the guidelines in every other category except over-the-top weirdos. Set up the character early. Give him a wider life, and more comprehensive personality, than just his villainy. Give him plausible self-justifications for his actions and consistent reactions to his crimes. Deepen stereotypes with unexpected twists. Surround your villain with as many accurate details as your hero.

VILLAIN CHECK: THE OTHER SIDE OF THE STORY

In short, creating a successful realistic antagonist takes the same level of work as creating a successful protagonist. Gary Cooper White, for instance, doesn't have nearly as many scenes as Theresa Dunn in *Looking for Mr. Goodbar*. But Rossner has taken care that the scenes White does have—his confession and the murder—are each packed with nuance and detail. We can see, hear, smell this guy. We are in his head (and a loathsome place it is). We know why he kills, and why he kills in the way he does. He is not just another cipher. He is Gary Cooper White, a dreary and horrifying moral vacuum.

Evil may be banal, but it shouldn't be insubstantial. Give it substance. To do that, employ all the same techniques you used to create your hero: appearance, dialogue, attitudes, hopes, fears, preferences, mannerisms, childhood background, dreams and desires.

One test of a good villain is: Could you write a book telling his side of the story? It would be a different book, surely, and you might not want to write it—but *could* you? Is your villain real enough, complicated enough, possessed of enough personal history so that you could tell his tale in addition to, or instead of, the hero's?

If not, think about the villain some more. Try to get into his head, hear his language, feel his fear (everybody's afraid of something—

more on this in a later chapter). Imagine his childhood. Think what he loves. Listen to what he tells himself just before he falls asleep at night. And try again.

When the answer is yes, everybody comes out ahead. Especially your reader.

SUMMARY: CREATING GOOD BAD GUYS

- Not all novels need villains.
- If you do have a villain, flesh him out as fully as you do the hero—unless he's an over-the-top weirdo in a fast-paced action book with no other literary goals.
- Make sure that over-the-top weirdos really *are*: outrageous, fresh and eye-catching.
- For accidental villains, set up the fatal flaw early and take care that the character is more than just his flaw.
- Provide villains with sufficient and heartfelt self-justification.
- Foreshadow surprise villains carefully enough so that readers will think back on the story and say, "Of course!"

DO I WANT TO KNOW YOU?
How to Create an Unsympathetic Protagonist Without Driving Your Readers Away

As we saw in the last chapter, a villain both is and is not a special case of characterization. He's *not* different from all your other fictional people in that he, too, needs to be well characterized. But he *is* different in that, depending on the type of villain he is, you may have to use some additional techniques to fully create him on the page.

The same is true of the protagonist who isn't really a villain, but isn't exactly someone you'd invite home to dinner, either. The unsympathetic protagonist.

Stories with unsympathetic protagonists often receive mixed reactions from readers. An aspiring novelist once wrote me a bewildered letter centering around this question:

> Can a short story survive if the narrator is disliked? My
> creative writing professor and a screenwriter I happen to

know both read a story of mine, and both were uncomfort-
able—disquieted?—by the depths of hate they felt for my
heroine . . . a bitter old woman.

It's a good question. Although both a story and a dinner party require us to spend time with unknown personalities, they are not the
same. We don't want to attend a dinner that features ugly surroundings, scanty food, social cruelty or poisoning the guests—but all these
things can be welcome in a good novel. Similarly, we're willing to
undergo intimate fictional encounters with people whom for various
reasons we might not invite into our homes: Don Corleone (too dangerous), Becky Sharp (too exploitive), George Babbitt (too boring),
Captain Queeg (too untrustworthy), Hannibal Lector (we don't wish
to *be* dinner).

Note that this list is widely eclectic. It includes characters that
some people might find sympathetic (Becky Sharp has her defenders,
including feminists that consider her to be making the best of the
hand Victorian women were dealt). It includes characters who are in
no way evil but merely unsympathetically limited and tedious (George
Babbitt). And it includes characters so unsympathetic (Hannibal
Lector) that they are in fact villains. There's no clear line between the
villain and the unsympathetic protagonist, just as there is no clear line
between the sympathetic and unsympathetic character. Each reader
draws those lines for himself. And each reader will differ in his reaction to spending four hundred pages with a person he does not like.
Some readers enjoy it. They like to dislike fictional characters.

On the other hand, no writer can afford to ignore that many people
read for identification. These readers want to experience vicariously
adventures they will never have in real life. They want the thrill of
falling into perfect love or solving a murder or making three million
dollars or escaping the villains in an unchartered boat. To experience
these things along with your protagonist, readers must first be able
to identify with your protagonist. And they won't want to do that if
your protagonist is as criminal as Don Corleone, as rapacious as Becky
Sharp, as wimpy as George Babbitt, as paranoid as Captain Queeg or
as monstrous as Hannibal Lector.

But on the other hand (we're running out of limbs here), *The
Godfather* (Mario Puzo), *Vanity Fair* (William Makepeace Thackeray),

Babbitt (Sinclair Lewis), *The Caine Mutiny* (Herman Wouk) and *The Silence of the Lambs* (Thomas Harris) were *all* bestsellers. When can you get away with an unsympathetic main character? There's no one straightforward answer—but there *are* some variables to consider. They take the form of seven questions to ask yourself before and as you write your fairly-off-putting-to-totally-repulsive character.

THE DESIGNATED READERS: WHAT AUDIENCE ARE YOU WRITING FOR?

Your intended audience is probably the most important factor determining how unsympathetic your main character can be. Certain kinds of commercial fiction—romance, "cozy" mysteries, romantic suspense, young adult—demand a sympathetic protagonist because of the identification phenomenon mentioned above. "Literary" fiction, however, which frequently aims to examine its characters rather than encourage identification with them, allows much more unpleasant protagonists. Even so, Thackeray, a very popular author in his day, was widely criticized for creating Becky Sharp. She was seen as an unflattering portrait of sacred womanhood. And Toni Morrison has not escaped criticism for providing very few portraits of black men that any black male reader would want to identify with.

The bottom line here is that your chances in commercial fiction are better with a sympathetic protagonist. You can save the unsympathetic characters for secondary roles. Until the movie version of his novel *The Silence of the Lambs*, Thomas Harris did not sell anywhere near as many copies—by an order of magnitude—as Danielle Steel, whose most prominent characters are always sympathetic. At the other end of the literary spectrum, the "little" magazines often seem to me to be bored by ordinary, nice, loving people as protagonists. Know your prospective audience when you plan your unsympathetic character.

THE NOVEL'S EYES: IS YOUR UNSYMPATHETIC PERSON THE ONLY POV CHARACTER?

It's easier to pull off an unpleasant protagonist if somebody more sympathetic is the POV character. This gives the reader someone else to identify with. For instance, we see Captain Queeg's story through the eyes of a likable young officer on his ship.

In a novel, you can also try a multiple POV. The amoral Becky

Sharp shares her multiviewpoint novel with the saintly Amelia Sedley. On the other hand, George Babbitt is both protagonist and POV character in his eponymous novel. However, Sinclair Lewis tells the story from a great enough distance, and with enough authorial comment, that we don't feel we're locked into this dim and tedious man's head all the time. The author becomes a second POV.

Can you tell your nasty character's story just as effectively from another POV, with a shared POV or using a fairly distant third person? Will what you lose in immediacy be redeemed by a more balanced perspective—and by some reader distance from a distasteful mind? Only you can make that decision.

THE ACCEPTABLE LIMITS: IS YOUR CHARACTER JUST TOO NASTY TO BE BELIEVABLE?

Sometimes the problem with an unsympathetic character isn't that she's a bitch but that she's not a believable bitch. Losers have just as complicated motives as anybody else. Bitter old women get that way because of real-life events. Children who pull wings off butterflies may be fiercely loyal to a friend or a pet dog. Ask yourself whether your unsympathetic character might become more plausible if you showed us her softer side, her history or her inner beliefs. Even if we still don't like her, believability may make us more willing to hear her story.

THE BIG CHANGE: WILL YOUR CHARACTER BECOME MORE SYMPATHETIC BY THE END OF YOUR STORY?

Many readers are willing to accept an unsympathetic protagonist if they sense that during the course of the story he's going to change. A character who learns great truths and becomes more human as a result can make a satisfying tale. I did this in my science fiction story "Mountain to Mohammed," in which a young doctor works illegally among the uninsured poor for the danger, self-aggrandizement and thrills. Only after he gets thrown out of the medical establishment does he realize the real rewards of practicing medicine.

To pull this off, your character has to be deluded or callow, not genuinely nasty, or the change won't be believable. Even so, you'll lose some readers unwilling to stick with the story long enough to discover that the protagonist changes. At least one reviewer has compared "Mountain to Mohammed" unfavorably to some of my other work because of its "unappealing protagonist."

JUST DESERTS: IS THIS A COMEUPPANCE STORY?

Many readers like stories about distasteful people—provided they get squashed in the end, restoring moral order to the universe. When the distasteful person is the protagonist, however, and not merely a supporting character, there are two pitfalls for the comeuppance story.

One is that, as with the protagonist-who-changes story, readers may not stick around long enough to find out there *will* be a comeuppance. To ensure they do, you have two choices. You can signal from the beginning that your unsympathetic protagonist not only is riding for a fall, but will get it. Do this through a prologue that hints at the ending, or through making it clear that the author also dislikes the villain, or through telling the story as a flashback, with the comeuppance a settled thing.

Or, you can make your unsympathetic protagonist seem harmless for the first part of the story, so that by the time we realize he's unsympathetic, we're already hooked on finding out what's going to happen. The second choice is more common.

A classic example is Edith Wharton's short story "Roman Fever." In the beginning its two middle-aged widows, Mrs. Slade and Mrs. Ansley, seem equally benevolent. They watch their two daughters, brilliant Barbara Ansley and mousy Jenny Slade, go off for an afternoon of pleasure in Rome. But as the ladies reminisce, we slowly realize that Mrs. Slade is an amoral and jealous woman who, twenty-five years ago, tried to have her friend killed because Grace Ansley was in love with Alida Slade's fiancé. Mrs. Slade mocks her friend, reminding her that Delphin Slade loved her and not Grace, that "I had him for twenty-five years, and you had nothing but that one letter he didn't write." She bullies Grace and admits she hates her, even though she believes Delphin never cared about Grace. It isn't until the last line of the story that Mrs. Slade gets her comeuppance: Taunted with having nothing of Delphin, Grace Ansley says quietly, "I had Barbara." It's a quietly devastating line.

The other danger of the comeuppance story is that it can seem contrived. Every adult knows that the universe doesn't always punish the bad guys. So if your universe is doing just that, it must seem to grow naturally out of the human forces opposing your bad guy, and not just from the author's desire to provide moral justice. Your unsympathetic character must stumble because he's too shortsighted or too ambitious or too cold to understand other people's strengths and alliances—not just because he's doing unsympathetic things.

THE STINGING EXAGGERATION: ARE YOU TRYING TO MAKE A BITING POINT ABOUT THE WORLD?

Sometimes the unsympathetic character isn't actually the protagonist; his world is, and he exists mostly to direct our attention to it. In this case, if the texture of the world is compelling enough, or relevant enough, or horrifying enough, many readers (not all) will accept the unsympathetic protagonist as an inevitable product of the environment you're showing them.

Consider two very different examples. George Babbitt, an uninteresting man in himself, succeeds as a character because Sinclair Lewis uses him to hold up a mirror to the (then contemporary) world of small-town American business. Lewis's aim is to show how boring, petty, stifling and mean-spirited that world was. Babbitt is its emblem, but it was the portrait of a way of life that made the book so hotly controversial, so much discussed—and so successful.

Similarly, Harlan Ellison's science fiction story "A Boy and His Dog" features a protagonist, Vic, as horrifying as Hannibal Lector—and for much the same reasons. But Vic is the logical product of a horrifying future, and that future is both the story's justification and its real protagonist.

A FINAL GOOD JUSTIFICATION FOR MR. REPULSIVE: DOES HE HOLD US RAPT?

This is the bottom line: If your character is unpleasant, unrepentant, unpunished, implausible, and atypical, is he just so sheerly fascinating that we'll want to read about him anyway? If so, it won't matter that he's unsympathetic; the story or book will sell. But he'd better be *really* fascinating.

And there's another caveat here: What's fascinating to one person may not be to another, no matter how well written. Case in point: Bret Easton Ellis's *American Psycho*, told from the POV of a psychopathic serial killer. The first publisher, alarmed by adverse publicity, dropped the book. But when it eventually came out, a great many people found the profoundly unsympathetic protagonist fascinating enough that they read the novel. Many others did not. Similarly if less dramatically, many readers praised John Updike for his four-novel series about Rabbit Angstrom, who is crude, selfish, misogynistic, and irresponsible. Others have disliked Rabbit from the beginning, refusing to spend one entire book with him, let alone four (one early reviewer called Rabbit "repulsive"). It's worth remembering that *unsympathetic* and *fascinating* are both subjective terms.

THE LAST WORD: TRADE-OFF

To return to the bewildered writer's question: *Can* a story or novel survive if the main character is disliked? Yes. Not only survive but flourish, provided the story gives us something else—perspective or change or justice or point or sheer fascination—to offset our dislike. As with so much else in writing fiction, an unsympathetic protagonist is a trade-off. Are you gaining more than you're losing?

If so, you don't have to invite him to dinner. Celebratory cocktails—say, in an editor's office—are quite enough.

SUMMARY: CREATING DISTASTEFUL PEOPLE WE'LL HAVE A TASTE FOR

- Unsympathetic protagonists work best in "literary" fiction, while unsympathetic secondary characters are a staple of commercial fiction. This is even more true if the unsympathetic protagonist is also the POV character.
- Unsympathetic characters need to be as fully developed as likable ones. Nastiness is not, in and of itself, sufficient characterization.
- In fact, unsympathetic characters probably need to be even *more* interesting than sympathetic ones, since the writer loses the interest-garnering technique of reader identification.
- If unsympathetic protagonists are going to get a comeuppance at the end, either disguise their nastiness early on, or hint that this is a just-wait-he'll-get-his story.
- If an unsympathetic protagonist is used to make a comment on a particular time and place, make sure the connection is very clear from the beginning.

chapter fifteen

THE INTELLIGENCE DOSSIER
A Wrap-Up System for Investigating Your Character

FBI agents need to know everything they can about the people who are key to their cases. So do novelists.

The FBI meets this need by keeping intelligence dossiers, adding to each as new information becomes apparent. Some writers do the same thing. They write biographies of their major characters before starting a book, add to these during the writing and refer to them often. To other writers, this whole idea is horrible. These are the seat-of-the-pants writers who rely on intuition, moment-to-moment inspiration and surprise to construct believable and interesting characters. They also rewrite extensively on the second draft, since they change their minds so often during the first one.

It doesn't matter which kind of writer you are. Different methods work for different people. But if you are the methodical, preplanning type, you might find this chapter useful before you begin writing a book. If you are the flying-blind type, this chapter can be used after you've finished the first draft and are ready to reconcile all your course changes into a single smooth trajectory.

What follows is one way to better understand your character: the dossier. It covers information that you should know about your protagonist, and probably should know about the other major characters as well. Different sections of the dossier concentrate on different kinds of knowledge. All sections have the same goal: to stimulate your thinking about your character. You may do only that with the dossier: think about some section(s) of it. Or you may decide to photocopy some, all or none of the sections as they seem to apply to your particular characters in your particular book, and fill them out. If you do, keep them for later reference.

PART 1
Just the Facts, Ma'am: Your Character's Basic Statistics

NAME _____

ALSO KNOWN AS (NICKNAMES) _____

AGE _____ BIRTHDATE _____ PLACE OF BIRTH _____

HEIGHT _____ WEIGHT _____ EYE COLOR _____

HAIR COLOR _____ STYLE _____

DISTINGUISHING MARKS _____

FATHER'S NAME _____

FATHER'S CURRENT STATUS ☐ LIVING ☐ DECEASED

MOTHER'S NAME _____

MOTHER'S CURRENT STATUS ☐ LIVING ☐ DECEASED

ETHNIC BACKGROUND _____

RELIGION _____

DEGREE OF RELIGIOUS PRACTICE _____

CURRENT ADDRESS _____

     ☐ RENTS ☐ OWNS

     BRIEF DESCRIPTION OF HOME _____

     _____

     OTHER OCCUPANTS OF CURRENT HOME _____

     _____

CURRENT OCCUPATION _____

CURRENT EMPLOYER _____

SIGNIFICANT PAST JOBS _____

INCOME LEVEL _____

EDUCATION _____

MARITAL STATUS

    ☐ NEVER MARRIED

    ☐ FIRST MARRIAGE—HOW LONG? _____

    ☐ SECOND MARRIAGE—HOW LONG? _____

    ☐ THIRD MARRIAGE—HOW LONG? _____

    ☐ DIVORCED—HOW LONG? _____

    ☐ SEPARATED—HOW LONG? _____

    ☐ WIDOW/WIDOWER—HOW LONG? _____

    ☐ OTHER _____

SPOUSE'S NAME _____

NAME BY WHICH CHARACTER ADDRESSES SPOUSE _____

SPOUSE'S OCCUPATION _____

CHILDREN

    _____ AGE _____

    _____ AGE _____

    _____ AGE _____

    _____ AGE _____

    _____ AGE _____

POLICE RECORD

    ☐ NO ARRESTS OR CONVICTIONS

    ☐ ARREST(S) FOR _____

    _____

    ☐ CONVICTION(S) FOR _____

    _____

    ☐ SENTENCE(S) SERVED _____

    _____

MEDICAL RECORD

GENERAL HEALTH

☐ EXCELLENT ☐ GOOD ☐ BELOW AVERAGE ☐ TERRIBLE

CHRONIC CONDITIONS _____

_____

CURRENT CONDITIONS _____

_____

PEOPLE OFTEN FOUND WITH OUTSIDE OF WORK _____

_____

_____

_____

ORGANIZATIONS OF WHICH HE/SHE IS A MEMBER _____

_____

_____

_____

PART 2
How Do I Recognize Him/Her? Preferences and Mannerisms

DRESS

☐ EXPENSIVE COUTURE CLOTHING, LONG-LASTING STYLES

EXAMPLE: _____

☐ EXPENSIVE COUTURE CLOTHING, TRENDY STYLES

EXAMPLE: _____

☐ GOOD QUALITY, CONSERVATIVE CLOTHING _____

_____

☐ GOOD QUALITY, UNCONSERVATIVE CLOTHING _____

_____

☐ WHATEVER EVERYBODY ELSE IN HIS/HER GROUP WEARS, WHICH IS

_____

☐ WHATEVER'S MOST COMFORTABLE; COMFORT IS MAIN VALUE

WHENEVER POSSIBLE _____

_____

☐ WHATEVER'S HANDY, DOESN'T REALLY CARE _____

_____

☐ DRESSING TO BE NOTICED—HOW AND WHY? _____

_____

☐ OTHER _____

_____

GROOMING

☐ EVERY-HAIR-PERFECT TYPE

☐ AVERAGE GROOMING AND CLEANLINESS FOR OWN GROUP

☐ CLEAN BUT SLOPPY

☐ DIRTY AND A SLOB

SPEECH

PACE ☐ TALKS FAST ☐ AVERAGE PACE ☐ TALKS SLOWLY

ACCENT/DIALECT _____

VOICE

☐ SHRILL

☐ AVERAGE

☐ DEEP

☐ UNUSUALLY MUSICAL

☐ UNUSUALLY AUTHORITATIVE

☐ OTHER_____

ANY FAVORITE PHRASES OR WORDS? _____

_____

USUAL CUSS WORDS, IF ANY _____

_____

MANNERISMS

GENERAL

☐ PROJECTS A CALM IMAGE

☐ VOLATILE—MOODS CHANGE, AND BODY LANGUAGE WITH IT

☐ USUALLY FIDGETY

☐ OTHER _____

POSTURE

☐ STIFF AND RIGID

☐ STANDS STRAIGHT BUT NOT STIFFLY

☐ AVERAGE—VARIES WITH MOOD

☐ SLUMPED AND DEFEATED-LOOKING

☐ FLEXIBLE AND GRACEFUL

☐ USUALLY RELAXED

☐ SLOUCHY AND CARELESS

☐ OTHER _____

GESTURES

☐ DOESN'T GESTURE MUCH

☐ GESTURES ARE DELIBERATE AND CONTROLLED

☐ GESTURES MOSTLY WHEN EXCITED/UPSET

☐ GESTURES MUCH OF THE TIME

☐ GESTURES WILDLY, EVEN WEIRDLY

FAVORITE GESTURE _____

WHEN DOES HE/SHE USE IT? _____

HABITS

SMOKER? ☐ NO ☐ FORMER SMOKER

☐ YES—WHAT AND HOW MUCH? _____

DRINKER? ☐ NO ☐ FORMER DRINKER

☐ YES—WHAT AND HOW MUCH? _____

DRUGS? ☐ NO ☐ FORMER USER

☐ YES—WHAT AND HOW MUCH? _____

MONEY

☐ PRUDENT, CAUTIOUS—SAVES MONEY

☐ AVERAGE—SOME DEBTS, SOME SAVINGS

☐ SPENDS WHATEVER HE/SHE HAS, SOON AFTER ACQUIRING IT

☐ DEEP IN DEBT

☐ INTO CRIMINAL ACTIVITIES FROM FINANCIAL NEED

VEHICLE

☐ DOES NOT OWN A PERSONAL VEHICLE BECAUSE _____

_____

☐ LUXURY CAR MAKE _____ YEAR _____

DETAILS _____

☐ STANDARD VEHICLE MAKE _____ YEAR _____

DETAILS _____

☐ OLD/DILAPIDATED VEHICLE MAKE _____

YEAR _____ DETAILS _____

☐ OTHER _____

LEISURE/CULTURAL PREFERENCES

ENJOYS SPORTS? ☐ NOT PARTICULARLY ☐ YES

HOW MUCH? ☐ MILDLY ☐ A LOT ☐ RABID FAN

WHAT KIND(S)? _____

ENJOYS MUSIC? ☐ NOT PARTICULARLY ☐ YES

HOW MUCH? ☐ MILDLY ☐ A LOT ☐ RABID FAN

WHAT KIND(S)? _____

ENJOYS READING? ☐ NOT PARTICULARLY ☐ YES

HOW MUCH? ☐ MILDLY ☐ A LOT ☐ RABID FAN

WHAT KIND(S) OF BOOKS? _____

ENJOYS DANCE? ☐ NOT PARTICULARLY ☐ YES

HOW MUCH? ☐ MILDLY ☐ A LOT ☐ RABID FAN

WHAT KIND(S)? _____

ENJOYS THEATER? ☐ NOT PARTICULARLY ☐ YES

HOW MUCH? ☐ MILDLY ☐ A LOT ☐ RABID FAN

WHAT KIND(S)? _____

ENJOYS MOVIES? ☐ NOT PARTICULARLY ☐ YES

HOW MUCH? ☐ MILDLY ☐ A LOT ☐ RABID FAN

WHAT KIND(S)? _____

ENJOYS THE OUTDOORS? ☐ NOT PARTICULARLY ☐ YES

HOW MUCH? ☐ MILDLY ☐ A LOT ☐ RABID FAN

DOING WHAT OUTSIDE? _____

ENJOYS GOING OUT? ☐ NOT PARTICULARLY ☐ YES

HOW MUCH? ☐ MILDLY ☐ A LOT ☐ SELDOM HOME

GOING WHERE? _____

IS GOOD FOOD IMPORTANT TO HIM/HER?

☐ NOT PARTICULARLY ☐ YES

HOW IMPORTANT? ☐ MILDLY ☐ A LOT ☐ TRUE GOURMET

WHAT KIND(S) OF FOOD? _____

CAN HE/SHE COOK? _____ HOW WELL? _____

ENJOYS SHOPPING? ☐ NOT PARTICULARLY ☐ YES

HOW MUCH? ☐ MILDLY ☐ A LOT ☐ ADDICTED

SHOPPING FOR WHAT? _____

WHERE? _____

HOME

WHERE DOES THE CHARACTER LIVE?

☐ BIG CITY ☐ SMALL TOWN

☐ RURAL AREA ☐ OTHER _____

WHERE WOULD HE/SHE PREFER TO LIVE?

☐ BIG CITY ☐ SMALL TOWN

☐ RURAL AREA ☐ OTHER _____

WHY DOESN'T HE/SHE LIVE THERE? _____

WHAT KIND OF HOME?

☐ APARTMENT ☐ HOUSE ☐ TRAILER ☐ OTHER _____

WHAT KIND OF HOME WOULD HE/SHE PREFER?

☐ APARTMENT ☐ HOUSE ☐ TRAILER ☐ OTHER _____

WHY DOESN'T HE/SHE LIVE THERE? _____

DECOR OF PERSONAL SPACE CONTROLLED BY *THIS* CHARACTER

CAREFULLY PLANNED? ☐ YES ☐ NO

EXPENSIVE? ☐ YES ☐ NO

NEAT? ☐ YES ☐ NO

CLEAN? ☐ YES ☐ NO

COMFORTABLE? ☐ YES ☐ NO

ATTRACTIVE? ☐ YES—TO WHOM? _____

☐ NO—TO WHOM? _____

CLUTTERED? ☐ YES ☐ NO

BASIC OVERALL STYLE/IMPRESSION _____

_____

PETS

DOES HE/SHE HAVE ANY? ☐ YES ☐ NO

IF NO, WHY NOT?_____

WOULD HE LIKE A PET? _____ WHAT? _____

IF YES, WHAT PETS DOES HE/SHE HAVE? _____

_____

WHY DID HE/SHE ACQUIRE THEM? _____

HOW IMPORTANT ARE THESE PETS TO HIM/HER? _____

HOW WELL DOES HE/SHE TREAT THE PETS? _____

PART 3
The People Around Your People: His/Her Social Ties

HOW DOES THE CHARACTER TREAT AND/OR GET ALONG WITH:

SPOUSE? _____

CHILDREN? _____

PARENTS? _____

SIBLINGS? _____

THE OPPOSITE SEX? _____

CHILDREN IN GENERAL? _____

NEIGHBORS? _____

FRIENDS? _____

PEOPLE MORE SUCCESSFUL THAN HE/SHE IS? _____

PEOPLE LESS SUCCESSFUL? _____

BOSS? _____

UNDERLINGS AT WORK? _____

COMPETITORS AT WORK? _____

THE LOCAL POLICE? _____

THE IRS? _____

ANYONE WHO CHALLENGES HIM/HER? _____

ANYONE WHO ANGERS HIM/HER? _____

ANYONE WHO HELPS HIM/HER? _____

ANYONE WHO ASKS FOR HELP? _____

PART 4
Everybody Gets Twenty-Four Hours:
How Does He/She Spend a Typical Day?

WAKING UP

WHO ELSE IS SLEEPING IN THE SAME BED? _____

WHAT TIME DOES HE/SHE WAKE UP? _____

WHAT WAKES HIM/HER UP—ALARM? DOG? WIFE? _____

_____

IS HE/SHE CHEERFUL IN THE MORNING? ☐ YES ☐ NO

DOES HE/SHE EAT BREAKFAST? WHAT? _____

WHAT DOES HE/SHE DO DURING BREAKFAST—READ, TALK, WATCH TV,

FEED KIDS, ETC.? _____

DRESSING

IS THIS A BIG DEAL, CONSUMING TIME AND THOUGHT? ☐ YES ☐ NO

WORK

HOW DOES HE/SHE GET THERE? _____

_____

DOES HE/SHE ANTICIPATE, DREAD, RESENT, ETC., THE WORK AHEAD?

☐ YES ☐ NO

DOES HE/SHE HE GIVE THE JOB GENUINE ATTENTION AND EFFORT?

☐ YES ☐ NO

DOES HE/SHE ENJOY THIS WORK? ☐ YES ☐ NO

WHY? _____

IS HE/SHE GOOD AT THIS JOB? ☐ YES ☐ NO

WOULD HE/SHE RATHER BE DOING SOMETHING ELSE? ☐ YES ☐ NO

WHAT? _____

HOW LONG AND HARD IS THE WORK DAY? _____

DOES HE/SHE STOP FOR LUNCH? ☐ YES ☐ NO

WHERE? _____

EATING WHAT, TYPICALLY? _____

WITH WHOM? _____

DINNER

WHO PREPARES HIS/HER MEAL? _____

WHO DOES HE/SHE EAT IT WITH? _____

WHAT DOES IT TYPICALLY CONSIST OF? _____

_____

DOES HE/SHE ENJOY THE MEAL? ☐ YES ☐ NO

WHY? _____

WHAT GOES ON DURING DINNER—TV, CONVERSATION, FIGHTING,

READING, ETC.? _____

_____

WHO CLEANS UP? _____

_____

EVENING

WHAT DOES YOUR CHARACTER DO ON A TYPICAL EVENING?

_____

WHERE? _____

WITH WHOM? _____

HOW MUCH DOES HE/SHE ENJOY IT? _____

WHAT WOULD HE/SHE PREFER TO BE DOING INSTEAD? _____

_____

WHY DOESN'T HE/SHE DO THAT? _____

IS THE EVENING ATMOSPHERE PLEASANT, CALM, TENSE, FRENETIC,

WARY, FUN, PRODUCTIVE, OTHER? _____

BEDTIME

DOES HE/SHE USUALLY GO TO BED AT A CONSISTENT TIME? ☐ YES ☐ NO

WHAT TIME? _____

WITH WHOM? _____

WHEN DOES BEDTIME OCCUR AT A DIFFERENT TIME? _____

_____

DOES HE/SHE USUALLY FALL ASLEEP RIGHT AWAY? ☐ YES ☐ NO

IF NO, WHAT IS HE DOING IN THE MEANTIME—READING, WATCHING TV,

SEX, TOSSING AND TURNING, ETC.? _____

HOW MUCH DOES HE/SHE ENJOY THIS ACTIVITY? _____

_____

DOES HE/SHE DREAM A LOT, LITTLE, OR NEVER? _____

ARE MOST OF HIS/HER DREAMS SCARY, PLEASANT, SEXUAL, ETC.? _____

_____

_____

IS ANY ONE DREAM RECURRENT? ☐ YES ☐ NO

WHAT? _____

DOES YOUR CHARACTER SLEEP PEACEFULLY THROUGH THE NIGHT,

RESTLESSLY, OR VERY BADLY? _____

PART 5
Deep Inside: Your Character's Inner Life

WHAT IS HIS/HER EARLIEST MEMORY? _____

_____

IF HE/SHE WERE SUDDENLY MUCH MUCH RICHER, WHAT WOULD HE/SHE DO

WITH THE MONEY? _____

WHAT IS HIS/HER STATED DREAM IN LIFE? _____

WHAT DOES HE/SHE REALLY LONG FOR, UNDERNEATH? _____

_____

WHAT EVENT IS HE/SHE MOST AFRAID MIGHT HAPPEN? _____

_____

WHO DOES HE/SHE, IN HIS/HER DEEPEST SOUL, REALLY LOVE BEST

IN THE WHOLE WORLD? _____

WHAT WOULD HE/SHE BE WILLING TO DIE FOR, IF ANYTHING? _____

_____

WHAT DOES HE/SHE BELIEVE ABOUT GOD? _____

ABOUT THE PURPOSE OF LIFE? _____

ABOUT AN AFTERLIFE? _____

WHAT DOES HE/SHE ACTIVELY WORK TO GAIN OR KEEP OR PROTECT—NOT

MERELY SAY IS IMPORTANT, BUT ACTUALLY INVEST TIME AND EMOTION

IN—MONEY, FAME, FAMILY, LOVE, COUNTRY, REVENGE, ETC.? _____

_____

HOW WOULD HE/SHE DESCRIBE HIMSELF/HERSELF, IF TOTALLY HONEST?

_____

_____

_____

IN A SINGLE WORD, HOW WOULD *YOU* THE AUTHOR SUM UP THIS CHARACTER'S

ATTITUDE TOWARD THE WORLD—INTERESTED, OPTIMISTIC, DEFEATED,

EXPLOITIVE, COMPASSIONATE, DISSATISFIED, POWER-MAD, CONTROLLING,

HAPPY, ETC.? _____

_____

WOULD YOUR CHARACTER AGREE WITH YOUR ASSESSMENT? ☐ YES ☐ NO

WHY OR WHY NOT? _____

_____

_____

NOW THAT I KNOW YOU . . .

You've compiled the dossier on your character—bit by bit or all at once, written down or not, in depth or just enough to suit his role in the novel. Now what? Besides referring to it as you work to make sure that he isn't forty-three years old in chapter eight and forty-nine in chapter seven, what do you do with the dossier? How can it help you?

It can help generate plot.

Ideally, this should happen as you fill it out (bit by bit or etc.). You come, for instance, to "Pets" and think, *Well, all right, does this guy have a pet?* Yes, he has a dog. And "How does he treat the pet?" Badly. He's neglectful, which fits with the rest of his character. He forgets to feed the dog. He doesn't give it water in the summer. The poor beast barks in misery. In fact, the dog barks and a neighbor comes over to check on him. Outraged, she calls the Humane Society. And their *hassling* of him comes to the attention of his ex-wife, who sees a chance to cause him trouble. . . . You've crossed over from characterization to plot. Moreover, the plot development is springing naturally from consistent characterization.

Another example: Thinking about the dossier, you ponder "What event is he most afraid might happen to him?" You realize you don't know. You give this question some time, thinking over everything your character has done so far, getting a better feel for his psyche. And finally you realize that he's afraid of public failure. He doesn't put this into words—but now you have. A public humiliation, with everyone laughing at him, would devastate this guy. And if it *did* happen, how would he react? With rage? With so much shame that he would leave town? Or would he, over time, grow past it and emerge a stronger person, more guided by inner values? Maybe that public humiliation should happen in the book. You see how to set it up. Then, afterward, the character could. . . .

You are committing plot.

More on this in the next chapter.

SUMMARY:
YOUR OWN PERSONAL INTELLIGENCE AGENCY

- A methodical approach to investigating your protagonist can make you aware of aspects of character you may not have thought about.

- The dossier should be used whenever it fits best into your particular writing process—before you begin, after the first draft, somewhere in the middle, etc.
- Think about the dossier questions more completely for your protagonist than for secondary characters, who may not need to be so fully developed.
- Use what you learn about your character(s) to generate plot developments for the novel.

part three

Character and Plot

chapter sixteen

THE YELLOW BRICK ROAD
How to Start Anywhere and Arrive at Plot

One definition of plot is that it's "just one damn thing after another."

Not, however, just *any* damn thing. In fact, in some ways, plot is perhaps the most critical aspect of fiction. "I want well-plotted stories," says the Eminent Editor. (Don't we all?) "What's it about?" asks Semi-interested Reader, holding a new novel in her hand and meaning "What's the plot about?" "But it doesn't have any real plot!" wails the devoted reader of Charles Dickens upon finishing a story by Grace Paley. Plot, plot, plot. It's enough to make you think we're all conspirators in an endless Machiavellian takeover.

And so we are. We all want—at least vicariously—drama, action, things to happen. But not just any things. Things that catch and hold our interest, which usually means things that have gotten screwed up. Nobody wants to read about things that are humming along in tranquillity. In our lives we want tranquillity; in our fiction we want an unholy mess, preferably getting unholier page by page.

Perhaps the definition of plot in the first paragraph of this chapter should read "one damn*ed* thing after another," because events that are damned—that bedevil our characters with physical or mental pitchforks—are what make up plot. That bedeviling is what we're really after when we read fiction.

In short, we want conflict.

HOW CHARACTER AFFECTS CONFLICT

Conflict is the place where character and plot intersect. A novel includes several such intersections. Four of the most important are conflict perception, character reaction, conflict resolution, and theme. Let's look at each.

Character Determines What Constitutes a Conflict

Different people—both real-life and fictional—consider different things to be a conflict. I know a man who can make a crisis out of anything: a passing remark, lost keys, a slight fall in the stock market. All of it portends doom and leads to endless confrontations, decisions, drama. I also know another man who is so calm by temperament that for him, nothing less than a death in the family would be considered a crisis. And even that wouldn't be a conflict, but only a grief.

What constitutes a conflict for your character should grow out of what he values, what he struggles for, what matters to him individually. For some characters, leaving home (physically, emotionally) is an immense struggle. Others just pack and go.

What is giving *your* character problems? To answer, you must know who he really is.

Character Determines How Your Protagonist Copes With the Conflict Once He Has It

The list of ways human beings meet conflict is endless. It includes:

- denial that there is a problem
- rational problem-solving
- becoming ill with stress
- relying on hope
- creating art

- seeking outside allies
- turning to professionals
- blaming someone else
- alcohol and/or drugs
- going crazy
- getting someone else to deal with the problem
- throwing a tantrum
- prayer
- homicide
- becoming depressed and withdrawing from life
- giving up and passively accepting fate
- forming a committee
- placating—peace at any price
- punishing anyone who points out that there is a problem ("Shoot the messenger.")

- trying harder
- leaving: the job, the scene of the crime, the marriage, the country
- turning pain into helping others
- torturing small animals
- hunting large animals
- trying to stay in control of everything
- learning better to avoid the same conflict again
- self-sacrifice to aid others
- negotiation and compromise
- suicide
- covering tracks to avoid blame
- revenge
- courage
- many more

How does your protagonist react to the conflict you've given him? The answer will depend on his individual character. And his reactions will in turn determine plot incidents.

Character Affects, if Not Determines, the Conflict Resolution

Sometimes the resolution, admittedly, is beyond your character's control. Frederick Henry in Ernest Hemingway's *A Farewell to Arms* could not control the fact that Catherine dies in childbirth. Francis Urquhart could not control the fact that he is brought down as Prime Minister of England in Michael Dobbs's novel *To Play the King* (although not in the television version).

In other books, however, the protagonist does resolve the conflict by summoning from within himself aspects of character that he himself may not have known he possessed. Jane Eyre, to take a classic example, refuses to marry Mr. Rochester for reasons of morality (he has a wife living) and self-respect (she will not live with him as less than his equal). This paves the way for Mr. Rochester to become a grieving recluse, who is alone with his mad wife when she sets the mansion afire. He, because of aspects of his character, tries to save her life, and in the process she jumps from the roof and he is blinded. This clears the stage for Jane to return to him. Had she not left in the first place, the book's resolution would have been much different.

Or, consider a more contemporary example: John Grisham's best-selling *The Firm*. Mitch McDeere, the protagonist, is not responsible for the fact that he is in life-and-death conflict with the Mob, the FBI and his employers. *They* have created this situation. But Mitch resolves it by outwitting all three antagonists. He does this by exercising certain aspects of his character: intelligence, daring, ambition and a certain disregard for the law—despite being a lawyer himself.

What aspects of your protagonist's character will affect how the conflict ultimately is resolved?

Character Decides How the Protagonist Feels About the Conflict Resolution

This is actually your story's theme, and so will be more fully discussed in chapter twenty-four. For now, let's look at just a brief, hypothetical example: Two novels are written about a woman's struggle to find love. In both books, she doesn't find it. In the first novel, she ends up defeated and bitter. In the other, she discovers that she is strong enough to stand alone, and even enjoy it. The resolutions are identical, but how the protagonist *feels* about each resolution is not. This means that the first book conveys the message "Love is destructive." The second conveys "Losing something can show a person positive paths."

How does your character feel about the plot resolution—based on her individual personality? What does that say about the worldview implied by the book as a whole?

So we're agreed: Character affects plot at several critical places. But how do you actually construct all this? How do you first choose a protagonist? After that, how do you weave conflict and character together? Where do you *start*?

Anywhere you can.

GETTING TO CHARACTER FROM ANYWHERE ELSE AT ALL

Let's say you have an interesting idea for a story. Or a setting. Or a character. Or maybe just an intense image. Ursula K. Le Guin began *The Left Hand of Darkness* with no more than that. So did William Faulkner, with *The Sound and the Fury*. Le Guin's image was two figures hauling a sledge across a remote sheet of ice. Faulkner's was a little girl with muddy underpants up in a pear tree.

But now what? How to go from image—or character or setting or idea—to an actual story?

The first step is to turn whatever you have into a character. Fiction (like life) happens to people. So you need questions to ask yourself that will give you a vivid character with many fictional possibilities.

If you're starting from a setting (for more on starting with setting, go back and reread chapter three), ask yourself:

- Who lives here?
- What does she want?
- Why does she want it?
- How hard is this goal to reach? (It should be hard. It may be impossible. The setting should contribute to its difficulties.)
- Who else lives here that might affect the protagonist's pursuit of her goal?

If you're starting from an idea (for instance, "I want to write a book about the effect of AIDS on a family," or, "I want to write a novel about a terrorist attack on the White House," or, "I want to write a romance about two people working for opposite sides on an oil-spill dispute"), ask yourself:

- Who will be affected by this idea? Make a list.
- Of the people on the list, which ones will be hurt the most? (These people, or their direct advocates, make good protagonists. They have the most at stake.)
- Why is this protagonist involved? What does he want?
- What can go wrong with this idea? (Remember, fiction is about things going wrong.)
- How does this character react to things going wrong with his plans?

If you're starting from an image, ask yourself:

- Is it an image of a person? If so, who is this person? What is she doing? Why? What is she trying to accomplish? What are her emotions at this particular moment? Why?
- If there's no person in the image (a deserted Aztec pyramid, a jeweled music box that plays a lost Mozart song), who can you put there? Who is interested in this image? Why? What does she want? What is she trying to accomplish? Why?

If you're starting with a character, so much the better. Now ask yourself who this person really is. Use the dossier in chapter fifteen to focus your thinking, if you wish. In fact, no matter where you start, the dossier can be of use in pointing your character creation in directions that may not have occurred to you.

So now you have a character. On to the next step.

GETTING TO PLOT FROM CHARACTER

Probably some plot elements have already occurred to you at this point; it's hard to picture a character in a total vacuum. Most likely he's doing *something*. But it's possible the plot is still rudimentary, fragmented or unsatisfactory. Now what?

You need something to further direct and focus your thinking. One way is to go to the source: the wellsprings of human behavior. Concentrate on those universal drives that power all of our actions, in all times and all cultures. Here lie rich motherlodes of fictional gold.

Let's illustrate how you can mine them using two of the strongest human emotions: fear and love. Psychologists tell us that these drives directly or indirectly motivate much behavior. They can also motivate your story by weaving together character and plot.

FEAR: THE BOGEYMAN WILL GET YOU

Human infants come with a few fears built in: fear of falling, fear of very loud noises. During the first year of life, the number of fears grows: fear of separation from Mommy, fear of strangers, fear of dogs or vacuum cleaners or elevators or lightning or dozens of other possibilities. Babies differ (a few aren't afraid of anything, which makes their *parents* afraid). In coming years, children will add fear of failure, fear of "looking dumb," fear of being different, fear of not being unique, fear of being unlovable, fear of death.

Over time, rather than face fear directly, the mind will also learn to fear *symbols* of its real anxieties. Thus, by the time we're adults, we're capable of fearing almost anything, for buried and twisted reasons of self-protection. And I mean anything. There are people who are morbidly afraid of spiders, or thunderstorms, or driving a car, or leaving their house, or comets or forks or asphyxiating constriction by their own underwear (really).

What does all this have to do with plot?

Knowing what your characters fear is a wonderful way to generate plot ideas and story resolutions. Think about two things: *what* your character fears, and *how* that fear is likely to make her react. You do this on not one but two levels: the immediate situation and her subconscious terrors. The latter drives the former.

This is getting complicated. Let's clarify it with some examples.

FEAR AND REACTION IN THE MATERNITY WARD

Suppose you are writing a story about a couple searching for a name for their new baby. This doesn't sound like a very dramatic or fearful situation—certainly not the equivalent of, say, a detective faced with a serial killer. Yet even in the quiet of a hospital maternity ward, fear can help you understand your characters and develop your plot.

What is the wife afraid of, deep down? Perhaps she's the kind of person who has always been afraid of being abandoned. She reacts to this fear, which she doesn't even know she has, by constantly trying to please other people. Do you know anybody like this? I certainly do. They're accommodating to the point of being doormats. People take advantage of them all the time. They just cling harder.

How is this likely to make her react to the search for baby's name? On the surface, such people react by saying, "Oh, I don't care. You choose." But perhaps the new mother is clinging to more than one person (this is common). She doesn't want to displease any of them. And her father wants his grandson to carry his name, since he has no sons to bear it. His only son was killed during Desert Storm.

The husband, meanwhile, has his own deep fears. He's afraid of not being in control. This is, in fact, why he married such an accommodating wife. His fear leads him to react by insisting on his own choice of names. First name *and* middle name.

Do you see a story shaping up here full of conflict over issues of family, identity and power? It could, in fact, be quite a good story. And all generated by fear.

Note that it doesn't really matter *why* the wife is afraid of being abandoned or the husband is afraid of being not in control. If you want to, you can invent childhoods for each to account for the persons they became. But you don't need to do this. You only need to understand what buried fears drive them. Nor do you ever need to name the fears in the story itself. In fact, you probably shouldn't. A story is not the same as a psychological case study. It's enough that you yourself understand your character's way of reacting to fear, and that you *show* it to us in convincing action and dialogue.

FEAR AND REACTION IN SCOTLAND YARD

"That's all right for quiet, subtle, character-driven fiction, you may say. But I write mysteries. Or science fiction. Or techno-thrillers. Or romance. Deeply buried fears aren't necessary for my characters. What I need is an exciting plot."

Deeply buried fears can help generate exciting plots.

Consider a few examples from the best-seller list. Granted, I don't *know* how Michael Crichton or Terry McMillan or P.D. James think up their plots. But I can easily imagine arriving at the plots of *Jurassic Park*, *Waiting to Exhale*, or *Devices and Desires* through thinking about what the characters fear and what they do to quell those fears.

Start with John Hammond, *Jurassic Park*'s billionaire founder. What might he fear? Aging, dying. How does he react? By building a monument to himself, a stupendous theme park in which he, like God, has (re-)created an entire species. And he won't let anything convince him to limit the park, this proof of his God-like immortality—not warnings from scientists or technical danger signs or even an escaped Tyrannosaurus Rex. From Hammond's megalomaniac drive spring all the plot events of the novel.

McMillan's *Waiting to Exhale* reflects its characters' fears in the very title. All four protagonists are holding their breath until they can find someone to love. They are afraid of being unloved, alone—even though some of them do learn during the course of the novel how to do that.

Adam Dalgliesh, P.D. James's detective, at first glance does not seem like a very fearful man. But consider. Detectives are driven—

some of them maniacally—to solve crimes and catch criminals. Why? Many of them fear not being in control. Others fear authority, and so deal with it by *becoming* the authority (this is especially true of those detectives who are in constant conflict with their own superiors). Others fear failure, and so are driven to test themselves against a problem—a juicy murder—over and over. How would such a character react to frustration by a wily killer? Perhaps with a sense of personal anger, carefully controlled—or not.

What does *your* character fear, in the deepest level of his soul? How does he deal with his fear—through avoidance, compulsion, acting out, anger, depression, desire to cling to someone stronger? Is his way of dealing with deep fears constructive (catching criminals, fighting disease, raising children) or destructive (beating his wife, shoplifting, spending money he doesn't have to impress others)? And can his characteristic way of handling fear be used to generate plot ideas?

I'm betting that it can.

LOVE: I'D DO ANYTHING FOR YOU

So can love.

The reasoning here is the same as for fear. Human beings are a social species. We're hardwired to form attachments to others. This can be expressed constructively: loving a partner, being loyal to a friend, sacrificing gladly for our children. Furthermore, the attachment drive can be elaborated in labyrinthine ways. We can love a country; an idea; a pet; a stamp collection; an object that, to us, symbolizes something *else* we love. Just yesterday, for example, I saw a newspaper article about a man who ran back into a burning house to try to save his grandmother's Bible. In fact, said essayist Charles Lamb two hundred years ago, the human mind is capable of falling in love with anything at all.

And what we love, we act to gain or keep. (Witness all those newspaper ads: LOST: School Ring. Great sentimental value. Reward.) This can generate all kinds of plot ideas.

Who, or what, does your character love? What is she willing to do to gain or keep it? What are the limits (if any) to how far she'll go? How does she react if something interferes with her gaining or keeping the thing she loves? (Consider the movie *Fatal Attraction*.) Plot galore.

THE YELLOW BRICK ROAD

Not to mention characterization that touches readers in a vulnerable spot—their own attachment to whatever it is that they love.

FEAR *AND* LOVE: THE TWISTED SKEIN

Finally, love and fear can be tightly intertwined emotions. When you love something, you fear you'll lose it. A mother, for instance, may go to enormous lengths to safeguard her children—lengths that ultimately may interfere with their ability to function well in the world without her. Is the mother driven by love of the kids, or by fear of being left alone?

Another example: A doctor goes to tremendous, heroic lengths to save a patient's life, expending great amounts of time, energy and ingenuity. Is the doctor driven by love of humanity or by fear of personal failure in not saving a life? Or both?

Out of these kinds of questions can come some truly complex characterization, and some very interesting fiction. So the next time you're trying to turn an idea into a plot—or are stuck in the middle of a story—ask yourself some questions. What does this character really fear, deep down? What does he love? In what ways, direct or indirect, does he behave to assuage his fear, express his love? Do these habitual behaviors intensify under stress? How? What kind of stress can you give him? What is he likely to do then?

"When I have fears that I may cease to be," wrote John Keats, "then on the shore/Of the wide world I stand alone, and think." Well, that's one way of reacting to fear. What does *your* character do?

SUMMARY: FROM CONCEPT TO CHARACTER TO PLOT

- A story can begin with anything: idea, image, character, setting, problem, technological breakthrough, natural disaster, etc.
- Go from the beginning point to the character by choosing someone with a stake in the action.
- Think about, feel your way into, fill out a dossier about this character until you understand him.
- Figure out what he would consider a conflict, how he would react to it, how he would affect the resolution and how he would feel about the events after they're over.
- Base this figuring-out on his deepest drives, such as fear and/or love.

chapter seventeen

FIGHT! FIGHT! FIGHT!
When Conflict Leads to Violence

Sex and violence.

Got your attention, didn't I? It seems that everyone, from the president to my grandmother, has an opinion on these two burgeoning aspects of modern storytelling. Not, of course, the same opinion. One subset of critics maintains that sex and violence should not be coupled together in the same debate. Sex and violence, goes this reasoning, are entirely different things, and one of them (take your pick) isn't even a problem at all.

There is one way, however, in which sex and violence definitely *do* belong in the same discussion. They're both natural outgrowths of those two conflict producers we examined in the last chapter, fear and love. Violence, especially, is implicit in many plots. Conflict escalates until it turns physical. And so Tybalt stabs Mercutio, Bill Sykes bludgeons Nancy, Costa Rica bombs Jurassic Park.

How *much* violence should your story's conflict lead to? That depends on the story. One critic famously remarked that there are "no brutalities in Jane Austen's novels—except the verbal," and that those are quite enough. In her context, they are. You, however, may need more physical fighting.

If so, what makes a fight scene work? Five things: necessity, detail, accuracy, plausibility and surprise.

NECESSITY: IS THIS VIOLENCE GRATUITOUS?

The big complaint about violence in storytelling of all kinds is that it is "gratuitous." The complaint is often true. Writers of novels, TV shows and movies throw in fight scenes to "keep things lively" and "increase tension." The results may be lively in that the audience follows the fight without falling asleep, but they're not necessarily involved. To feel genuinely involved with a fight scene, the reader needs more than flashy descriptions of attacks and counterattacks. Reader involvement comes from two things that happen well before the fight: *motivation* and *timing*.

Motivation means that both opponents have been provided with a reason to fight. (The intertwining of plot and character, yet again.) And not just any reason. Something must be at stake that matters not only to the characters but to the reader. This requires careful preparation. We must have had dramatized for us what the protagonist cares about, why he cares about it and why this particular fight is necessary to gain or keep it. Otherwise, even the most spectacular kick-boxing will feel mechanical.

Consider, for example, a fight from Pulitzer Prize-winning author Conrad Richter's novel *The Sea of Grass*. This fight is very brief, but the reasons for it are as complicated as the nineteenth-century West that Richter evokes so well. Two small boys, brothers, are having a routine fistfight. They are egged on by idle grown men, one of whom calls out: "I'm a-bettin' on the Chamberlain young 'un." But there is no Chamberlain young 'un. Both boys are sons of the protagonist Hal's uncle, the fiercely proud Colonel Brewton, and his mercurial wife Lutie, whom Hal has secretly loved for years. At the suggestion that Lutie has committed adultery—and with his uncle's political enemy—Hal loses it:

For a split fraction of a second as his meaning broke over me, I saw Lutie Brewton clear and beautiful as I had ever seen her in the life. And when the nester turned and grinned toward a sand-box, it was almost as if he had spat in her face. I was aware of the grave silence of the cowmen and of a curious wild hate sweeping over me like prairie fire. I had thought myself a medical student soon to go out in the world and save human lives. Now I found that the thin veneer of Eastern schools had cracked and I was only a savage young Brewton from an untamed sea of grass, moving through the little gate where customers' rifles and pistols stood or lay in their accustomed places on the back bar. I was aware of the cowmen backing out of range and of the bar-keeper ducking. And then I almost wanted to kill Dr. Reid, too, one of whose white hands had with surprising force suddenly thrown up my barrel so that oil from a brass hanging lamp started to pour on the walnut bar.

Brief action—but layers and layers of motivation. Hal acts violently, which is uncharacteristic for him, out of jealousy, anger, family pride, shame and unfulfilled longing. The fight is a truly dramatic moment— even though only one shot is fired, and nobody is injured, and the violence lasts only a few seconds.

Timing also counts. This fight has dramatic impact partly because it occurs four-fifths of the way through the book, after we've had plenty of time to get to know all the characters' values. Thus, an affront to those values has meaning for us. Contrast this with the fight-as-opening-scene ploy (fantasy is especially guilty of this), which so often fails because we don't know either side well enough to understand them. What is it they're fighting over? Who's supposed to be the good guy? Does it matter that the short guy got killed? Who cares?

Save your fight scenes until the story is well launched.

DETAIL: TELL ME MORE

In general, you should describe fight scenes in more detail than you think you need. Why is this?

Because the fight, as we've already established, must be important to the characters. That, plus the fact that it's full of action, gives it the character of a miniclimax. Something important is being decided, by physical force. And a climactic scene shouldn't be rushed, because in written storytelling, one way you give a scene importance is to spend enough words on it. Verbiage is a flag to the reader: *This counts.*

So give us details. Don't write: "I pushed her, and she fell, hit her head on the cement birdbath, and slumped unconscious," even if that's all that actually happened. Give us detail, external or internal. Describe how she looked going down: the surprised expression on her face, the slow-motion way she fell. Or describe how he felt as his palm connected with her cheek, his emotions as he realized what he did. Or describe in detail the reactions of everyone watching. Make the moment last.

In the above excerpt from *The Sea of Grass*, for instance, Richter draws out a single ineffective gunshot by dwelling on Hal's heightened awareness: of the moment, of the past, of his own reactions. Detail gives the fight its dramatic weight.

One exception to this: It's sometimes effective to use a single summary sentence of a crucial fight as the ending of a chapter. In that case, the lack of detail is balanced by the fact that whatever comes at a chapter's end automatically has climactic drama.

ACCURACY AND PLAUSIBILITY: GETTING IT RIGHT

In order for a fight scene to be successful, readers must believe it is actually happening to the characters. This is true of the entire story, of course, but often scenes of violence put a particular strain on the suspension of disbelief. This happens in two ways: wrong details, or superhuman reactions.

Accuracy refers to correct details of weapons and fighting techniques. Many, many readers are knowledgeable about such things, and mistakes will bounce them right out of your story. What's more, they will write you about it, with great indignation. (This is especially true of gun aficionados.) So if you don't know the number of rounds in a Smith & Wesson Model 439 9mm, or the correct place to drive a knife into the chest, or how silent a revolver silencer actually is, *find out.* Ask an expert. Delve the Internet. Read a reference book. (Writer's Digest Books publishes the Howdunit series, which ably addresses these issues. Each book is written by a forensics expert.) However you get the information, get it right.

Plausibility, a fuzzier area, refers to the effects of the fight on the fighters. It's fuzzier because people differ greatly in both their fighting ability and their capacity to absorb physical punishment and keep on fighting. Still, there is a limit, and unless you're writing satire, exceeding that limit will undercut the plausibility of your story. "Oh, come *on!*" the reader will exclaim. "He's got a broken arm, two cracked ribs and a concussion, and he can still chase the villain across the catwalk after knocking off four of his henchmen? I don't think so!"

To avoid this reaction, you must convince us of your fighter's general strength, level of training, experience, toughness and/or desperation. The less expected these things are, the more explanation we need, either before or after the fight. If, for instance, a young FBI agent takes out two men, withstanding a few severe blows but no broken bones or internal damage, we'll accept this. If a hundred-pound, seventeen-year-old female baby-sitter does it, you will have to work much harder to convince us that she is able to do what you say she's doing.

Keep the injury level, fighting expertise and odds against the winner all plausible.

SURPRISE: OH MY GOD!

Surprise, perhaps surprisingly, is the least necessary element to a good fight scene. Many fights are not surprising, and shouldn't be. We know the characters well enough to know what they're capable of; we can see the physical conflict coming; we know what weapons are likely. We may even have a good idea who will win. For some types of fiction, that's fine. The point of the violence is not to surprise us, but to dramatize an inevitable confrontation settled in an inevitably direct way.

In other stories, however, the outcome is not inevitable, and the whole tone of the book has led us to expect a spectacular and breathless confrontation. This often involves unexpected weapons, complicated maneuvers, desperate cunning: real edge-of-the-seat stuff. To pull it off, you must surprise us with some novel way of winning the battle.

It may be novel weapons. Ian Fleming certainly contributed his share of deadly fountain pens and cigarette lighters in his James Bond series. But more likely, the surprise will be how an overmatched protagonist uses his wits to convert whatever is around him to a weapon, a plan of attack or an escape route.

Give this a lot of thought. You are competing with some very inventive writers here. Charles Sheffield, to take just one example, once made his desperate hero use an entire zoo to fight off the villain, in the thriller *My Brother's Keeper*. What is in the environment, or in your hero's head, that he can use to gain a fighting advantage? How can you surprise the reader with his attack, and still have it seem logical?

One way is to foreshadow the protagonist's special knowledge. Sheffield's hero's hobby was visiting zoos all around the world. If your character will surprise us by using live steam to win a fight, make him an engineer or maintenance man. If she will surprise us with her amateur cunning in planning a killing, make her a mathematician with a methodical, obsessive mind (Scott Turow did this in *Presumed Innocent*). Surprises are best when our first reaction ("Oh my God!") is followed by uncritical acceptance ("But of course!").

A FINAL WORD: THE WITTY FIGHT

For some writers, there is a great temptation to embellish fight scenes with wit. The protagonist hurls the bad guy, whose name is John Cunningham, in front of a rolling roadgrader, under which Cunningham is squashed flat. Our hero dusts off his hands and says, "One more for the road, Jack!" The problem with this sort of wisecrack is that it immediately converts the fight from a genuine plot event into a send-up of a plot event. It's not conflict; it's vaudeville.

You should resist this, if you want us to take both your character and your conflict seriously. Sometimes, however, you don't want that. The whole book may be a send-up of a genre, as Piers Anthony's Xanth books are a send-up of heroic fantasy. Or it may be that the book is serious, but the narrator/protagonist is incapable of taking macho fighting very seriously. In that case, writing a tongue-in-cheek description of a fight will convey that self-satire very nicely. Here is Humbert Humbert in Vladimir Nabokov's *Lolita*, fighting another middle-aged, out-of-shape man for possession of a gun improbably named Chum:

> Fussily, busybodily, cunningly, he had risen again while he talked. I groped under the chest trying at the same time to

keep an eye on him. All of a sudden I noticed that he had noticed that I did not seem to have noticed Chum protruding from beneath the other corner of the chest. We fell to wrestling again. We rolled all over the floor, in each other's arms, like two huge helpless children. He was naked and goatish under his robe, and I felt suffocated as he rolled over me. I rolled over him. We rolled over me. They rolled over him. We rolled over us.

To make a fight look ridiculous, you can't do better than to begin declining the fighting verbs in the middle of the action.

If, however, you *don't* want your fight to appear ridiculous, refrain from both witty exposition and wisecracking dialogue.

Fights are exciting. When your characters' conflict explodes into violence, make it necessary, detailed, accurate, plausible and (perhaps) surprising. Readers will gladly pay for ringside tickets.

SUMMARY: CHARACTERS AND VIOLENCE

- Keep violence necessary to the plot and consistent with the characters.
- Write fight scenes in more detail than you think you need.
- Be accurate about weapons, martial techniques and bodily injuries.
- For flamboyant, action-oriented fiction, write flamboyant and surprising fight scenes.
- Put wisecracks in fight scenes only if you're willing to undermine the seriousness of both plot and character.

chapter eighteen

WHOSE STORY IS IT, ANYWAY?
How Point of View Begins With Character and Leads to Plot

No man is an island. Neither is any story.

That sounds very poetic (at least, John Donne thought so), but in writing terms, what does it *mean*? It means that every story with more than one character in it is actually more than one story. *N* characters = *n* stories. This fact is well known to policemen, judges and parents of nine-year-olds. ("So what's *your* side of what happened between you and your brother?") There are two (or more) versions of every story.

As a writer, however, you usually get to fully tell only one version, no matter how many other characters you've invented or how well you understand their plots. Which one do you choose?

It depends. Often the writer chooses the first version that occurs to him. But that may actually not be the most interesting version. The purpose of this chapter is to get you to widen your sense of the possibilities. Before you choose a version to write, consider how many are available, what each has to offer and what effect each will have on the reader. Your key to all this is—surprise!—characterization. More specifically, the key is making a careful, cool survey of the options.

CASTING DECISION NUMBER ONE: WHO STARS?

It's easy to understand that many versions exist of any given story. A wedding, for instance, appears quite different to the bride (who's pregnant), the groom (who's secretly in love with someone else), the father of the bride (on the verge of bankruptcy), the maid of honor (the groom's true beloved), the groom's grandmother (sentimental and misty-eyed), the groom's sister (enjoying the party) and the photographer (just doing a job). The star is whoever's actions and reactions you, the writer, choose to focus on. Whose story do you want it to be?

There is no single right answer.

Lately, for example, a sort of cottage industry has sprung up around retelling famous stories from a point of view different from the original. Valerie Martin wrote *Mary Reilly*, which gives us the tale of Dr. Jekyll and Mr. Hyde from the viewpoint of Dr. Jekyll's housemaid. Joan Aiken wrote *Jane Fairfax*, an account of how the events of Jane Austen's *Emma* looked to secondary character Jane Fairfax. Editors Ellen Datlow and Terri Windling have published four collections of retold fairy tales, in which such classics as "Cinderella," "Thumbelina" and "The Frog Prince" are retold through the eyes of an ugly stepsister, the tiny girl's foster mother, and the frog himself. (The collections are called *Snow White, Blood Red*; *Black Thorn, White Rose*; *Ruby Slippers, Golden Tears*; *and Black Swan, White Raven*.) Each variation makes a secondary character into the star. Each is an interesting story in its own right.

So if anyone can be the star of your story, how do you choose? The same way casting directors do: by auditioning all the aspirants.

Suppose, for instance, that your novel is about race relations in an inner-city high school. The five major characters will be a white junior named Mary; the black senior with whom she has a romance (Darryl); the Hispanic principal who used to be a math teacher and is groping his way through his first administrative position (Mr. Chavez); a black student teacher (Tish Sullivan); and a young white security guard (Mike) newly hired by the district and only a few years older than Mary and Darryl. Whose story should it be?

- It might be Mary's book. She's naive, good-hearted, too romantic for her own good. This could be a novel about how the contemporary world destroys innocence.
- It might be Darryl's book. He's torn between Mary and pressure from a militant group of brothers to not date white girls. He also has a mother he's helping to support, a cop gunning for him and a scholarship to Princeton—which scares him a lot. This could be a novel about making good choices before you're old enough to understand their consequences.
- It might be Mr. Chavez's book. He was a great teacher but a terrible administrator. This might be a novel about an educational system that values everything but good teaching.
- It might be Tish Sullivan's book. She attended this high school four years ago; there's nothing the students can try that she hasn't already seen. Tough, realistic, unsentimental, she's far more effective than her supervising teacher—who resents her for that. This could be a novel about generational clashes.
- It could be Mike's novel. He didn't finish high school himself, and is one confused and angry young man. When the security firm he works for wins the contract to implement a new program to control school violence, Mike is assigned to hall patrol. It's a dangerous position for someone so young and furious himself. This could be a novel about power and its tragic misuses.

All potentially interesting characters—and interesting stories! Before you choose, consider another important decision.

CASTING DECISION NUMBER TWO: WHO NARRATES?

Usually, the protagonist and the narrator will be identical. That is, whoever is the star of the story will also be the person through whose eyes we view the action (the POV character). Usually—but not necessarily. It's also possible to have one character be the real star of the story, while a different, secondary character narrates the events. Some famous examples:

- *To Kill a Mockingbird*, by Harper Lee. This is the story of Atticus Finch, small-town Southern lawyer, fighting for justice against the forces of bigotry. But the story is narrated in the first person by his eight-year-old daughter, Scout.

- *The Moon and Sixpence*, by W. Somerset Maugham, is his take on the life of painter Paul Gauguin ("Charles Strickland"). The narrator, however, is not Strickland but an acquaintance of his who functions as a detached observer throughout the novel.
- *Rebecca*, by Daphne du Maurier. Rebecca, the dead aristocratic beauty, is the star and focal point. We view her story through the eyes of her successor, a young and awkward second wife.
- *The Great Gatsby*, by F. Scott Fitzgerald. It's Jay Gatsby's story, as narrated by his next-door neighbor, Nick Carraway.

This approach (like everything else in writing) comes with both advantages and disadvantages. A disadvantage is that we will experience the star's story secondhand and, hence, not as viscerally or completely. Although sometimes, of course, that's the effect you want. In that case, splitting the roles of actor and explainer can be very effective indeed.

It lets the star remain mysterious, shadowy at first, his history revealed only in stages (*Rebecca, The Great Gatsby*). It can add an intimate voice for moral judgment when that quality is missing in the star (*The Moon and Sixpence, Rebecca*). It can present a story through eyes more innocent than those of the main participants, thus compelling readers to also see it freshly (*To Kill a Mockingbird*).

So where does that leave us? Each of the five major characters in our high-school novel could be not only the star but the narrator. This yields twenty-five possible ways to write the novel; see the chart on page 179.

From the chart, can you see how varying the protagonist and the POV character could lead to an entirely different approach to the novel? Different incidents, different slants, different book.

So which one would you want to write?

Maybe you already know. One combination or another may have leaped out at you. If not, you can provoke your dozing Muse by applying a few key questions to each combination:

- Does this protagonist interest me, as a person? Why?
- What might this person want?
- What might stand in the way of his getting it?
- What could go wrong with this situation?
- Who could end up a winner or a loser here?

Narrator

	Protagonist				
	MARY	DARRYL	MR. CHAVEZ	TISH SULLIVAN	MIKE
MARY	Mary's story, as told through her own eyes	Darryl's story, as viewed and reported by his girlfriend	a new principal's story, as viewed and reported by a female student	a student teacher's story, as viewed and reported by a student of the same sex, different race	a new security guard's story, as viewed and reported by a female student he must control
DARRYL	Mary's story, as viewed and reported by her boyfriend	Darryl's story, as told through his own eyes	a new principal's story, as viewed and reported by a male student	a student teacher's story, as viewed and reported by a male student of the same race	a new security guard's story, as viewed and reported by a male student he must control
MR. CHAVEZ	a female student's story, as viewed and reported by a new principal	a male student's story, as viewed and reported by a new principal	a new principal's story, as told through his own eyes	a student teacher's story, as viewed and reported by her supervisor	a new security guard's story, as viewed and reported by the building boss
TISH SULLIVAN	a white student's story, as viewed and reported by a new black student teacher	a black student's story, as viewed and reported by a new black student teacher	a new principal's story, as viewed and reported by a student teacher	a student teacher's story, as told through her own eyes	a new security guard's story, as viewed and reported by another newcomer
MIKE	a white girl's story, as viewed and reported by a new security guard	a black kid's story, as viewed and reported by a new security guard	a new principal's story, as viewed and reported by a new security guard	a student teacher's story, as viewed and reported by a new security guard	a scared young guard's story, as told through his own eyes

If none of those questions spark plot ideas for any one of the twenty-five combinations . . . then give up. You were not meant to write this book. Start over with another idea and another chart.

CASTING DECISION NUMBER THREE: WHERE DO WE FILM THE STAR FROM?

As if we didn't already have a wealth of choices—a cornucopia, a treasury—each of the twenty-five possibilities is actually two possibilities. You could write the story in the first person or in the third person. If you choose first person, you record the story in your narrator's words, through her eyes. You gain intimate opportunities for the narrator to editorialize on her views of the action.

If you choose third person, you situate your camera outside both narrator and protagonist. You gain increased license to describe character and action from the outside, in *your* POV.

To get a feel for the difference, consider these two possible opening paragraphs:

> The first time I saw Tish Sullivan, I thought she was hot. 'Course, I didn't know then that she was a student teacher. I thought she was just one of the black kids, standing there in her short skirt with them long legs in black tights. I didn't know then that the scowl on her face wasn't no tough-kid cool. I didn't know she was twenty-six, and a ex-sergeant. I didn't know she was smart as a mean whip. I didn't know nothing.
>
> —Tish Sullivan's story, narrated by
> Mike the security guard, in first person

> The first time Mike Oldham saw Tish Sullivan, he thought she was another student. Another black girl, prettier than most, but with the same set scowl that broadcast, *Don't mess with me*. Mike didn't pay too much attention to Tish, no more than a cursory male glance. He had other things on his mind. It was his first day on the job, and already, after twenty-two minutes, he was in trouble. How the shit did trouble turn up so *fast*?
>
> —Tish Sullivan's story, narrated by
> Mike the security guard, in third person

Diction changes, distance changes, what you the writer can tell and show us changes. Which do you prefer? Either one could make a good novel.

Total possibilities: fifty. Fifty different emphases, fifty different slants about race and education. All generated by your choice of protagonist, narrator and viewpoint—all of which are, of course, character choices. And—here's the main point—from those character choices will flow fifty different sets of plot incidents, depending on who's the star and who's the camera lens.

Look again at the outline for your novel. How many novels do you really have in front of you? And which one do you really want to write? The choice is yours.

SUMMARY: HOW VIEWPOINT CONNECTS CHARACTER AND PLOT

- Nearly any character can be the star of any story.
- Nearly any character can narrate any story.
- Choosing different stars and different narrators will lead to a different choice of plot incidents.
- To generate the plot that excites you the most, consider several possible combinations of star and narrator. What incidents does each suggest?

chapter nineteen

ALSO FEATURING . . .
Secondary Characters and Plot Construction

In the last chapter, we discussed your protagonist and your point-of-view character as if they were the only two people in your book. This is, of course, untrue. You also have all those secondary characters, antagonists and spear carriers. What can they do for your story? And how do you tie their characterization to the book's plot?

By working backward. You figure out what the climax will be, and then you provide everybody else but main players with just enough characterization to end up wherever you want.

This needs explanation. Didn't I already spend all of part one detailing how a writer starts with a complex character and gets to plot? How can I then say that sometimes you should start instead with plot and fill in only enough characterization to serve the needs of that plot?

Because you *have* to limit the amount of characterization that you give your secondary characters. If you don't, if you try to make every single person in the book full and rounded and contradictory, your novel will fail. It will do so for three reasons:

• *The book will be too long.* It takes sheer wordage to adequately develop full, round characters. If you try to do this for not only the key characters but also the protagonist's boss, his wife's best friend and the waitress at their favorite restaurant, the book will have to go on for volumes. Which might not be too bad except:

• *The book will be too slow.* The details that build character do not usually move as fast as those of plot. If they're details of background, events that have happened before the story begins (sometimes called *backfill*), they're even slower. Developing all your players will cause the story to creep forward at a glacial pace, and everyone will become chilled and stop reading.

• *The book will be muddy.* In real life, *everyone* is complicated. Each person on the planet (all five billion of us) is the complex center of his or her own life story, which also features important secondary characters, people with third or fourth billing and bit players. But fiction is not real life. Fiction traces patterns through the infinitely complicated morass of real life. The patterns may be simple or complex, but they are always simpler and more clear-cut than real life (more on this in chapter twenty-four). You must highlight what's important to your book's particular pattern, and downplay the rest. You do this by concentrating on the stories of your protagonists—one, or two, or at most a handful—and demoting everyone else to permanent bit-player status, without fully developed characterizations that might detract from your main story line.

SHE'S SECONDARY BUT SHE'S CERTAINLY COLORFUL

So where does that leave us? With four categories of characters:

• *Main characters*, who will be fully developed, with backgrounds and contradictions and the capacity for change (whether or not they actually do change). Often (but not always) they are POV characters.

• *Secondary characters* who, although not fully developed, are nonetheless more than briefly animated pieces of plot furniture. The readers know, or can guess, something about their lives beyond the events of the plot. However, these people don't change during the novel and don't give any indication that they could. They come in two versions: "ordinary folk" types, undeveloped in part because they already seem like familiar and comfortable friends, and:

• Colorful *secondary individuals* who may be fascinating to read about, but who nonetheless offer more arresting quirks than deep characterization.

• *Bit players*, who appear once or twice and essentially *are* furniture.

It's important to note that these categories may overlap somewhat. The reason I'm trying to set them up, despite their slipperiness, is that I think different categories benefit from different approaches by you, the writer—especially at the climax of your book.

Let's get some clarification here from a specific example. We need a well-known novel with familiar characters. Once more we'll call on F. Scott Fitzgerald's classic, *The Great Gatsby.*

Main characters are the narrator, Nick Carraway, who changes as a result of the novel events, deciding to break up with girlfriend Jordan Baker and return to his native Midwest. Also major, although they don't change, are Jay Gatsby, Daisy Buchanan and Tom Buchanan. For all four, the author gives us details of growing up, of current beliefs only peripheral to the plot (such as Tom's racism) and of complexities and contradictions of personality (Daisy is torn between her romanticism and her hardheaded need for money to support a lifestyle she knows she will never abandon for love).

Colorful secondary characters include Jordan Baker, the society beauty who cheats at golf; Myrtle, Tom's mistress; and Wolfsheim, the mobster. We get no background for these people, but each appears in more than one scene, each is essential to the plot and each is flashy and memorable. Jordan is scornful, beautiful and dishonest—all flashy qualities. Myrtle is pretentious, comic, and pathetic, with her too-elaborate dresses and her disdain for her temporary servants. She makes a memorable figure. And Wolfsheim—it would be hard to imagine a flashier figure, nose hairs "quivering tragically," cuff links of human molars, illegal "gonnections" offered without discretion.

I stress the colorfulness of these characters because, as a general guideline, the more colorful you make a secondary character, the greater your obligation to account for him at the end of the book. The reason is simple: Readers will remember colorful characters. Remember, and wonder what became of them. If the answers are never provided, readers are likely to feel cheated.

Thus, Fitzgerald accounts for Jordan and Wolfsheim, even though neither accounting is essential to the main plot (Myrtle, whose fate *is* essential, is of course dead). Nick goes to Wolfsheim's office to urge him to go to Gatsby's funeral. Wolfsheim refuses, and we get a clear glimpse of what will happen to him: more endless shady deals, just as if Gatsby had never lived and died. Similarly, we see from Nick's last scene with Jordan (the third-last scene in the book) that she will just go on dating her various beaux until one of the romances turns into a convenient marriage—but not with Nick.

In contrast, less colorful secondary characters often don't have to be accounted for at a book's end. The reader may not even remember that they existed, even though they appeared in more than one scene. Or, the reader may just assume that since this character was presented as ordinary and unremarkable, that's what he'll go on being, and such a fate doesn't need accounting for.

In *The Great Gatsby*, Daisy's daughter Pammy is just such a secondary character. She affects the plot in that she certainly would have complicated any decision Daisy might have made about Gatsby, had Gatsby lived. In addition, Daisy delivers one of her key speeches to Nick on the subject of the child's birth and the painful circumstances surrounding it. Yet the ending of the novel doesn't account for Pammy—never even mentions her. And readers don't notice the omission. Pammy is an ordinary little girl of her class, and it's assumed she goes on living the life that implies, even though her mother and father are both responsible for manslaughter.

Finally, *Gatsby* abounds with minor characters, some colorful and some not: Myrtle's sister Catherine, the "boarder" Klipspringer, the reporter checking out the rumors around Gatsby, Michaelis, the McKees. They are all furniture, there to facilitate the doings of the main characters.

It's not, of course, possible for us to know exactly what was in F. Scott Fitzgerald's mind as he wrote Wolfsheim, Jordan, Klipspringer, Daisy and Pammy. However, it's not hard to deduce that he must have had a pretty clear idea of what would happen to Daisy, Tom, Gatsby and Myrtle—otherwise he wouldn't have had a book. Perhaps he knew their fates before he wrote even the first word of the novel.

Perhaps their fates became clear to him part way through the writing. Or perhaps he wrote a first draft, exclaimed at the end of it, "Good Lord! Wilson shoots Gatsby!" and wrote that.

It doesn't matter. There are all sorts of ways to arrive at the end of a first draft. But sometimes (often) that's just the beginning.

FIXING PLOT PROBLEMS THROUGH SECONDARY CHARACTERS

After the first draft is finished, most writers feel a flush of triumph. Then they reread the manuscript.

At this point, nearly every writer will find at least some loose ends unraveling during or after the climax. Some common problems:

- Characters will be unaccounted for. (Whatever happened to Good Old George?)
- Actions you need for your climax seem, on second reading, undermotivated. *Why* are these people doing these things?
- Some situations aren't as plausible as you would like. How can you make them feel more inevitable?
- The climax occurs too abruptly. You need more and/or better foreshadowing.
- A few sections of the book seem a little thin. Not enough action, or not enough character development, or not enough tension.
- A key scene reads, alas, too much like a cliché.
- A subplot doesn't feel closely enough tied to the main story line.

What to do about these problems?

Work backward, through your secondary characters.

Secondary characters are usually more easily revised than are primary ones. It is a major undertaking to strengthen plot holes by changing your protagonist from Irish to Vietnamese, from a plumber to an engineer, from thirty to sixty, from cheerful to bitter and devious. But it's not nearly as difficult to change her *cousin*. The cousin appears in only three scenes. And you hadn't imagined an entire history and personality for him anyway. Thus, it's not so difficult to alter him to whatever your evolving plot requires him to be.

But aren't the problems bulleted above traceable not to secondary characters, but to major ones? Can you solve such major plot difficulties without major changes in your protagonists? Actually, yes, some-times you can. Let's look again at each problem.

PROBLEM NUMBER ONE: CHARACTERS UNACCOUNTED FOR

Let's say you've finished a first draft and you're actually pretty pleased with the last three chapters. All the forces you've been setting up have come together effectively at the climax, and a complex plot has been brought to a satisfactory conclusion. However, one problem remains. One of the main characters cannot, for plot reasons, be present in the climactic scene. He *must* be elsewhere. Following the climax are only two more short scenes, both of which read very well, but he's not in those scenes either. And you don't want to add him, because he's supposed to be two thousand miles away, and there's no good reason to bring him, at this late date, to the location of the climax. Neither do you want to add a third scene after the climax; the book feels emotionally right just as it is, and another scene would only dilute the effect. Still, this missing character was important and colorful; readers are going to want to know how he ended up. What to do?

Use a secondary character.

This secondary character—we'll call her Pamela—can be the means to let the reader know what happened to the unaccounted-for main character (George). Pamela can receive a phone call from George. Or a birthday card, with a scrawled bit of news in it. Or see George's name in the newspaper. Or she can have a conversation about George with another character. Each of these can be brief—so brief they don't require another scene. Yet they will satisfy the readers' desire to know whatever happened to good old George.

But what if Pamela doesn't know George—and neither does any-body else present at the end of the book, when you're doing your wrap-up? That's where you plot backward with minor characters. Change Pamela's life so that she does know George. It's not hard to do; she's not that fully developed, and not in very many scenes anyway. So decide that Pamela and George are cousins, or ex-spouses, or in the same work field, or from the same town, or whatever. Then go back and plant that in a few earlier scenes—it's not hard. When the second-last scene rolls around and Pamela tells Justin that she re-ceived a gloomy note from George (Can you *believe* it, under *these* circumstances! George could be gloomy about winning the lottery, but then he was always like that even when we were kids), it will feel natural. And you the writer will have accounted for George.

Mystery writers do this often to account for suspects who turn out not to have committed the crime after all. Claudia Bishop, for example, in her book *A Taste for Murder*, has as a suspect a boorish business-man staying at the scene of the crime, an upscale inn. One of the two amateur sleuths suspects him. But he's not the killer, and he leaves the inn before the end of the novel. To account for his fate, Bishop ends the book with a restaurant review he wrote of the inn. He was actually a food writer traveling incognito. Had the cook known, she would have cooked much better for him! The tiny incident is funny, brief enough to not slow down the book's ending, and satisfying in accounting for someone physically not present at the novel's end.

PROBLEM NUMBER TWO: ACTIONS YOU NEED FOR YOUR CLIMAX ARE UNDERMOTIVATED

This problem is common: At the book's climax, a major character (Mike) is required to take a sudden decisive action. This action sur-prises everyone. The problem is, it also surprises *you*. You didn't antici-pate that Mike would be doing this at the climax, and as a result you've never shown him to be decisive. In fact, he comes across as a sort of wimp. How can you better set up Mike as capable of this plot development?

Again, look to your secondary characters.

Obviously, Mike has a decisive side that comes out only in certain kinds of situations, and just as obviously, the other major characters have never seen Mike operate in those situations (or they wouldn't be so surprised at the climax). But you need to let us see this side of Mike, to prepare us to accept his change. To do this, consider carefully each of your secondary characters. Which ones might be altered so they have dealings with Mike, either in story time or in the past? Which ones could become his cousin, or exspouse, or business part-ner, or fellow expatriate of Tiny Falls, Iowa, or whatever? Again, sec-ondary characters are easier to alter than Mike is. He's too important and complete to reimagine from scratch. Instead, reimagine a few of the secondary characters so that they have plausible reasons to see Mike's decisive side, and go back and insert those scenes as necessary. Then Mike's action at the climax will seem in character—and you won't have to rewrite major chunks of the book for that to happen.

PROBLEM NUMBER THREE: SOME SITUATIONS AREN'T AS PLAUSIBLE AS YOU WOULD LIKE

The third problem is not that the characters are violating what you've shown us, but that the situation itself does not feel inevitable. It may not even feel possible.

In some cases, of course, this is just the result of a bad story. Too many coincidences, too far-fetched a premise, lapses in story logic. Nothing can save a truly dumb plot. But in other cases, concentrating on the characterization of secondary personae can help an astonishing amount.

Let's take an example with a truly far-out premise: Ira Levin's *The Stepford Wives*. In this best-seller, the climax comes when the protagonist and point-of-view character, Joanna, discovers that the women in the town of Stepford are being systematically killed and replaced by look-alike robots more submissive to their husbands. Not a very likely idea. Yet Levin makes Joanna—and us—believe it by concentrating throughout the novel on his secondary characters. Without realizing the significance of the information, we learn that many men in Joanna's new neighborhood work in high-tech areas. We see a robotics expert, a computer voice-recognition researcher, a graphic artist, a doctor skilled in skin grafts. We are shown that these men are self-centered and ruthless. None of these men is a major character, and none is fully developed. But the backgrounds and sketchy personalities that the author does give these secondary characters are what make a silly plot seem horrifying and plausible (at least until we finish the novel).

Nothing will rescue an unworkable plot. But if yours is passable (though flawed), try strengthening the flawed areas by giving your secondary characters lives that enhance the plausibility of what happens to the protagonists.

PROBLEM NUMBER FOUR: YOU NEED MORE AND/OR BETTER FORESHADOWING

In the fourth problem, the climax of the book doesn't seem implausible. Upon reflection, the reader can see how such an event could come about. But so could a couple of other possible endings, given the plot that has gone before. So why did it happen *this* way, instead of *that* way? It seems the author has just arbitrarily chosen one of any number of possible endings, because she found it convenient.

What you need to do in this case is strengthen the feeling of inevitability: Yes, the story *had* to end this way. You do this by going back and inserting more scenes earlier in the book. These additional scenes have the purpose of foreshadowing the outcome, making it seem like the most logical one. In other words, you are loading the dice, adding weight to one face of the falling cube, so that the number you want will end up staring the observer in the face.

You do this—surprise!—by building additional scenes around your secondary characters.

This makes sense, if you think about it. The main plotline is already set. What you want is not to alter that main plot, but to nudge it here and there in a given direction. You want to close off certain possible actions, make others easier for your protagonist. Secondary characters are born to nudge, close off and facilitate.

Suppose, for instance, that your main character is trying to make her way in seventeenth-century England by her wits, beauty and unscrupulous willingness to do whatever is necessary to advance herself. This is the situation in Kathleen Winsor's perennially popular romance, *Forever Amber*. Amber St. Clare rises to be mistress to King Charles II, but cannot win the one man she ever really loved. After she rises as high as possible, Amber then is shown beginning her inevitable descent into obscurity (unscrupulous courtesans always seem to end up miserable or alone: Consider Mata Hari, Mary Anne Clarke and Gennifer Flowers). In order for this descent to occur, more prosperous pathways must be cut off from Amber.

She can't, for instance, just return to the king, or find another bewitched rich lover, or be allowed to go on trysting with her beloved Bruce Carlton every few years, or retire in wealthy dignity with her illegitimate son. Any of those endings would not provide a satisfying retribution for Amber's appalling behavior, which has pretty much included breaking all ten commandments.

Instead, author Winsor uses secondary characters to close off all possible ways in which Amber might have escaped a climax of humiliation and despair.

Another mistress of the king, a minor character, cuts Amber off from renewed royal mistresshood by threatening to leave him if he ever sleeps again with Amber. That path is closed.

Another secondary character, a duke with his own reasons to dislike Amber, arranges for her to be tricked into leaving the country, far from anyplace she could easily acquire another titled keeper.

The author creates another secondary character to marry Bruce. His new wife is a gentle woman he does not want to hurt; this closes off the possibility that Amber will win her lifelong struggle to keep Bruce for herself.

She can't retire with her son because yet another secondary character persuaded her years ago to let Bruce adopt the boy.

All these secondary characters exist only fully enough to do their jobs of making Amber's fate seem inevitable. That's all the existence they need.

What secondary characters could you use, or alter, or create to do the same for your plot?

PROBLEM NUMBER FIVE: SOME SECTIONS OF THE BOOK SEEM THIN

Parts of the novel don't have enough action, or enough character development, or enough tension. Yet you need those scenes for plot development.

This is perhaps where interesting secondary characters are the most use of all. Like a magician's patter and hand-waving, they can entertain the audience while the illusion is prepared for unveiling.

Charles Dickens was the master of this technique. We could find examples in any of his novels; let's take *David Copperfield*. The first part of the book consists of David's childhood, allowing Dickens the time he needs to explore his protagonist's character and set him up for the major adult choices he will eventually have to make. While this childhood is progressing, David is necessarily more acted upon than acting. Yet the book never seems passive or preachy or even unrelievedly earnest, because the secondary characters whom David encounters, and who shape his personality, are such a fascinating and colorful lot. The improvident Mr. Micawber, the charming and cold-blooded Steerforth, little Emily, Aunt Betsey and her enemy donkeys, the faithful Ham—all entertain us mightily. That they are also serving important plot purposes recedes into the background; we're too absorbed in their interesting eccentricities. What might have been a relatively thin section of the book, mere setup for what comes later, instead takes on richness and fascination.

None of us is Charles Dickens. But we can still look hard at our secondary characters, considering whether they couldn't be given an expanded role in those thin sections of our books. Can they have crises of their own, choices of their own, successes of their own? Can these crises and successes be used not only to interest readers but also to deepen our sense of the protagonist and his world?

If so, plot backward to make your secondary characters do whatever will add to the book as a whole. That's what they're there for.

PROBLEM NUMBER SIX: A KEY SCENE READS TOO MUCH LIKE A CLICHÉ

A nineteenth-century Western horseman rides sadly out of town forever. A woman divorced against her choice squares her shoulders and just decides to get on with her life. A detective discovers that he himself is being set up for the crime he's supposed to be solving. A leader is trapped into turning on a loyal lieutenant.

You have to have this scene in the book, but even as you type it, you're wincing because it seems like such well-trodden ground. Well, maybe it is. But even if the protagonists and situation are overly familiar, secondary characters can still add freshness. Take, for instance, that last cliché (leader trapped, etc.), and then add a plot familiar for over half a century: the legend of King Arthur. Old, old stuff.

But not the way T.H. White reworked the story in his wonderful novel *The Once and Future King*. The incidents are from the fifteenth-century work by Sir Thomas Malory, but the tone is pure twentieth century: rueful, funny, humanly sad rather than heroically tragic, touching. And much of that tone is derived from the secondary characters.

Here is the scene in which the leader, King Arthur, is being trapped into declaring war on his loyal lieutenant and best friend, Sir Lancelot. Present are knights Gawaine, Gareth, Gaheris and Agravaine, plus Mordred. The latter two persuade Arthur that, under the new laws of justice that the king himself has devised, the queen must be tried for treason if she is discovered to be guilty of adultery with Lancelot:

Gareth threw himself on his knee.

"It has nothing to do with us!"

Gawaine, lumbering to one knee more slowly, joined him on the floor.

"Sir, I came ben hoping to control my brothers, but they willna listen. I dinna wish to hear what they may say."

Gaheris was the last to kneel.

"We want to go before they speak!"

Arthur came into the room and lifted Gawaine gently. . . .

Agravaine smiled.

"We don't know much about the new law," he said smoothly, "but we thought that when an assertion could be proved, in one of these new law-courts of yours, then the need for personal combat did not arise. Of course, we may be wrong."

"Trial by Jury," observed Mordred contemptuously, "is that what you call it? Some pie-powder affair."

Agravaine, exulting in his cold mind, thought: "Hoist with his own petard!" . . . "So you will go on the hunting party, Uncle Arthur, and we have permission to break into the Queen's room, if Lancelot is there?"

The elation in his voice was so indecent that even Mordred was disgusted. The king stood, pulling his gown around him, as if for warmth.

"We will go."

"And you will not tell them beforehand?" The man's voice tripped over itself with excitement. "You will not warn them after we have made the accusation? It would not be fair!"

"Fair?" he asked.

He looked at them from an immense distance, seeming to weigh truth, justice, evil, and the affairs of men.

Note that Arthur's reactions are downplayed, presented as mild, even dispassionate. All the color comes from the wildly contrasting emotions of the secondary characters: Gawaine's anguished shame over his brother's behavior, Gaheris's and Gareth's passionate refusal to be involved, Agravaine's cruel glee, Mordred's contempt. The situation is old—leader is trapped into turning on a loyal lieutenant—but the scene is fresh and original because of the fresh and original secondary characters.

PROBLEM NUMBER SEVEN: A SUBPLOT DOESN'T FEEL CLOSELY ENOUGH TIED TO THE MAIN STORY LINE

When a subplot is the problem, secondary characters provide an ideal remedy. You can easily alter their histories and actions to create closer ties among competing subplots.

Let's say, for instance, that your main story line concerns a lost family heirloom of great sentimental and monetary value. There's a subplot about the complicated relationship between an unrelated mother and her grown daughter. There's also another subplot about a police investigation in another city, which will turn out near the end of the book to have relevance to the lost heirloom.

However, the end of the book is a long way off. While you're developing these necessary subplots, how can you make them seem as if they all belong in the same book?

Again, use your secondary characters. Forge ties among them. The grown daughter can be a cousin to the police detective. The family hunting for the heirloom lives next door to the woman's mother; they share the fruit from an apple tree growing exactly on the property line. A young brother in the family is studying at the police academy in the other city and comes home for vacations. This not only ties your subplots together, it may also suggest plot developments and/or thematic complexities. What is the brother learning at the academy that might change the way his family searches for the heirloom? What does sharing apples from the same tree suggest about the fruits of one's actions?

You don't, of course, want to make these connections between secondary characters seem coincidental: The detective just *happens* to turn out to be the mother's cousin. Or, in Charles Dickens's nineteenth-century version in *A Tale of Two Cities*, the turnkey at Lucie's husband's prison just *happens* to be Lucie's governess's long-lost brother. That worked in the nineteenth century, but no longer.

The way to avoid such implausible coincidences is to build in the relationships from chapter one, not spring them on the reader in chapter forty-two. In other words, don't keep the connections among characters hidden. They aren't secrets; they're just facts.

THE FOUNDATION vs. THE WALLS

To sum up this whole chapter: Your main characters are the foundation of your novel. The poured concrete, the weight-bearing girders. Once such things are in place, they are difficult to move. The whole structure relies on their solidity to hold itself together.

Secondary characters, on the other hand, are non-weight-bearing walls. Certainly they help determine the final plan of the rooms: their shape, size, relationship, uses. But non-weight-bearing walls can be altered while a building is being built or remodeled, without causing structural collapse. You can move a wall, subdivide a major room, eliminate partitions—whatever seems to yield the most pleasing arrangement as the building goes up.

Secondary characters, plus spear carriers, can also be the colorful aspects of a building that determine its finished look: plaster, paint, wallpaper, carpets, window treatments. Should they be flashy or be neutral background? Ornate or severe? Sensual or cold marble? These are the things about a room that an observer notices first—but they are also the easiest things to change. Many writers, in fact, "build" their novels on the first draft, but leave nearly all the colorful decorating until revision time.

When you remodel, decorate or redecorate, look first to your secondary characters. It's much easier than moving a foundation that may be perfectly sound anyway.

However—and it's a big *however*—if your novel has serious problems in its basic architecture, fiddling with your secondary characters is not the answer. Realigning a wall will not cure a crack in the foundation. In that case, you need to rethink your major characters—starting back at chapter one.

SUMMARY: USING SECONDARY CHARACTERS EFFECTIVELY

- Secondary characters are not, by definition, as fully developed as main characters. There isn't room.
- Secondary characters, precisely because they have fewer dimensions than main characters, can often be more colorful and over-the-top.
- The more colorful a secondary character is, the greater will be the reader's interest in what happens to her at the novel's end.

- Secondary characters are much easier to revise than are complex main characters, whose emotional growth is tied into the story's main plotline.
- Because they are easier to alter, secondary characters can be used to solve a number of second-draft problems, including unaccounted-for characters, undermotivated actions, insufficiently plausible situations, a less-than-inevitable climax, thin developmental sections, cliché scenes and unattached subplots.
- However, secondary characters are not gods. If your story has *several* of the above problems, you need to seriously rethink its basic foundations.

chapter twenty

THE CHARACTERS, THEY ARE A-CHANGING
How to Make Character Change a Strong Element of Plot

"Plus ça change," say the French, *"plus c'est la même chose."* Which means, "The more things change, the more they stay the same"—or, in a slightly rougher translation, "You can't fight city hall." But in a short story or novel, *change* is precisely what you must have if the fiction is to work, even though some story elements may stay the same. Change, as mentioned in the last chapter, is one thing that distinguishes main characters from spear carriers. And maybe fighting city hall is exactly what propels your characters toward change.

In other words, you the novelist not only have to know who your protagonist is, you also have to figure out who he becomes.

But is it really necessary that characters change? Well, no. *Something* has to change, but it doesn't necessarily have to be the characters. There are three possibilities: the situation-change novel, the reader-change novel and the character-change novel. Each has a different relationship to plot, and each requires different handling.

RETURNING NEXT WEEK: THE SITUATION–CHANGE NOVEL

The situation-change story opens with a problem for the characters, or else the problem develops shortly after the story begins. The detective is handed a murder case; the colonists on Titan discover an air leak in the security dome; the beautiful architect learns that someone has stolen her building designs. By the end of the book, the problem has been solved, and that solution is what makes the ending situation different from the opening one. The protagonists, however, are fundamentally unchanged.

This is the simplest kind of fiction. For that reason, it's usually the kind presented by TV series, since at the end of the story everyone important is left unaltered for next week's episode. Before television, much magazine fiction was also of this type: unchanging series characters recycled through endlessly different situations. The form still exists in some series fiction, although for the most part, TV took over the static major character, and print fiction moved on to concentrate on stories in which characters do personally grow and develop as a result of the events in the story.

Still, it's possible to write a nonseries novel in which character change is absent and plot is all. To do so, you need to invent characters interesting enough to hold our attention without any interior conflict; a plot complicated and fast-paced enough to absorb us by itself; and a setting or style outrageous enough that we don't need to take the whole thing very seriously.

A good example is Carl Hiaasen's hilarious 1993 novel, *Strip Tease*. Good-hearted exotic dancer Erin Grant, wheelchair-stealing scumbag Darrell Grant, cynical detective Al García and lusty noodle-headed congressman David Dilbeck are, at the end of the book, just as good-hearted, cynical, lusty and noodle-headed as at the beginning (Darrell would be just as scumbaggy, except he's dead). The book's closing situation is different in several ways, including the fact that half the cast has been murdered. But the survivors are unchanged. The book is an outrageous romp, with only minimal relevance to real life, and that's enough. If your work is of this type, put your energies into exciting, over-the-top situations that make us gasp, and don't worry about character change. However, we'd better actually *gasp*.

LIFE ARTFULLY OBSERVED: THE READER-CHANGE STORY

Much "literary" fiction, in direct contrast to a book like *Strip Tease*, tries to portray real life as real people actually experience it—but it may still feature characters that don't change. This is because literary authors have observed that, sadly, most people in real life don't change. They go on doing over and over again whatever has messed up their lives before: tunnel vision, denial, passivity, alcoholism, impulsivity, whatever. The difference between this kind of story and Hiaasen's is that *something* besides plot situation is meant to change between the opening and closing. That something is the reader. Through careful piling of detail upon detail, the literary author hopes to change how the reader perceives the character(s) or their world, even though that world itself remains unaltered.

Consider a famous, much anthologized short story: James Thurber's "The Secret Life of Walter Mitty." Hapless daydreamer Walter Mitty, sent on Saturday errands by his domineering and unpleasant wife, starts by imagining himself an ace pilot navigating a dangerous storm. At the end of the story he's still escaping his dreary afternoon through exciting daydreams. Walter Mitty has not changed. But the reader has gained insight into why Mitty daydreams and—more important—into the poignant contrast possible between a man's outer life and the hidden, vital power of his secret imagination. And who, asks the story, is to say that one is more "real" than the other? The story nudges the reader to face that question. And afterward the reader looks a little differently at bland, colorless men doing errands on Saturday afternoons.

It's harder to sustain this no-change structure throughout a novel, because a novel is so much longer. If we spend five hundred pages with a character, we're likely to want to see some growth from him. However, novels do exist in which the whole point is that the character has refused a chance (perhaps his last chance) for meaningful change, but the *reader* ends up with more insight about reality.

One famous example is Sinclair Lewis's *Babbitt*. George Babbitt, a self-satisfied, provincial, superficial and unthinking businessman, is thrust into circumstances that could make him less satisfied, less provincial, less superficial and more thinking. He actually progresses a way—a tiny way—down this path, starting to look more closely at the reality of his world. But the glimpse is too frightening. And the price of looking more closely is too high: George Babbitt would become different from those around him and, so, alone. He can't do it. He scurries back into safe modes of thinking, refusing change. At the end of the novel he's exactly the same as he was at the beginning, a point Lewis underlines by duplicating the book's first scene as its last.

Writing this kind of novel requires a keen appreciation of the complexity of the human mind. It also requires better-than-average prose (to compensate for the lack of flashy events). Put your energies into small faithful details, revealing and symbolic, that suggest ambiguities of character. When done right, such details lead to a change in perception in the reader; in other words, we think differently about the character at the end of the story than we did at the beginning. Under such circumstances, the protagonist can remain static. It's not, however, easy to pull off at book length.

A SADDER BUT WISER MAN: THE CHARACTER-CHANGE STORY

Because the reader-change story is not easy, most novels do feature characters that grow and change, sometimes for the better, sometimes not. Mitch McDeere (*The Firm*, by John Grisham) discovers he has abilities to cope with a world more treacherous than he suspected. Tom Rath (*The Man in the Gray Flannel Suit*, by Sloan Wilson) learns there are more important values than corporate success. The narrator of *Bright Lights, Big City* (by Jay McInerney) discovers you can't evade grief forever, no matter how hard and frantically you run. But *how* do these characters change with their discoveries? And how can you create plausible changes for your protagonist?

It's a four-step process: preparation, pressure, realization, validation.

PREPARATION: RIPENESS IS ALL

Preparation refers to making us believe that this character is capable of change in the first place. You can do that one of two ways: Show us he has qualities in the present that could lead him to change, or show us he did have such qualities in the past.

Consider, for example, the famous transformation of Ebenezer Scrooge in Charles Dickens's *A Christmas Carol*. Scrooge starts out miserly, mean and isolated. By the end of the story he's become generous and joyful, giving away turkeys and hip operations. But Dickens prepares us early for this change. During Scrooge's first nocturnal trip, with the Ghost of Christmas Past, we see that Scrooge wasn't always as soul-shriveled as he is now. In the past he enjoyed himself. He danced at his employer's parties. He loved his sister, Fan. He was a person capable of inspiring in Fan a return love. When Scrooge finally becomes a "new man" at the end of the story, we find it plausible because it isn't really new; it's a return to qualities he once displayed.

You can do the same with your character. Show us that once she was different, closer to how she will be after the change in your story. You don't need a Christmas Ghost to do this. Show us through snatches of memory, brief allusions in other characters' dialogue, objects left over from a different life, old photographs—anything that will establish that another side of your character once existed. Then build on that submerged side to make plausible her subsequent change.

The same techniques can be used to show us present qualities that prepare for change. The airhead who comes through in a crisis will be more believable if she isn't completely an airhead. She's unexpectedly good at handling money, for instance. Or at sensing what other people feel. Or she never forgets a face.

PRESSURE: I CAN'T TAKE IT ANYMORE

Preparation, however, isn't enough by itself to make character changes believable. The next step is to add enough *pressure* to force your character to change. Why the pressure? Because change is threatening to most people, and they won't do it unless something drives them to it, usually pain or conflict. This truth is well known to psychiatrists, drug counselors and confirmed bachelors.

Scrooge is an especially hard case. It takes four ghosts, counting Marley, and a glimpse of his own tombstone in order to effect a change in him. Probably your protagonist will respond to somewhat less pressure. The pressure should be of a type appropriate to the story circumstances and to the character.

Some people, for instance, are most easily reached through concern for others—which might mean that your alcoholic young mother changes only after you dramatize how her drinking is making her child miserable. Other people are motivated to change by guilt, or boredom, or hitting bottom, or love, or danger. Pick your pressure and apply liberally, until something has to give.

All right, now your character has reached the moment of change. She realizes that something has to be different from here on in. How can you best portray this crucial inner transformation?

REALIZATION: IF I DON'T TRY SOMETHING DIFFERENT, THAT'S ALL SHE WROTE

Oddly, the best technique is to downplay the moment of change. If you've done a convincing job with preparation and pressure, we readers will be expecting some sort of change. If you then drag out the moment of *realization* by having the changee review what she's been doing so far, why it hasn't worked, what she could do differently and how resolved she is to turn things around—if you prolong the moment with all that intellectualizing—it will lose its electric force. Instead, it's more effective to indicate that *something* has happened and let us deduce what it is from the character's next actions.

Scrooge, for instance, does not sit on his bed on Christmas morning ruminating about his past sins and future reformation. Instead, the moment he awakes, he flings open the window and engages in exuberant conversation with a passing, astonished lad.

Similarly, consider the moment of significant change in *Bright Lights, Big City*. The second-person narrator has spent a couple hundred pages drinking, drugging, partying and behaving badly in order to try to evade looking at his life. He's been led in this by Tad, his wild and basically heartless best friend. At a crazy party in which he's introduced to his ex-wife Amanda's gigolo fiancé, the narrator has finally had enough: of his destructive friends, his destructive life, his own self-destruction. He's ready to change. McInerney indicates this in a brief, understated exchange:

> "Thanks." You stand up.
> "Take it easy, Coach." [Tad] puts his arm around your shoulders.
> "I just realized something."

"What's that?"

"You and Amanda would make a terrific couple."

The narrator has, of course, realized much more than that. But under-playing the moment of change saves the passage from melodrama and leads naturally to step four: validation.

VALIDATION: THINGS WILL BE DIFFERENT NOW

Validation refers to concrete actions the character performs that let us know for sure that she's changed—and in what way. It's never enough for the author to tell us that a person has grown. It's not even enough for the person to tell herself (how often have friends said, "I've really changed," when you can see quite clearly that they're doing the same old things?). Words are easy. Only actions have the force to convince. Seeing is believing.

Scrooge's transformation is validated by a whole string of actions: gifts for the Cratchit family. Donations to the poor. Benevolence to-ward his nephew and niece-in-law. Dickens takes the time to dramatize each of these fully, validating for us that more has happened with Scrooge than just a passing mood of relief at avoiding immediate death.

McInerney also shows us two validating actions, each fully drama-tized. After the narrator's moment of realization with Tad, he finds a phone and calls Vicky, the one sane person in his life. For the first time, he is honest with her about who he is, what he's been through and what he's feeling. He then walks home across Manhattan, finally letting himself remember his dead mother and feel his grief about her death. She used to bake bread; he stops to buy a bag of fresh-baked rolls and to accept that his life is going to be different from now on:

> You get down on your knees and tear open the bag. The smell of warm dough envelops you. The first bite sticks in your throat and you almost gag. You will have to go slowly. You will have to learn everything all over again.

The book ends there.

To make the change in your character genuinely convincing to readers, finish your story with one or two validating actions. These may be as simple as mailing a letter or closing a door. In an action-oriented novel, the character may have larger and more dramatic actions to perform after he changes, in order to undo whatever chaos existed *before* he changed.

Readers enjoy watching characters grow. To give us that pleasure, dramatize the entire change process: preparation, pressure, realization, validation. Then we'll believe what's happening inside your protagonist—and inside us as we discover her. This is the very heart of successful fiction, the lifeblood of most novels. In the next chapter, we'll look at it in even more detail.

SUMMARY: CHARACTERS WHO CHANGE

- Not all protagonists need to change. Exempt are the protagonists of satires, series action novels, outrageous romps, and books whose point is that human beings are hopelessly stuck.
- If your character does change, give us evidence beforehand that he is capable of being more than he is.
- Put sufficient pressure on him to change.
- Dramatize the moment of change through what he does, not just says or thinks.
- Give us some reason to believe the character change will last once the immediate crisis is over.

chapter twenty-one

SEEING IS BELIEVING
A Concrete Example of How Character, Change and Plot Intertwine

In the last chapter we rushed through the complex process of character change, a process important enough to label it "the very heart of successful fiction," in less than 3,000 words. That's quite a sprint. Hearts deserve more time. So in this chapter, we'll look again at the four steps of effective character change, this time in considerable and concrete detail. We'll do this by examining how one recent novel intertwines character, change and plot: *Higher Education*, by Charles Sheffield and Jerry Pournelle.

This novel is science fiction for young adults, but the techniques it embodies apply to other types of fiction as well. Whether characters change on Mars, in Regency England, in contemporary New York or deep in the heart of Texas, the four basic steps apply. Let's see how.

Higher Education is the story of Rick Luban, a sixteen-year-old troublemaker in a future public-school system even more beleaguered than inner-city schools are now. Academic standards have been watered down to the point where most kids can barely read; between voice-activated computers and other media entertainment, there's little need. Rick doesn't see the need to prepare for a meaningful job because few jobs are available, and they don't go to people like him. At home, his parents don't exhibit much concern about him. Rick gains prestige among his peers by being obnoxious to teachers, sexually predatory with girls and cynical about life.

In short, not a candidate for Most Likely to Succeed.

But Rick *does* succeed—because he changes. To make the change believable, Sheffield and Pournelle carefully and unobtrusively take Rick through the four steps discussed in the last chapter.

PREPARATION: THE CHARACTER BEHIND THE CONDOM CAPER

The way to prepare us for a character change is to show us that either at some point in the past the character behaved differently, or in the story present he possesses the qualities necessary for change. Rick, at sixteen, does not possess much past. Therefore, Sheffield and Pournelle concentrate on the second approach.

In the novel's opening scene, Rick and his two buddies are engaged in a favorite occupation: harassing teachers. Rick sneaks out of the auditorium during assembly, ducks back into the classroom and arranges a water-filled condom over the door to drench the teacher who unlocks it. What do we learn from this introduction to the character?

That Rick Luban is obnoxious, contemptuous of authority, willing to lie and to humiliate others, a show-off among his peers. All that, yes. He also gets into fights and callously "scores" with girls. But Sheffield and Pournelle also show us that Rick is capable of planning, of attention to detail and of a certain perverse discipline:

> He stayed in his seat until everyone except Mr. Preebane had left the room, then he moved out and held the door for the teacher. Preebane nodded his thanks. Rick closed the door; was careful not to lock it; and hurried after the rest of the class.
>
> First he headed away from Room 33, keeping his eyes open for working videocameras. The contraceptive dis-

pensers were down by the cafeteria entrance. They needed a student name and ID code before they would operate, but Rick was prepared for that. He entered "Daniel J. Rackett" and "XKY-586," waited as the valedictorian's ID was confirmed, and took the packet of three condoms. He did it twice more.

The corridors were deserted as he hurried back toward Room 33, opened the door, and slipped through. The tricky piece now was to disable the classroom videocamera without being seen by it. The cable ran along the ceiling, well out of reach. Rick scaled the open door and balanced precariously on top of it. He had no knife on him—anything that might form a weapon would never get past the school entrance—but his nail clippers were enough for this job. He crouched on top of the door, reached up, and delicately snipped the thin gray cable.

There is intelligence behind this stupid prank, but not enough to save Rick. The water bomb hits not the teacher but his aunt, a visiting congresswoman on the board of education. Rick is expelled.

A kind teacher takes the time to talk with Rick on a bench outside the school. The conversation propels plot; the teacher urges Rick to take application tests for the apprentice program of Vanguard Mining, which mines asteroids in space. However, Sheffield and Pournelle also use this long conversation for more preparation for later character change, by showing us several more latent or underutilized aspects of Rick's character. We learn that he has a natural aptitude for math.

"So now what happens to you?"

"I don't know. Sit around and watch the tube, I guess, until they throw me out. Mick's goin' to kill me. The education incentive was nine-forty a month and we only get sixty-two hundred altogether."

"So your education is a good part of the money. Of course you don't get it yourself."

"Naw. Mick takes it. He's gonna hate losing that nine-forty. Fifteen percent—"

"It is that. You do percentages in your head?"

"Sure. That's useful, you need it to play the numbers."

We are also shown that, unlike many teens, Rick is able to control his temper when it's to his own advantage, even in the face of direct insult:

> Rick stood up. . . . "Why are you doing this for me?"
> Hamel paused. "Certainly it's not because I like you, Luban. I do not. As I said, you are a fool. And you are—"
> "Ignorant, cynical, amoral, and unthinking. I heard you."

Rick is also capable of such softer emotions as gratitude, although he has trouble expressing it:

> He wanted somehow to thank Mr. Hamel, but he did not know how.

This ability to recognize another person's actions and motives will become critical later in the book.

Finally, when Rick goes to take the application tests for the mining job, we see that he has a street-smart ability to size up a situation, rather than act on his first impulse:

> There was a temptation to lie, or put things in a way more favorable to Rick. Some instinct warned him that would be a mistake. He recounted the whole episode. . . . After the fact it sounded so stupid and pointless and unfunny. Rick was sure that any hope of employment with Vanguard Mining was evaporating with every word he said.

Finally, that Rick goes for the job interview at all—and, when he passes, goes first to New Mexico for training and then into space— dramatically illustrates that he possesses courage, initiative and some degree of adaptability. Sheffield and Pournelle will build on all these qualities later, as Rick changes.

It's important to emphasize that each of these qualities is shown more than once. Throughout the first six chapters, Rick reveals again and again that he can assess reality, face it bravely and react with self-preserving intelligence. These qualities are convincingly mixed in with his macho fights, predatory attitudes toward women, suspicious anger, and disregard for any rules he thinks he can get away with breaking. He is still a punk. But he's a punk that his creators have endowed with qualities upon which change can be convincingly built. The authors are preparing for the next developments in their plot.

It can also work the other way. If you start with a character (many writers do), you can use her complexities to generate plot ideas. Ask yourself:

- What qualities does this person have that her current circumstances don't allow her to fully express?
- What circumstances might allow—or even force—her to express them?
- Does that indicate where my plot should go?

Adequate preparation is critical to our believing your character *can* change. Next you need to show us *why* he does so.

PRESSURE: THE FACTS OF LIFE IN SPACE

Rick Luban is already under powerful pressure as soon as he gets expelled from school: He has nowhere to go. If he goes home, his stepfather will beat him because he has lost the supplementary welfare that the government pays households with children attending school. He applies to Vanguard Mining out of desperation, a convincing pressure. It's also a common one in fiction. It drives characters as different from Rick Luban as Scarlett O'Hara, Robinson Crusoe, Mitch McDeere, Becky Sharp and Oliver Twist.

A need for somewhere to go is not the only pressure that Sheffield and Pournelle bring to bear on Rick. If it were, the novel would be over as soon as he signed up with Vanguard Mining. Instead, as soon as one pressure is satisfied, the authors introduce another. And another, and another. . . . This makes sense because pressure *is* plot. Pressure is things happening that tighten the screws on your character and force him to fight back. In other words, conflict plus action plus trouble equals plot. No pressure, no plot. Many pressures, much plot.

One pressure on Rick is macho competitiveness. From the first moment he arrives at the Vanguard training facility, another recruit, Vido Valdez, is determined to show up Rick and eliminate him from the program. Their competitiveness is reinforced by the trainees' discovery that not everyone recruited will actually be offered a job with Vanguard. They are in competition with each other for a limited number of job slots.

A second pressure is death (always a good motivator). Space mining is dangerous. The recruits are told to learn their training material, and learn it well, whether or not they object to the hated terms *school* and *rules*.

> "So let's agree that this isn't a school. Let's say it's a survival course for off-Earth mining operations. The Belt is a dangerous place. You can screw up bigtime out there, eat vacuum, O/D on radiation, blow yourself up, get flattened by an ore crusher, get stranded and starve to death. No legal liability for Vanguard Mining—read your contract. But Vanguard doesn't want you dead, because we already have an investment in you. You think all those tests you took don't cost money? So it's my job to make sure that by the time you leave here you know how to avoid killing yourself. That means learning a few new rules. Anybody object to the idea of *surviving*?"

No one does. Effective pressure to change one's attitude.

A third pressure on Rick is also survival-related, and deemed necessary in dealing with a bunch of tough adolescents. An instructor explains to a recruit named Gladys:

> "These are meal vouchers. You need one to obtain food from the cafeteria service system. When you complete your assignment satisfactorily—by this evening, or tomorrow morning, or tomorrow midday, or whenever—you will receive one voucher. But if you fail to complete your assignment to my satisfaction, you will not."
>
> "You can't do that to me!"
>
> "I'm afraid I can. Read your contract. Vanguard Mining, in loco parentis, decides the manner and extent of trainee nutrition. Now, Gladys. Are you going to leave? Or would you like to stay here with the rest of the trainees while I explain today's assignment? Dinner is lasagna with mushrooms, peppers, and garlic bread. The choice is yours."

Not all the pressures on Rick Luban come from the mining company. In addition to the competition for jobs, there are social forces from his peers. Rick has been used to intimidating girls into responding to him; he considers this a courtship technique. But the females at Vanguard Mining all receive training in handling male intimidation.

His first counterattack from a woman—a painful and nearly crippling knee in the groin, followed by a kick to the jaw—is sufficient pressure to change his approach to girls.

Finally, Sheffield and Pournelle show an important internal pressure on Rick—the desire to complete a job well. This pressure can't kick in until Rick actually has some real-world, meaningful successes, something his old school never provided. But once he discovers that school subjects he once scorned actually have important adult uses, he is driven by the human desire for practical mastery:

> "So what do we do?"
>
> Rick did not answer. He had called up a section of the ship's manual onto the display. More than anything he had ever wanted in his life, he wanted to read that manual. And he couldn't. The words were too long and unfamiliar, the sentences seemed too complex. He strained to understand, *willing* the words to make sense. And still he couldn't read them. The ship was drifting along, but CM-2 was not directly ahead. Their present course would miss the planetoid.

Again, pressure to learn to read well comes about as a result of plot developments (the training ship is rotating wrong) and in turn fuels more plot (intense studying—a new phenomenon for Rick Luban).

So the pressures to change are many for Rick Luban: a need for somewhere to go, competitiveness, physical danger, obtaining food, negative responses to sexual overtures and—eventually—a desire to succeed for the sake of success alone. As with showing us Rick's initial capacity to change, the authors of *Higher Education* don't merely mention each of these various pressures once. Each is dramatized over and over. Such dramatizations, along with Rick's responses, make up the plot.

What pressures will you bring to bear on your characters, driving them toward change? The list of possibilities is endless, since it includes everything a human being wants to obtain, wants to keep, wants to avoid, wants to conquer or wants to eliminate. Some common pressures in fiction follow.

- Someone wants to harm the protagonist.
- Someone wants to harm a loved one of the protagonist.

- A pressing need for money, or more money.
- A pressing desire to be loved.
- The ravages of war (from either civilian or soldier POV).
- The human need to explore.
- Internal pressure to avoid being alone and unconnected.
- Parental pressure to achieve or to be something specific.
- Desire to please God.
- Fear of displeasing God.
- Peer pressure to belong.
- Pressure from the boss to do something (or not do something).
- Pressure from a spouse, ditto.
- Pressure from the need(s) of one's child(ren).
- Pressure to conform to one's society, religion or subgroup.
- Pressure from internal guilt over some action one has taken.
- Pressure from the law.
- Internal pressure to look good through impressing others.
- Pressure from one's conscience or ethical values.
- Etc., etc.

You can also play these pressures against each other, creating even *more* pressure on the protagonist. For example, Rick Luban is under pressure from Vanguard Mining to avoid fistfights during training, or he'll be tossed out of the program. He's also under pressure from fellow recruit Vido Valdez to get into a fight, in order to establish the adolescent-male pecking order and not be thought a wimp by his peers. Whatever Rick does, he thinks, will be wrong—a good definition of pressure.

And a good generator of plot incidents.

REALIZATION: TESTS AND GIRLS AND STAYING ALIVE

In addition to creating plot, pressure also serves another purpose. It's a reason for a character to do something differently than he did it before. If what he did before was working, he wouldn't be in trouble. But he *is* in trouble (or you don't have a book). Therefore, the protagonist will often respond to pressure by trying something else. If the something else works, the stage is set for the character to realize he must change.

There is another version of this, in which the realization precedes the change. Characters who are self-aware, used to intellectualizing, thoughtful about themselves and others—such people sometimes perceive on their own that they need to change what they're doing. So they do. Change is conscious and self-chosen.

Rick Luban, however, is not an introspective guy (nothing in his environment has ever even shown him the possibility). But he is intelligent, and he can adapt. When all the pressures detailed above act on Rick, he acts differently (he has little choice). And when his new behaviors prove effective, he naturally continues them. Thus, his actions change.

In what specific ways?

He's careful to follow mining-company rules—because he wants to avoid accidents. He studies hard—because he wants to stay in space. He cooperates with the other recruits in studies and assigned projects—because there's no way he can complete them if he doesn't. He keeps his hands off the girls—because they'll take him apart otherwise.

These changes are all motivated by selfishness. Rick changes his behavior because it's in his own best interests to do so. But then an interesting thing occurs. His changed behavior causes others to respond differently to him. He in turn changes his behavior toward them a little more—and out of these second-order changes comes a different internal attitude toward other people. Rick finally learns to see them as real, separate individuals with their own agendas and feelings, which should be respected.

For the first time, Rick realizes that his actions impact others—and he accepts responsibility for that impact:

> "That's our answer." Deedee had turned. "We can go right around the outside. Don't waste time with that door, Rick. Come on! We're down to twenty-one minutes."
>
> She led the way, zooming at maximum suit speed for the open entrance of the mine loading chamber. Rick, close behind, did the calculation. They had to make their way right around CM-2 to almost the opposite side of the planetoid. Say, three kilometers. If they could average ten per hour, they would do it. If not. . . .
>
> All Rick could think of was that early this morning he

had made Deedee sit down and eat breakfast when she was hyped up and raring to go. If they were too late now, it was his fault.

Rick's improved attitude toward women leads to a reciprocal genuine liking between him and Deedee. And out of that change comes an understanding of how bad his old enemy, Vido Valdez, must feel when Vido's girlfriend flunks out of the program and is sent back to Earth. This empathy ends the feud between Rick and Vido. It's new behavior for Rick:

> Rick hesitated again. He wasn't sure what he had to say would please Vido, but he knew he had to say it. "Vido, it wasn't you. I talked to Monkey a long time that day before you came along. When it comes to math, she just doesn't get it. Not at all. I could have taught her every day, so could you, and it wouldn't have made any difference. She'd never have passed that theory final in a hundred years. She just didn't seem able to get the basic ideas. You know her a lot better than me. Surely you saw that?"
>
> "I thought it was me. I thought I wasn't explaining right."
>
> "It wasn't you. It was Monkey. I'm really sorry, Vido." Rick finally reached out and patted the other's shoulder, knowing it was something no sixteen-year-old male did to another male in his old school without risking mockery. But the hell with that, things were different in space.

By the end of the novel, Rick's actions have changed considerably. In response to the pressures on him, he has become more responsible, more sensitive, more trustworthy and much more hardworking. All of which has been *dramatized*—not merely talked about—by the authors.

VALIDATION: JIGGER TAIT SAYS IT'S SO

Validation is whatever the author does to let us know that this character change is real and permanent; the character will not revert to his old behavior the next time the wind changes directions. You can do this in several ways.

- Show the character engaging in concrete action(s) that clearly demonstrate that the change is now an entrenched part of his behavior (this is the most common method).

- Show the character making future plans that reflect his change(s).
- Show another person accepting the character as genuinely changed.
- Show the character resisting old temptations.
- Show the character leaving his old haunts to start over, differently, elsewhere.
- Repeat a version of the first scene, with the character acting much differently this second time around.

Sheffield and Pournelle combine three methods of validation: the third, fifth and sixth.

Rick Luban's changes are validated by his training instructor, Jigger Tait. Throughout the novel, Jigger Tait's judgment has been established as sound, so we can believe his evaluation.

> "You may wonder what the hell all this is about," Jigger began, even before the door was closed. "I'll get to the point right away, Rick. I want to talk about your future. . . . I want to ask you to consider a career with Security."
>
> The idea caught Rick totally unprepared. "Security?" He stared at Jigger. "Why me?"
>
> "I think—and Gina and Barney agree—you probably have a talent for it."

We understand that Jigger, a member of Security himself, is offering high praise—and an objective confirmation of how much Rick has changed from the cynical wise guy he was in chapter one.

In addition, we see Rick preparing for his next post with Vanguard Mining: packing his things, applying for special expeditions, and we understand that he is going forward, not backward, with what he's learned. His preparations for the future validate that he intends to continue those new behaviors that make that future possible.

Finally, the novel employs a truncated version of the sixth method of validation, in which a version of the first scene is repeated to show the character acting much differently this time. Sheffield and Pournelle don't actually repeat the entire first scene (the prank in the high school). Instead, they show Jigger telling Rick that the entire education system must change radically, and that eventually recruits from the more effective private training programs, such as Vanguard, will need to be the means for change. Young-looking recruits will need to "infiltrate the education system, and either transform it or destroy the whole mess." The book ends this way:

> "We need older people, like Turkey Gossage and Coral Wogan—they've both volunteered—but we also need younger people, too, like me and Gina and—"
>
> "No. Absolutely no. I'm not interested." Rick backed toward the door. "I don't want to talk about it any more."
>
> . . . Rick closed the door and entered the second chamber of the airlock. He went through, but at the inner hatch he paused and stood motionless for a long time. He had not thought about Mr. Hamel for months, until today; but suddenly his mind was full of their final meeting, the small stooped figure sitting on the bench in the fading light of late afternoon. He heard again that dry, dusty voice: *Not an easy job, but a worthwhile one. The most rewarding jobs are always the most difficult ones.*
>
> Could that be true? On Earth, in space, everywhere?
>
> Maybe, but not for Rick Luban. Not tomorrow, not ever. And certainly not today, with Deedee waiting for him.
>
> He moved to operate the hatch.
>
> Beyond it, the party was getting into its stride. From where Rick was standing the sound coming through the closed door was no more than a confused hubbub, like the first distant swell of a revolution.

The book ends with the implication that there *will* be a revolution in education on Earth, and that Rick will indeed (despite his current teenage denial) be a part of it. He will go back to his old high school, or one like it. And, as an agent of the revolution, he will behave much differently this second time around than he did when the novel's first scene unfolded. This final scene sets the stage for a possible sequel. It also validates that what has happened to Rick is permanent and real.

More introspective characters may give us more direct reinforcement of what they've learned, through either dialogue or thoughts.

Here are three famous examples of novel-end soliloquies that validate a genuine change in attitude:

> He realized that he had deceived himself; it was no self-sacrifice that had driven him to think of marrying, but a desire for a wife and home and love; and now that it all seemed to slip through his fingers he was seized with despair. He wanted that more than anything in the world. What did he care for Spain and its cities, Cordova, Toledo, Leon; what to him were the pagodas of Burmah and the lagoons of South Sea islands? America was here and now. It seemed to him that all his life he had followed the ideals that other people, by their words and their writings, had instilled in him, and never the desires of his own heart . . . had he not seen that the simplest pattern, that in which a man was born, worked, married, had children, and died, was likewise the most perfect? It might be that to surrender to happiness was to accept defeat, but it was a defeat better than many victories.
>
> —PHILIP CAREY, IN W. SOMERSET MAUGHAM'S *OF HUMAN BONDAGE*

> Now Catherine would die. That was what you did. You died. You did not know what it was about. You never had time to learn. They threw you in and told you the rules and the first time they caught you off-base they killed you. Or they killed you gratuitously, like Aymo. Or gave you the syphilis like Rinaldi. But they killed you in the end. You could count on that. Stay around and they would kill you.
>
> —FREDERICK HENRY, IN ERNEST HEMINGWAY'S *A FAREWELL TO ARMS*

> I felt a little peculiar around the children. For one thing, they were grown. And I see they think me and Nettie and Shug and Albert and Samuel and Harpo and Sofia and Jack and Odessa real old and don't know much what's going on. But I don't think us feel old at all. And us so happy. Matter of fact, I think this the youngest us ever felt.
>
> —CELIE, IN ALICE WALKER'S *THE COLOR PURPLE*

Rick Luban is not nearly as eloquent as Philip, Lieutenant Henry or Celie (he is, after all, only sixteen). But he is just as changed.

SUMMARY: DESTINY ON AN ASTEROID

This is anonymous, and very old:

> Watch your thoughts; they become words.
> Watch your words; they become actions.
> Watch your actions; they become habits.
> Watch your habits; they become character.
> Watch your character; it becomes destiny.

Although probably written to apply to real people rather than fictional ones, the verse nonetheless encapsulates everything in this chapter:

- Like Rick Luban, your character should demonstrate qualities that foreshadow change (*thoughts* and/or *words*).
- He should be pressured by story events into behaving differently (*actions*, which make up plot).
- The new behavior should be validated for us so we know it is now part of him (*character*).
- And then he can go on, a changed man, to his *destiny*.

chapter twenty-two

"...BUT IT REALLY HAPPENED!"
Basing Plots on Real-Life Events

A few months ago my local newspaper reported the story of a drunk driver who accidentally hit the car of his own fiancée, killing her. He was convicted of manslaughter. The sentence was reduced to probation, however, when the dead woman's family pleaded for leniency.

Another news story described the divorce proceedings of a man who moved across the country to a city where he knew no one and accidentally married his long-lost half sister.

If a beginning writer puts either of these events into fiction, someone will say, "Oh, come on now! I don't believe that!" And then the writer will say, "But it really happened!" Which, unfortunately, is no defense at all.

Fiction is not about what really happened. It's about what seems so real that it's happening *now*, as you read the story. Real life is sometimes capricious, occasionally mysterious, once in a while totally inexplicable, nearly always messy. Fiction, on the other hand, has the task of making the capricious, the mysterious, the inexplicable and the messy into something much more coherent. It gives shape and meaning to events that in real life may have none, thereby satisfying a deep human hunger for order. Fiction patterns life for us.

Does that mean that you can't base fiction on real events? Not at all. In chapter eight, we considered ways to adapt real people to fiction. In this chapter, we'll do the same for real plots. Three general guidelines follow.

"ANYTHING BUT THE FACTS, MA'AM"

The most important rule is this: *Don't* stick to the facts.

Fact, as we established above, is different from fiction. It's messier. The facts might be that the man who moved across country really didn't know anyone in the new city, really did meet his half sister purely by chance and really did marry her in total ignorance. But you aren't bound by the facts (no, not even if they happened to you). Instead, create nonfacts that will make a better story.

Perhaps the relocated man knew that his father had once lived in this new city, a long time ago. His father, once a champion pool player and now dead, deserted the family when the boy was four. There was another woman. He finds himself hanging around pool halls, half resentful, trying to learn about the life his father must have led here. He meets a girl, herself a champion pool player. Her father taught her. The clues are there, but he can't put them together—or won't.

What have you gained here? Quite a lot. You've transformed a random coincidence into a story of submerged longing and painfully buried memory. Your augmentation of the facts has given the entire chain of incidents both pattern and meaning.

An important note: In recommending that you play fast and loose with the facts, I'm talking about writing fiction, not about writing dramatic journalism. When Shana Alexander, to take one superb example, writes about a real-life murder of a rich man by his own grandson (*Nutcracker*), she's not composing a novel. *Nutcracker* also tries to find pattern and meaning in what at first appears to be an inexplicable act of violence—but the book is not fiction. It's journalism and, as such, must stick to what really happened.

You don't. Add, drop and invent events as necessary. Treat reality like clay, not stone.

WHY WOULD ANYONE *DO* THAT?

The most important thing you can invent is motives for all the major characters in your borrowed story. In real life, we sometimes don't know why other people behave as they do. In fiction, motives lay the foundation for reader acceptance of everything else. The characters may not understand themselves, but the reader should understand them, at least enough to sense that even the most demented has consistent demons driving him in consistent ways.

Consider an example. Judith Rossner based her famous novel *Looking for Mr. Goodbar* on an actual 1973 murder in Manhattan. Katherine Cleary, a young schoolteacher devoted to her small pupils, was brutally killed in her own apartment by a man she'd picked up in a bar. Journalists ferreted out many facts about the victim, the murderer and the circumstances (one comprehensive treatment is Lacey Fosburgh's *Closing Time*). But when Rossner wrote her novel, she ignored or changed many of these facts, and she spent no more than a few pages on the movements of the killer. Instead, she built coherent patterns of behavior that showed readers how a pretty, educated young woman from a good Irish Catholic family could put herself in such a situation. Rossner concentrated on her character's *motives*.

Note the plural of that word. The schoolteacher, here named Theresa Dunn, is not merely a victim; she's the complicated yet understandable protagonist that good fiction requires. She arrives at that seedy bar, ready for sex with a thug she doesn't know, because of everything that has happened to her throughout her whole life. Rossner uses her novel to show us what drives Theresa.

At least two motives are factual. Both real-life Katherine Cleary and fictional Theresa Dunn have spines deformed by polio, which leaves them feeling less than perfect. And both are rather isolated individuals, without close friendships.

To these facts, however, Rossner adds other motives for Theresa Dunn. Journalist Fosburgh tells us that "little is known of Katherine Cleary's childhood." This doesn't stop Rossner. She invents for Theresa a brother killed in Vietnam, a gorgeous older sister to whom Theresa could never measure up and a contented younger sister who marries early and happily. In college, Theresa is callously rejected by a married professor after a four-year affair she believes is true love. Rossner also throws in a burning desire in Theresa to escape repeating her mother's life, which Theresa sees as made burdensome by marriage and family, including Theresa's own long illness:

> Still, if you weren't careful, you could end up with a house in New Jersey and six screaming kids. Or maybe five, and one who was too sick to scream and just lay in the bed and stared at you.

Terrified of domesticity and the "nice" men who lead one into it, hating her own body, feeling inferior always to her sisters, Theresa grows into a woman who feels she doesn't deserve to be loved, and who even needs to be roughed up in order to feel sexual desire. By the time she picks up her killer in an Upper West Side bar, we understand all her tragic motives for being there. *Not* because those motives were true of her real-life counterpart, Katherine Cleary, but because Rossner has concentrated throughout her novel on showing us Theresa's acting out of the demons she herself refuses to recognize.

What does all this mean to you? That if you're going to base your story on real-life incidents, first ask yourself the following questions:

- What does my character think about these events? Why?
- What does my character feel about these events? Why?
- What formed his thoughts and feelings?
- How can I dramatize his motives clearly to my readers?
- What facts do I need to change to make those motives even stronger?

The answers will transform opaque life into illuminating fiction.

I WAS ON THE VERY EDGE OF MY SEAT!

Fiction must not only be illuminating, it should also be exciting. This is where tension comes in. Tension is the other great transformer of life into art.

Tension means that the pressure in a situation mounts and mounts, until finally there's a climactic scene where the pressure in some way explodes. We all know that in real life, it doesn't always work that way. In real life, a given difficult situation might wax and wane, instead of building steadily. A climactic explosion might come with no advance warning. Or it might build and build—and then suddenly collapse into nothingness, like a hurricane that bypasses a town at the last minute. Or it might just wind down slowly, with no real climax at all.

Fiction, however, demands a pattern of mounting tension. Thus, if you are shaping real-life events into fiction, you must rearrange them into the kind of pattern we discussed in the last two chapters—a pattern that puts ever increasing pressure on your protagonist.

To see how this works, let's return to *Looking for Mr. Goodbar.* The factual Katherine Cleary was killed by a bar pickup in a situation no different from her other bar pickups. She had been doing this for several years, and that night offered no more significance for her than any other—until the man killed her. But that random pattern doesn't satisfy the needs of fiction for mounting pressure or significant choices.

So Judith Rossner rearranged events to provide pressure and choice, starting at the very beginning of the novel. We see how deeply Theresa is emotionally involved with her first lover, an older professor. We see her choices of men worsen steadily, as she despises herself more and also feels more need to despise them. Theresa's fall into danger has a clear trajectory, lower and lower.

Another pattern is provided by Rossner's inventing a serious suitor for Theresa. Katherine Cleary had no decent boyfriend in her life. But Rossner gives Theresa a decent man, James, who wants to marry her. James finds out about Theresa's sexual activities with rough strangers and gives her a choice: them or him. He issues his ultimatum on the very night she's killed. In fact, it's this choice that sends Theresa out to Mr. Goodbar. She just can't deal with the pressure.

Further pattern comes from the time-honored use of foils. These are paired characters who are opposites in some crucial aspect, thereby throwing that quality into sharp relief in both of them. Theresa, for instance, cannot face her inner pain. Whenever it tries to break through, she runs away: out of the room, into drink or drugs, into mindless sex. James, on the other hand, calmly faces pain and gives it words. He explains to Theresa why he believes in God:

> "The truth," he said, "is that I have chosen to believe in
> Him. I'm not sure even that's true. I believe in Him and I

choose not to challenge my own belief. Because if I found that my challenge was successful . . . I would feel myself totally alone. And then I would know despair."

And then I would know despair.

She looked at him in wonder.

I would be alone and then I would know despair.

Theresa can't bear to think about it. Immediately she starts a quarrel with James, to avoid having to think. That's her pattern, a perfect foil to his.

Pattern and pressure—the two elements that create tension. Neither was present in the facts about Katherine Cleary, but Rossner didn't let her story be bounded by facts. In inventing pressures, she created something different: a choice for Theresa with greatly heightened implications. Theresa makes her choice. And dies for it, in a climax that seems to follow inevitably from all that went before.

You can—in fact, you must—do the same with your factual material. Rearrange existing events and invent new ones to form a pattern of mounting pressure. Then let that pressure explode into a climax we're holding our breath waiting for.

THE FIRST OBLIGATION

Your main goal as a fiction writer should be to create emotional truth, not literal truth, in an interesting and exciting way. If that means changing real-life events until they're nearly unrecognizable, go right ahead. Make life serve your plot. Stanley Elkin understood this completely in his wonderful surreal novel *The Living End*. The protagonist, a modern-day loser as beleaguered as Job by tragedy and bad luck, finally makes his way to God to ask, "*Why? Why* did You put so much suffering in the world?"

And God answers simply, "Because it makes a better story."

SUMMARY: BASING PLOTS ON REAL EVENTS

- Change whatever facts are necessary to make a better story.
- Concentrate on inventing and dramatizing motives for real-life events.
- Rearrange incidents into a pattern of mounting pressure culminating in a definite climax.

chapter twenty-three

ARCHETYPAL ATTRACTIONS
Using Rich Old Plots in Rich New Ways

This chapter could just as easily have been titled "Common Plot Patterns—and the People Who Live Them." That's what archetypes are: the original pattern or model after which a thing is made. In other words: the basic, universal characters, the basic, universal plots.

Are there such things? And if there are, haven't they been worn into useless clichés?

Yes, archetypal plots and characters both exist. And no, they aren't useless clichés—if they're handled with a fresh approach. That usually means original characters inhabiting a time-tested plot, or time-tested characters inhabiting a fresh plot. Let's look at some examples.

AN OLD, OLD STORY: THE ARCHETYPAL PLOT
Some researchers into the human brain have concluded that it reasons not by analyzing data, but by recalling stories. We have cultural stories

embedded in the very fabric of our thinking, goes this argument, and those stories influence what we notice in a given situation, how we interpret it and how we choose to react. Moreover, some stories seem to transcend individual cultures. They are universal archetypes. The form may look different in different tellings, but the underlying plot is the same.

Here is one such plot: A character becomes discontented with where he lives. He journeys to some other place, which at first seems much better. But over time, the defects of the second place make themselves known. The character returns home, better able to appreciate what he had.

This is a very old plot. It's also an extremely versatile one, adapting amazingly well to different characters and situations, with each new version fresh and absorbing. These versions include:

- "City Mouse, Country Mouse," a seventeenth-century European folk tale. Country Mouse is visited by her cousin, City Mouse, and tempted to the city by tales of rich human houses with lavish table scraps. But the city household also contains a cat, and after a brush with death, Country Mouse decides she prefers her humble but safe nest and simple diet.
- *The Wizard of Oz*, by L. Frank Baum, in which Dorothy runs away, is taken to miraculous Oz, but eventually decides "there's no place like home."
- *Bright Lights, Big City*, by Jay McInerney, in which the narrator, unable to cope with the grief in his home after his mother dies and his marriage ends, immerses himself in the big-city club scene of drugs, drink, easy sex, nonstop hedonism. Eventually he returns home to take up the grief and sanity he left behind.
- *Maybe I'll Go Home Next Month*, a young adult novel by Robert Carter, in which Sam, fifteen, runs away from parents who are "always on his case" and teachers who "just put him down." A summer on the mean streets of New York City helps him decide to return to his family and his education.
- *The Dispossessed*, by Ursula K. Le Guin. In the far future on another planet, Shevek leaves his peaceful, spartan, anarchistic society on the moon to enter the richer and more intellectually varied one on the planet Urras. Eventually its injustices drive him back home.

Past, present, future. Fable, realism, science fiction. Children, teens, adult readers. This archetypal plot works for each new mood, set of characters and audience. It—and the other archetypal plots discussed later in this chapter—can work for you, too.

I'VE MET YOU BEFORE: THE ARCHETYPAL CHARACTER

When the character is an archetype, the plot may be new, but the character is recognizable. *Not* because he's a stereotype or a cliché, but because he's an aspect of human nature we all share. We know him because, in some sense, he is us. He embodies some deep part of ourselves that we remember, or fear, or treasure, or hate.

Here is such an archetypal character: the person possessed by some desire who eventually transgresses laws and morals. We all know such a person. She's an alcoholic who can't stop drinking. Or a woman so consumed by the desire for love that she commits terrible acts in her frenzied search for it. (The Glenn Close character in the movie *Fatal Attraction* comes to mind. So does real-life Susan Smith.) Or a man so desirous of financial success that he sacrifices integrity to get it, breaks the law and ends up in jail.

The obsessed person may also be more than an acquaintance. Even if you personally have never gone over the line in your pursuit of some desire, you may recognize in yourself the capacity to do so. Perhaps you've held that capacity in check, through common sense or decency or good luck. But are you sure that you always could, given extremely provocative circumstances? *Completely* sure?

Because the archetype of the character possessed by overwhelming desire is so universal, it fuels an enormous number of different plots. Usually the character ends up destroyed by the laws and ethics he's smashed while pursuing his desire. But even within these shared traits and fates, this archetype lends itself to an astonishing range of individual, fully realized protagonists, including:

• Macbeth, whose desire for power leads him to kill his king, initiating a string of other murders until eventually Macbeth himself is killed. (Shakespeare, *Macbeth*)
• Captain Philip Queeg, whose very human desire is to never make a mistake—or at least to never admit to one. His increasingly convoluted cover-ups and threats lead to the mutiny of his World War II

minesweeper's crew, which in turn destroys Queeg's naval career (along with those of several mutineers). (Herman Wouk, *The Caine Mutiny*)

• Count Almásy, driven by passion for a married woman and by his desire to keep his promise to her. He betrays his country and, indirectly, dies for it. (Michael Ondaatje, *The English Patient*)

The character driven by desire beyond human laws doesn't always end up destroyed. It's the character who is the archetype, not the plot. Sometimes such characters triumph, getting clean away with their transgressions. Some examples:

• King Midas, obsessed with gold. His greed turns his beloved daughter into a gold statue. He escapes tragedy because Dionysus, god of wine, just happens to be a cheerful type who turns the statue back into a girl. (Greek mythology)

• Becky Sharp, nineteenth-century adventuress, who engages in adultery, fraud and betrayal—whatever it takes to go on living well and luxuriously. At the end of the book she's still at it, fresh prey targeted in her scheming sites. (William Makepeace Thackeray, *Vanity Fair*)

• Michael Corleone, driven by a desire to avenge his father's shooting. He commits multiple murders—including that of his brother-in-law—and ends up a respected and powerful Mafia don. (Mario Puzo, *The Godfather*)

• An endless number of detectives who become consumed by the desire to solve a particular case, no matter what the cost in (pick one) broken department regulations, disapproval of superiors, objections by wives and girlfriends, sneaky tactics. Almost always, the detectives' obsessions pay off.

Whether your character obsessed by desire comes out a winner or a loser is up to you. The archetype is strong enough to support all sorts of outcomes, all sorts of situations, all sorts of individual characteristics.

Can other archetypes also do that? Absolutely. Many writers and critics have amused themselves putting together lists of "all possible plots." I've seen a list with thirty-six categories of plots, a list with twenty categories, a list with three. Such categories are always idiosyncratic. But that's not necessarily bad. If something on the list sparks your own thinking, it doesn't matter in the least whether or not you agree with the way categories are carved up. The point of the archetypal plot is inspiration, not straitjacketing. Use anything you find in the rest of this chapter as a jumping-off point for *your* individual characters and their individual situations.

THREE BASIC PLOTS: HEINLEIN'S THEORY

Author Robert Heinlein was convinced that there are only three basic plots for fiction. All three revolve around character change. He named each plot according to what prompts the change:

- "Boy Meets Girl," in which the protagonist changes primarily as a result of his interactions with another human being (who doesn't necessarily have to be a love interest; it could be a child, a mentor, a corrupter, a friend). Examples include *A Separate Peace*, in which Gene Forrester is changed forever by his complex encounters with Phineas, and *The Great Gatsby*, which leaves Nick Carraway's life altered by having known Jay Gatsby.
- "The Little Tailor," in which a character changes as a result of facing some great challenge. In response to this challenge, he discovers in himself capabilities he didn't know he possessed, and uses them to triumph. This is the plot of John Grisham's popular *The Firm*. Mitch McDeere discovers he is able to outwit the Mob, the FBI and the banking system, and retires rich and anonymous on a Caribbean island.
- "Man Learns Better," which is the inverse of the second plot. In this, the protagonist does something, or observes something done, that leaves him "sadder but wiser." He loses, but he (and the reader) learn something about how the world works. In Michael Crichton's *Jurassic Park*, for instance, characters and readers both learn that it's not a good idea to play God and re-create vanished species. In Joseph Conrad's dark classic, *Lord Jim*, the protagonist learns that not even a lifetime of atonement may be enough to balance a moment of selfish cowardice.

Are Heinlein's plot categories of any use to *you*? To find out, compare the broad outlines of the story you're contemplating to the broad outlines of his formulations. Do the archetypal plots open any doors in your mind, spark any ideas? If so, fine. If not, move on to the next approach.

A number of plots are so time-honored they have become classics, rich stories that can still taste fresh on the palate. There exist several different approaches for bottling and labeling these classic plots. The following eight-category grouping is the house brand. One may suit *your* ripening ideas.

CLASSIC PLOT NUMBER ONE—CHASE PLOTS: SEARCHING HARD FOR HARRY

In the chase plot, someone or some group is pursuing someone else or some other group. The story can be told from the point of view of the pursuers, the pursued or both in alternate sections. Either one can be the good guys. The outcome can feature a capture or an escape. Combining these possibilities gives you many different structures.

For instance, Tom Clancy's *The Hunt for Red October*, with the Americans as pursuer and the Russian sub as prey, is a classic chase plot. So is Thomas Perry's *The Butcher's Boy*, in which Justice agent Elizabeth Waring is pursuing the Mafia hit man known only as "the butcher's boy." That novel is told from both of their points of view, in alternating sections. In contrast, the movie *Butch Cassidy and the Sundance Kid* concentrates solely on the point of view of the pursued, who earn our sympathy despite being outlaws. So does Jean Valjean in Victor Hugo's *Les Misérables*, relentlessly pursued by Inspector Javert throughout eleven hundred pages.

Chase novels don't have to involve lawbreaking, murder or national security. You might have an adopted teenager tracking down her biological mother, or a husband on the trail of his runaway wife. In such personal chase stories, the pursuit structure is the same, but the emotions and events will be much different.

A variation on the chase plot is the *rescue plot*. Here, the protagonists not only have to find someone, they also have to either rescue him or rescue someone from him. The game has become three-handed: pursuer, pursued and helpless victim. Victims can be anyone: a child lost in the wilderness and pursued by wolves, civilians taken hostage by fleeing terrorists, a lover kidnapped by the bad guys. One example is Marilyn Durham's *The Man Who Loved Cat Dancing*, which was also made into a popular movie. It's a sort of double chase plot; the hero is pursuing his half-Indian son, and is in turn pursued by the husband of his female accomplice.

If you decide to hang your novel on a chase plot, here are some questions to stimulate your thought processes:

- Who is looking for whom?
- Why?
- Which point(s) of view will you use?
- With whom would you like your readers to sympathize/identify?
- Will the pursued end up getting caught? How?
- After they do (or don't) get caught, what will happen to them? Will this outcome be depicted directly, as part of your novel, or will you just imply it?

Once you have the basic chase structure clear in your mind, you can concentrate on creating for it fascinating characters and inventive incidents.

CLASSIC PLOT NUMBER TWO—QUEST PLOTS: SEARCHING HARD FOR HARRY'S LEGACY

In the *quest plot*, what is being sought is not a person but a thing. There are several variations.

Sometimes the quest is for a specific object, which may be a magic sword or ring, a buried treasure, something valuable mentioned in an ancestor's will or a cultural artifact. In these stories, the characters know what they're after, have some clues (vague or not) to follow, and usually get in each other's way as they look. Within this framework, a wide variety of moods is possible. Object-quest stories include *Treasure Island* (Robert Louis Stevenson), *The Shell Seekers* (Rosamund Pilcher), *Raiders of the Lost Ark* (the Steven Spielberg movie), *The Word* (Irving Wallace) and the King Arthur legends of searching for the Holy Grail (various authors). A rich diversity indeed.

In some object-quest novels, the object being sought may not even be that important in and of itself. How much was a white whale *really* worth to Ahab, in the value of its oil and ambergris, over whales of other colors? But, as Herman Melville well knew, objects take on symbolic significance to the human mind. *Moby Dick* really isn't just about the quest for a white whale. It's about the quest for mastery of nature, for imposing one's will upon the enormous Other. Captain Ahab—like a great many other protagonists of quest novels—is obsessed with his search. He's willing to destroy everything for his obsession. And he does.

If your ideas lend themselves to a quest plot, ask yourself:

- What is being sought? Why?
- What are the obstacles to finding it?
- How many different groups are looking for it? Who are they?
- Is the object going to be found? Where? Is this where it was expected to be?
- Who's going to triumph in the quest?
- How will the other groups react?
- Where does the object end up at the conclusion of your story?

Each of these questions can be used to create surprises for the reader. In *Raiders of the Lost Ark*, for example, the Ark of the Covenant has been found by Indiana Jones on behalf of the American government. It ends up as just one more crate among thousands in a government warehouse.

But the search for a specific object is not the only kind of quest novel. In another type, character(s) search for a place. This might be a refuge, a semimythical location or just a new way of life. In such books, the character(s) pack up and move, and most of the book shows them either looking for the new place or exploring its ins and outs after they arrive.

Again, the place-quest plot has infinite variations. Tom Joad, of John Steinbeck's *The Grapes of Wrath*, is looking for a place where his "Okie" family can settle down and make a better life than in dustbowl Oklahoma. The Country Mouse is also looking for a place where life would be easier. So is Nora Silk, of Alice Hoffman's *Seventh Heaven* (the place she's questing for is Ideal Suburbia). On the other hand, Louis Wu, of Larry Niven's *Ringworld*, is looking for a place where life would be more exciting (he found it). In my own first novel, the long-out-of-print *Prince of Morning Bells*, the heroine quests for a mythical place called the Heart of the World. Several different times she believes she's found it. In the end, she actually does—and it's a much different place than she expected.

A variation on the place-quest plot is the place-exploration plot. The characters pack up and go somewhere exotic—the South Pole, Narnia, twenty thousand leagues under the sea—in quest of nothing more than adventure. This, however, is not a real plot by itself. Once the characters are there, and the strangeness has been described, there had better be another type of plot developed. Some other quest, or chase, or conflict had better develop, or you will end up with a travelogue rather than a novel.

If your people are questing for a place, consider:

- Why do they want to go there? (Again, the inseparability of character and plot.)
- What obstacles stand in their way?
- Will you let them get there?
- What will they find when they do? What will it mean to them by then? How will they cope?
- Do they stay, or go home again (the City Mouse/Country Mouse plot)?

Finally, characters can be questing for something intangible: a piece of knowledge, the answer to a question that consumes them. (What question? Your answer will be a strong part of their characterization.) Diogenes searched the world for an honest man. Larry Darrell, in W. Somerset Maugham's *The Razor's Edge*, covered much of that same world looking for mystical enlightenment. The scientist heroes of Gregory Benford's *Timescape* devoted all their dwindling resources to the search for a method to send a message into the past. The hero of Miguel de Cervantes's *Don Quixote de la Mancha* was on a quest, however misguided, for the good and the true and the beautiful, which he planned to defend as needed.

It's not always easy to make a search for abstract knowledge dramatically vivid. But it's certainly possible, as the above novels attest. If you try, keep in mind:

- Why does the character want this knowledge? What's really at stake here?
- What price will he have to pay for it? (Without a price, there's not usually much story). Is the price worth it?
- What does he plan to do with it when he gets it?
- What's the actual effect on himself of his getting it? On everybody else in the story?

CLASSIC PLOT NUMBER THREE—THE COMPETITION PLOT: HARRY vs. THE OTHER GUY

Quest plots can be competitive, but they don't have to be. Only one Ahab is out there looking for Moby Dick; only one group of scientists are looking for the answer to tachyons. But in the *competition plot*, rivalry is the whole point. Two sides compete for the same goal. It's a fight, and may the best man win.

The competition may be over a lover (many romance novels), or a sports championship (*Chariots of Fire*), or control of English monasteries (Jean Anouilh's *Becket*), or control of the entire globe (World War II novels). It may even be competition between two ways of life, as Conrad Richter portrayed so poignantly in *The Sea of Grass*: the free range vs. the coming of towns and agriculture.

Sometimes, as in *Becket*, the two protagonists are pretty evenly matched. Both Henry, King of England, and Thomas, Archbishop of Canterbury, are men of power, wealth and influence. Henry has barons on his side; Thomas has God. Who subdues whom in the end is an interesting point—and makes for an exciting rivalry. So does the rivalry between *The Sea of Grass*'s Jim Brewton, raw free-range rancher, and Brice Chamberlain, "civilized" and sophisticated lawyer. They vie both for control of the western frontier and for Lutie Brewton, Jim's wife. The outcome carries symbolic gains and losses.

Sometimes, however, rivals are not evenly matched. This variation is the *underdog plot*, and it immediately enlists our sympathy on the side of the character fighting with fewer resources. David was no match for Goliath. Nor were the mental patients in Ken Kesey's *One Flew Over the Cuckoo's Nest* for the sadistic Nurse Ratched. Yet both David and at least one of Kesey's underdogs triumph.

Does your story idea lend itself to a competition plot? Ask yourself:

- What is the prize here? (It should be clearly defined.)
- Who are the rivals? Why does each one want this? (It's interesting if they have different reasons. King Henry, for instance, wants control of the monasteries because he is outraged at the thought of an English entity not under his command. Becket wants control of them for the glory of God.)
- How far will each go to win? (This question should generate all sorts of plot incidents.)

- Who will win? At what cost?
- How will you make the other rival end up?

A competition plot does not have to involve violent control of entire countries. Romantic rivalry, to name just one example, can scaffold a plot without a single drop of blood being shed. Will Elinor Dashwood get Edward Ferrars, or will Lucy Steele (*Sense and Sensibility*, by Jane Austen)? All the above questions still apply: nature of the prize, motives for wanting it, extent of stratagems, winner and loser, costs paid.

A modern variation of the competition plot is the courtroom drama, in which the rivals are represented by professional champions (lawyers). Here, too, is something at stake (usually a murder conviction), stratagems and reversals, struggles and surprises, and of course a winner and a loser. Both Scott Turow and Jane Austen knew that readers can get very involved in fictional rivalries. In very different ways, they made the competition plot work for them. So can you.

CLASSIC PLOT NUMBER FOUR—THE ROMANCE PLOT: HARRY IN LOVE

Not all *romance plots*, of course, are competition plots. All, however, must have some kind of obstacles set between the lovers. The range of these is limited only by your imagination. Writers have used all these as obstacles:

- parental disapproval (Shakespeare, *Romeo and Juliet*)
- a pre-existing engagement (Jane Austen, *Sense and Sensibility*)
- a pre-existing marriage (Edith Wharton, *Ethan Frome*)
- class differences (Willa Cather, *My Ántonia*)
- disagreements about having children (Avery Corman, *Fifty*)
- indifference on the part of one party (W. Somerset Maugham, *Of Human Bondage*)
- too-similar natures (Georgette Heyer, *Bath Tangle*)
- too-dissimilar natures (Philip Roth, *Goodbye, Columbus*)
- strange personal scruples (Thomas Hardy, *Jude the Obscure*)
- war (Elswyth Thane, *Yankee Stranger*)
- revolution (Charles Dickens, *A Tale of Two Cities*)
- murder (Daphne du Maurier, *Jamaica Inn*)
- disease (Erich Segal, *Love Story*)

- abduction by pirates (Anya Seton, *Avalon*)
- abduction by Bolsheviks (Boris Pasternak, *Doctor Zhivago*)
- abduction by space aliens (Catherine Asaro, *Catch the Lightning*)

You name it, it's been used as an obstacle to a love affair—which doesn't mean it can't be used again, by you, for your characters.

In fact, you'd better have *some* obstacle to divide the lovers, because without it you don't have a story. They'll just get together, and that's that. Obstacles are one requirement of the romance plot.

A happy ending is not. Some of the lovers in the above novels end up together, some do not. Some start together, seemingly without obstacles early in the book, and then break apart as the obstacles manifest themselves (Brenda and Neil, for example, in *Goodbye, Columbus*). Some end up together but would be better off if they hadn't (Ethan and Mattie in *Ethan Frome*). The romance plot, more flexible than some commercial publishing lines would seem to indicate, can end up wherever you wish. It doesn't have to be happy, or sentimental, or sweet.

It doesn't even have to include a man and a woman. Any fiction which features as its main storyline two people strongly bound together by love, against obstacles, is a romance plot. *Kramer Versus Kramer* (Avery Corman) is a romance plot about Ted and his son Billy, who learn to genuinely love each other only when Ted's wife walks out on them both. The obstacle comes when she returns and wants Billy back—but not Ted.

Evelyn Waugh's bitter and brilliant novel *Brideshead Revisited* is a sort of double romance. Charles Ryder falls in love with Sebastian Flyte; the obstacle is Sebastian's erratic, alcoholic nature. Years later, Charles falls in love with Sebastian's sister, Julia. This time the obstacle is Julia's deeply ingrained Catholicism. She has already married once, and cannot bring herself to the excommunication a second marriage would entail.

Using the romance plot for your characters means knowing the answers to these questions:

- Who are the lovers?
- What obstacle is keeping them apart?
- Do they overcome it? If so, how? If not, why not?
- How do they end up?

These simple questions make the romance plot sound as if it were the easiest archetypal plot to write. In fact, it's the hardest—precisely because the questions are so simple. To keep the romance plot from being banal, or clichéd, or melodramatic, you must create characters that are more believable and interesting than you need for, say, the average action thriller. An exotic setting or snappy dialogue will not save a romance plot with boring characters. These people's emotions *are* your plot, and they must be absorbing enough to carry it pretty much by themselves.

If you can do that—try a romance plot.

CLASSIC PLOT NUMBER FIVE—THE SACRIFICE PLOT: HARRY GIVES UNTIL IT HURTS

Related to the romance plot, but not identical to it by any means, is the *sacrifice plot*. In this archetypal plot, the protagonist is motivated to give up something of great value for the sake of others.

The motivation may be love of another person. Sydney Carton, in Charles Dickens's *A Tale of Two Cities*, dies in order to save Charles Darnay, beloved of Carton's beloved, Lucie Manette. Carton goes to the guillotine uttering the famous anthem of the sacrifice plot: "It is a far, far better thing that I do, than I have ever done; it is a far, far better rest that I go to, than I have ever known." There wasn't a dry eye in Victorian England.

Other motivations besides love are possible for the sacrifice plot. Norma Rae, in the Sally Field movie of the same name, sacrifices comfort and safety to get the textile mill where she works unionized. Her motivations are better working conditions for herself and others, a sense of fairness and justice, and a personal stubborn cantankerousness, in about equal proportions. The mixture makes her interesting and saves the movie from preachy saintliness, which is a major pitfall of the sacrifice plot. You want to move readers, not preach at them.

Human nature being what it is, there's a dystopian version of the sacrifice plot. In this version, a character makes a major sacrifice—sometimes even death—and it makes no difference. Things go on just as before. The child named Father Time, in Thomas Hardy's *Jude the Obscure,* makes his shocking sacrifice to lessen the burdens on his parents—which instead are only increased. This may be the ultimate depressing plot.

Depressing or uplifting, sacrifice plots need these answers:

- Who will make the sacrifice? Of what?
- Why is she doing it?
- What is gained for the other characters? Is it a real gain?
- How will the sacrificer be remembered by the others—or won't she be?
- How would you like your readers to regard this sacrifice—as a noble act? A simple requirement of being human? A waste? (We are definitely into *theme* here. See the next chapter.)

CLASSIC PLOT NUMBER SIX—THE REVENGE PLOT: SOMEONE DONE HARRY WRONG

The *revenge plot* has two parts. First you show the character being dumped on. Then you show him getting even. There is something very satisfying (if forbidden) in the whole idea of revenge, so this plot is a perennial favorite.

Stephen King's *Carrie*, his first novel, is a spectacular revenge plot. So is Shakespeare's *Hamlet*. Prince Hamlet is shown by the ghost that he has a grievance: His uncle killed the king, thereby depriving Hamlet of both his father and his rightful kingship. Hamlet then spends five acts brooding on the situation and trying to trap the uncle into admitting guilt, until finally Hamlet just goes for revenge and the stage is awash in blood.

Sometimes the revenge plot ends more happily. Alfred Bester's classic science fiction novel *The Stars My Destination* gives us Gully Foyle, abandoned and left to die in space by the passing ship *Vorga*. Gully rescues himself and then makes it his life's business to become rich and powerful enough to bring ruin upon the owners of the *Vorga*. Except that when he's finally in a position to do that, he no longer wants to. As he transformed himself for revenge, revenge became a less worthy goal, even to him. The stage does not end awash in blood.

However you conclude your revenge plot, here are the elements you must build into it:

- Who gets dumped on? How? Why? The more dramatic this is—while still being plausible—the more we'll be rooting for your character to even the score. Nearly the entire length of *Carrie* is taken up by detailed descriptions of the cruel pranks played by her classmates on Carrie White, the dumpy girl with the unsuspected powers of telekinesis.

- What does he decide to do to get even? How does he set up his revenge? Show us; don't just tell us.
- Does he go through with it?
- At what cost? Whether or not the revenge is gone through with, there must be a cost. Hamlet pays with his life. So does Carrie. Gully Foyle pays with the increased vulnerability of his world to the forces he's loosed upon it.
- How do both revenger and target end up? Is the possibility still open for another round, even if only by implication?

An inverse variation on the revenge plot is the *atonement plot.* In this, the protagonist is the one who does the dumping on someone else, causing considerable harm. He then spends the rest of the novel trying to make up for that harm. Examples include Anne Tyler's *Saint Maybe,* in which Ian Bedloe believes he caused his brother's death and so devotes his life to raising his brother's children. Joseph Conrad's *Lord Jim* is also an atonement novel. For his one moment of cowardice, the protagonist pays with the rest of his life.

The elements of the atonement novel are the same as for the revenge novel: dumper, dumpee, plan to even the score, carrying out of the plan, personal costs and general results. The difference is that in the atonement story, you show us redemptive action from the point of view of the sinner, rather than punitive action from the point of view of the sinned against.

CLASSIC PLOT NUMBER SEVEN—THE TRANSFORMATION PLOT: HARRY CHANGES INSIDE

The *transformation plot* is what we dissected at such length in chapters twenty and twenty-one. A character encounters some heavy weather in his life, and as a result he changes.

Each of the previous six plot categories can feature character change. But it's not a *requirement.* Harry can conclude his chase, complete his quest, win his competition, lose the love of his life, make his sacrifice or take his revenge without being any different at the end of the book than he was at the beginning. The butcher's boy, Sir Galahad, Jim Brewton, Romeo, Norma Rae and Dirty Harry don't change during their respective stories.

In the transformation plot, on the other hand, internal change is the whole point of the fiction. It *is* the story. If you need to refresh your memory on how, when and with whom to construct this type of plot, reread chapters twenty and twenty-one.

CLASSIC PLOT NUMBER EIGHT—THE RISE-AND-FALL PLOT: HARRY GETS AN ENTIRE LIFE

The *rise-and-fall plot* is a large-scale plot, covering years (or even decades). Its basic outline is this: A character starts life near the bottom of whatever social heap you're considering. Through talent, corruption, betrayal, ruthlessness and/or sheer determination, he rises far in his world. But eventually his past sins and/or attitudes catch up with him. They bring about either a spectacular downfall or a spiritual emptiness that haunts his superficial success.

The rise-and-fall plot includes the Aristotelian tragedy, in which the protagonist is felled by a fatal flaw in an otherwise sympathetic character. It also includes the completely nonsympathetic protagonist who is a heel from the opening scene—but a crafty heel. The main point about the plot is that it has the shape of a long arc: rising trajectory, apex, falling trajectory. The shape itself has a satisfying symmetry for readers.

Within that basic shape, the variations of actual character, tone and events are legion. A sampler:

• *Elmer Gantry* (Sinclair Lewis), in which Gantry rises to become a successful preacher, based both on hypocritical oratory and an intense attractiveness to women. The latter brings about his fall.

• *Richard III* (Shakespeare), about a king who schemes and murders his way to the throne, and ends up murdered himself by a rival backed by Richard's more outraged subjects.

• *The House of Mirth* (Edith Wharton), concerned with the nineteenth-century social rise of Lily Bart, who starts out a penniless orphan. The fickle venality of Lily's world, plus certain aspects of her own character, bring about her fall; she descends into poverty and dies in a charity ward.

• *The English Patient* (Michael Ondaatje), an elliptically told version of the rise-and-fall plot. Throughout the 1930s, Count Almásy is a successful, respected explorer of the Libyan desert, living with great contentment the hard and solitary life he has fashioned for himself. When he falls in love with a married woman, he rises to heights of passion and intensity he never suspected existed. Then, as his beloved desert falls into the horror and chaos of World War II's African campaign, Almásy's life, too, declines into despair, then treason, then death and disfigurement.

It would be hard to imagine four more different characters than Elmer Gantry, Richard Lackland, Lily Bart and Count Almásy. Nor are the specific events of their books the same. But all share that same curving trajectory to their fascinating lives. If that plot shape sparks your imagination, some things to consider are:

- Do you want to cover a hefty chunk of time? Rise-and-fall plots don't occur in just a few weeks. You will, at least in flashback, be dealing with years (even decades).
- Can you set your trajectory against a larger social background? All of the above rise-and-fall stories do this (using, respectively, nineteenth-century religious fervor, the demise of the Plantagenet dynasty, "old New York" upper-crust elitism and World War II). Weaving your plot from historical circumstances gives it scope, interest and significance. The arc of your character's personal life becomes a comment on the world around him.
- Where will your character start out? Usually this is somewhere near the bottom (illegitimate poverty, backroom local politics). However, it may be only at the start of his career (Almásy), or at a place that looks privileged to the rest of us but inadequate and demeaning to the character (Richard, after all, was born son to a king). Wherever he starts, depict it for us vividly, either chronologically or in flashback. We need dramatization of his beginnings in order to fully appreciate how far he's come.
- What will be the apex of his achievement? Can you create a single strong event to make this concrete? What did he have to do to get here?
- What causes his downfall? Whatever it is should be dramatized sufficiently so that the fall doesn't seem even faintly arbitrary. The protagonist caused it by his own choices.
- Where does he end up? Show us vividly, in some detail.
- Does anyone else profit by his fall? Who, and how? If it's another

person just like him, that says one thing about the world you've depicted. If it's a better sort of person, that says quite another (Shakespeare, for instance, brings down Richard III in favor of the new Tudor dynasty—of which his reigning monarch was a member).

YET ANOTHER VIEW OF PLOT: STARTING WITH DESIRE

Perhaps none of these classic plots speaks to you. It's not that you dispute their existence, or don't see how they might shape other writers' thinking; they just don't grab *you*. You still have characters in search of a structure. Are there any other schemata that might appeal more to you?

There are hundreds. And, as you've undoubtedly already noticed in this chapter, it's possible to view the same novel from the vantage point of several different conceptual schemes. We'll consider just one more, in the hopes that it better fits your embryonic material. This time, we'll focus on a basic question we've encountered before: What does the protagonist want? Coupled with what he already has, the answer suggests a plot form. Actually, five plot forms, all starting from the protagonist's desire, as follows.

HARRY VICTORIOUS

Harry decides he wants something. It could be anything: a woman, a job, a million dollars, revenge, escape from his family, the presidency, a cure for cancer, to be left alone. He sets out to get it, encountering many and varied obstacles along the way. Eventually he overcomes these obstacles, gets his desire and retires from the battlefield satisfied.

This is the so-called *plot skeleton*, and it fuels much commercial fiction. Danielle Steel's heroine ends up getting the right man. James Bond ends up vanquishing the dastardly spy from the other side. Luke Skywalker and Han Solo end up defeating the evil Empire, awarded victory medals by Princess Leia herself. Readers crave heroes, and this plot gives it to them.

So, ask yourself:

• What does my character want?
• What's standing in his way?

- How can he overcome the obstacle(s)? The more inventive you are about this, the better.
- How will I make his victory graphic and satisfying?

Once you know these answers, you'll have your basic plot structure and can concentrate on the memorable and individual characters who will inhabit it.

HARRY DEFEATED

In the second plot from, Harry wants something, fights all obstacles to get it, and either comes very close or, more commonly, does get what he wanted. But he can't keep it. At the end, he loses his heart's desire.

Why should anyone want to read—or write—such a downer? Several reasons. Sometimes, Harry deserves to lose (the rise-and-fall plot we discussed earlier). Readers are pleased that Richard III and Elmer Gantry don't triumph. We're rooting for the obstacles instead.

Sometimes Harry loses, but on such a magnificent scale that the experience is not depressing so much as cathartic. Defeat rises to the level of tragedy. This is what keeps readers returning for centuries to such tales of total loss as Euripides' *The Trojan Women* and Shakespeare's *Romeo and Juliet*. More contemporary examples such as Michael Ondaatje's *The English Patient* or Kazuo Ishiguro's *The Remains of the Day* also end in total failure of the protagonists to attain what they wanted. But, again, the emotional workout for the reader, and the wonderful writing, made both novels prizewinners.

And sometimes Harry's defeat isn't total. He loses his major desire, but gains something else in compensation—either something better, or some hard-won simpler contentment, or some abstract quality of wisdom. Charlie Gordon, for instance, in Daniel Keyes's *Flowers for Algernon* (made into the movie *Charly*), wants to be smarter. His IQ is subnormal, and he's willing to undergo a risky, experimental operation to raise it. The operation succeeds; in fact, Charlie Gordon becomes a genius. But he also discovers a world of unhappiness and complex double-dealings he never before suspected. When the gains from the operation fade away, Charlie reverts to what he was. He can't hang on to what he so desperately wanted, but at least in compensation he gains a simpler contentment.

If your character will lose his heart's desire, make sure you build into your plot some compelling reward for the reader who must suffer along with him.

HARRY WINS, SORT OF: THE PYRRHIC VICTORY

Here Harry fights the obstacles and achieves his heart's desire. But it turns out to be not as wonderful as he thought, either because the cost was too high or because he never really understood the situation in the first place.

A famous example is Scarlett O'Hara, of Margaret Mitchell's *Gone With the Wind*. From the opening scene, Scarlett wants Ashley Wilkes. Twelve years and one war later, she finally gets him, at which point she realizes he isn't her true love after all, and never really was.

Count Vronsky, on the other hand, *is* Anna Karenina's true love. And she gets him. But the cost is too high: her child, her reputation, her self-respect.

Will your material lend itself to an I-got-it-but-then-didn't-want-it-at-that-price plot? If so, one suggestion: Consider balancing the disappointment of your protagonist with the fulfillment of some secondary character(s). That way, you present a more even, accurate view of the world—as well as some sweetener for readers. Scarlett O'Hara, for instance, ends up discontented with what she has striven so hard to get, but Melanie Wilkes dies fulfilled. Anna Karenina throws herself under a train, but Kitty and Levin, the book's other lovers, flourish.

Of course, if your view of the world is so unrelentingly bleak that you'd rather not soften it, don't. But you will then have to compensate for the book's more limited audience with some other attraction: dazzling writing or startling plot or cutting social observations so telling that publishers can't resist the novel.

HARRY LOSES BY WINNING

The fourth plot form is a sophisticated way of writing about human desires. Harry wants something desperately. He strives to overcome all obstacles, attains it and is victorious. Then, after he has his heart's desire, we see him unknowingly set about trying to change it into exactly what he had before, which is the only thing he really knows how to deal with.

This is the plot of Dan Wakefield's *Starting Over*. Phil Potter wants a new start in life: new city, new job, new relationship. He gets all three. The novel details his move from New York City to Boston, his switch from public relations to teaching, his search for the "right woman." Eventually he becomes a good teacher and falls in love. By the end of the book, his new wife has persuaded Potter to return to public relations, and the reader sees clearly that Potter's second marriage is doomed to exactly the same fate as his first, and for the same reasons. *Plus ça change, plus c'est la même chose.*

Your material might lend itself to this treatment if it's either satirical and funny (*Starting Over* is), or else so brilliantly despairing that it will shock us into a new awareness of the futility of trying to change. Without one of those two virtues, this plot structure could end up just being dreary. Tread cautiously.

HARRY WINS BY LOSING

The fifth plot form is the desire plot turned inside-out, like a sock. Harry doesn't want something to happen. He fights determinedly against it. It happens anyway—and slowly he discovers that the new situation is turning out far better than he thought. Sometimes it's even wonderful.

Georgette Heyer used this structure in her Regency romance *A Civil Contract*. Adam Deveril, newly returned from war after his father's death, finds the estate heavily in debt and his true love married to someone else. Adam tries every way he can think of to hang onto his family property, but the only way to do it is one that at first he fights against: marriage to a plain, unappealing heiress. Finally, Adam gives in and marries Jenny Chawleigh. The rest of the book relates how Adam and Jenny reach a strong partnership and build a happy life for themselves—happier than his first love would have made Adam, despite the intensity of his feelings for her compared to what he feels for Jenny.

Not only romances use the winning-by-losing plot. Anne Tyler's *Saint Maybe* features Ian Bedloe, who tries to bury his guilt over contributing to his brother Danny's death. (Ian had told Danny that Danny's wife was unfaithful, after which Danny crashed his car into a stone wall, either deliberately or in his rush to confront his wife.) Ian can't attain the absolution he so desperately desires. No matter what he does, he feels guilty. Finally he gives up his search for absolution and settles into raising Danny's children as atonement (the wife, who may not have been unfaithful after all, has killed herself). Decades later, he realizes that the raising of these three kids has made him happy—*and* brought him the absolution he had given up on. Ian, the pitied and unappreciated, ends up a winner.

The winning-by-losing plot is an appealing one, because we all like to believe in hope. To adapt it to your material, you need to decide:

- What does my character want?
- What insuperable obstacles make it impossible for him to get it? (Dramatize these enough so we believe there really is no way for the protagonist to attain what he wants.)
- What does he choose, or settle for, instead? What are the big drawbacks of this substitute? (There must be drawbacks. At this point, the character must appear to be losing.)
- What are the hidden advantages of this substitute? How can you dramatize them so that both character and reader slowly see that this is a good deal after all?

Basic, premade plots aren't for everyone. If nothing in this entire chapter has started your mind churning, maybe you'd better abandon the tried-and-true plot and custom-build your own. Go back to chapter three and start again to think about your characters. That, too, can be a rich source of plot incidents. It doesn't really matter where you start. It only matters where you are when you type *The End.*

Plus, of course, where your characters are.

SUMMARY: USING PREMADE PLOTS

- A premade plot doesn't have to lead to hackneyed work. The basic structure may be tried-and-true, but the novel will stand or fall on the freshness, depth and truth of your particular version with your particular characters.
- Basic plots lend themselves to a huge range of interpretations, moods and worldviews.
- There are many different ways to devise categories of basic plots.
- To spark a flagging imagination, consider the categories offered in this chapter, with the aim of seeing whether one fits well with the ideas incubating in your mind.

chapter twenty-four

I SEE A PATTERN EMERGING
The Connections Among Characters, Plot and Theme

Theme.

The most fraught word in literature. Even if you rename it *central concern* or *reader resonance* or some such thing, it still conjures memories of ninth-grade English: *What is the book's theme? Concisely state the theme, and be sure to support your statement with specific examples in a well-written essay with topic sentence and—*

No wonder so many writers go out of their way to announce that their fiction has no theme. They don't want students forced to reduce their works to twenty-five-words-or-less platitudes.

Nonetheless, every work of fiction does indeed have a theme. It's the third leg of the basic literary tripod: character, plot, theme. And, as a writer, you often benefit from knowing what yours is.

Three paragraphs into this chapter, and I know I'm already in trouble with hordes of would-be dissenters. Yes, I know that writers often are not particularly articulate about the larger implications of their own work. Yes, I know that the text itself is what matters. Yes, I know that a story can "mean" different things to different people. But I'm going to discuss theme anyway, because knowing your theme can help clarify your view of both characters and plot.

But if it defuses the controversy, let's not call it *theme*. Let's call it *worldview*, for reasons that I hope come clear as we go along. And let's see why you need to think about it—if not during the first draft, then later—in order to make your work successful.

YES, VIRGINIA, THERE IS A PATTERN

First, it's impossible to write a story—or even a few significant paragraphs—without implying a world view. This is because the writer has *always* chosen to include some events and some details, and to leave others out. Furthermore, the writer has—wittingly or not—chosen a *tone* in which to present those details, and that tone, too, implies a worldview.

Here, for example, are two descriptions of the same person. The first is from a police report. The second is from Eudora Welty's story "Old Mr. Marblehall":

> Caucasian female, 38, 5'1", 175 pounds. Mole on left cheek, near eye. Described by neighbors as possessing thick shoulders, small round head. Last seen by neighbor, on own front porch, wearing sleeveless loose brown cotton dress, green bedroom slippers size 4.

> There's his other wife, standing on the night-stained porch by a potted fern, screaming things to a neighbor. This wife is really worse than the other one. She is more solid, fatter, shorter, and while not so ugly, funnier looking. She looks like funny furniture—an unornamented stair post in one of these funny houses, with her small monotonous round stupid head—or sometimes like a woodcut of a Bavarian witch, forefinger pointing, with scratches in the air all around her. But she's so static she scarcely moves, from her thick shoulders down past her cylindered brown dress to her short, stubby house slippers. She stands still and screams to the neighbors.

The police report, through its tone and choice of details, says these things about the world: Reality can be objectively observed and numerically described. The physical world is our common ground in interacting with each other. Missing persons are sometimes able to be located and therefore it is rational to devise paperwork and procedures to do so.

On the other hand, the Welty description—like the story from which it's taken—implies a different view of the world: The best way to understand something is through subjective contrast and metaphor ("like funny furniture," "like a woodcut of a Bavarian witch," "so static" even while screaming). Ways of interacting are grounded in some unseen judgment ("This wife is really worse than the other one") that carries with it a tone of both contempt and mystery. A factual account of what the wife is shouting at the neighbors is never explained; it's the overall subjective impression that counts.

It's not hard to imagine a third way of describing the second Mrs. Marblehall that would be different from both of these. Her view of herself as a wronged woman, perhaps. Or the view of her through the eyes of her six-year-old son, as "Mama," warm and loving and dependable. Each of these would imply yet another view of the world by choosing different aspects of reality to emphasize.

What does all this have to do with character and plot in *your* writing? Hang on; we're getting there.

It's not only description that implies a view of the world. So does the choice of story events, and the way they work out in your work.

Detective stories, for example, almost always end with the murderer being identified. If they did not, most readers would get quite upset. The choice of events—investigation, deduction, resolution—carries the metaview that the world is rational, and the further theme that crime doesn't pay. Romances, on the other hand, all offer the reassuring theme that although the road to winning love may be rocky, love is possible and also is worth it. This is true even when the lovers end up losing each other, as in Robert James Waller's best-selling *The Bridges of Madison County*.

It's possible, however, to visualize a different choice of ending for the Waller novel. Suppose his two lovers had still ended up parting, but after Robert leaves, Francesca's husband discovers their affair. Shocked and betrayed, he divorces her. Francesca then hunts down

Robert who, nomad that he is, has meanwhile taken himself to Argentina and fallen in love with a Spanish girl named Rosaria. There is a confrontation, and Rosaria shoots Francesca. In *that* book, the view of love—the theme—would be much different than in what Waller actually wrote.

So, on a macrolevel, the events you choose to include in your story form an overall pattern that implies a worldview. If you know what worldview you're actually creating, it can help you invent plot events that support it, descriptions with telling details and evocative tone, and characters who bear out your beliefs. All this gives your fiction a wholeness, a consistency born as much of patterned emotion as of rationality, that can vastly improve the end result.

But there's more. Pattern operates in a story on a microlevel as well as a macrolevel, and there, too, you have more control than you may think.

CHEKHOV'S GUN AND TYLER'S CASSEROLES

A famous writing maxim attributed to Anton Chekhov says that if you have a gun going off in the third act of a play, it had better sit on the mantelpiece during the first two acts. Conversely, if a gun is clearly visible on the mantelpiece for two acts, it had better go off during the third. In other words, critical plot developments and critical characters must be clearly foreshadowed, not dragged in from left field at the end of your novel. And if you spend time and verbiage on something early on, we can reasonably expect that thing to figure in the climax or denouement.

Suppose, for instance, you give an entire early chapter of your novel to Aunt Mary shoplifting at Macy's. She stole a candy dish and a bath towel, with enough advance planning and elaborate cover-ups to carry out D day. The chapter is amusing, well written and characterizing. Is that enough? No. You're letting us know that this incident will be part of the overall pattern of your story, and so it had better turn out to be just that. You'd better use that candy dish, that towel or some other aspect of the escapade at Macy's as an important element of your overall plot. A book, like an Oriental carpet, is a pattern, and everything in it is supposed to contribute to the design. Although that's especially true of a short story, it also holds true for a novel.

Threads are supposed to be woven the whole length of warp or woof, not just abruptly unravel halfway.

However—and here's the critical point—not all patterns are equally tightly woven. Your theme gains or loses credibility partly on the basis of the weave you create.

Let me explain. In commercial fiction, especially, *everything* in the book usually contributes directly to the plot. Objects that receive more than a mention or two, secondary characters, symbols, events—all eventually relate to the main plot, in a clear pattern that can be satisfying because it imposes order on life. Such fiction pleases us at least partly because it says to us that life contains patterns, order, design. It all adds up.

But all of us know, in our heart of hearts, that life doesn't really add up so neatly. A real person's day (or week, or year) includes hundreds of small things unrelated in any pleasing, orderly way. Real life is messily patterned, if it's patterned at all. Aunt Mary's shoplifting occurs right in the middle of a daughter's illness, a cousin's wedding, a business triumph, a lawn-care crisis, and it's unrelated to any of them. It's not a pattern, it's a distraction. Real life is disorderly.

As a result, fiction that is too neatly patterned will not feel real. When everything in a story works out exactly, and each detail we saw has a neat place in the overall scheme, we may enjoy the story but we don't really believe it. It has a sterile, manufactured feel.

Some writers—especially "literary" writers—compensate for this by including elements that are connected indirectly, often thematically, but not directly woven into the main plot. Anne Tyler is especially good at this. Her novel *The Accidental Tourist*, to take just one example, abounds with subplots and digressions connected only loosely to the main plot of Macon's romances. One such recurring element is Macon's sister Rose's cooking. Rose cooks casseroles, desserts, a turkey, in some detail. All of this could have been left out, but it serves several purposes. It deepens our understanding of Macon's background. It creates thematic design; much of the book concerns how people nurture each other (or don't). And—more relevant to this discussion—it gives the book the feel of the multidistraction that is real life.

However, fiction in which there is no order whatsoever—in which things just seem to happen without connection or thematic implication—isn't satisfying either. Why should it be? It may look like life, but we want something more from fiction. We already have life.

The result is that every writer walks a tightrope between arranging the elements of his story in too tight a pattern and too loose a pattern. Too tight, and the novel feels contrived. Too loose, and it feels pointless. And, to complicate matters even more, different kinds of fiction define *too tight* and *too loose* in different ways. Romance novels usually require tight patterning; literary stories may allow very loose design.

This is one way to look at theme. *Theme* is how much order, how stringently, you've imposed on your fictional universe. It's also what kind of order: happy, malevolent, despairing, random, hidden-but-there, etc. What do you want your fictional world to say about the real world?

PUT THE ENGINE IN REVERSE: GOING FROM THEME TO PLOT

The reader's perception, of course, is that plot comes first, and theme emerges from it. Some writers find that they don't know their themes until they've finished the first draft (I am one). They then rewrite with an eye toward balancing on that tightrope: not too contrived, not too rambling, does what I'm observing about the world below my rope actually add up to anything? Other writers pay attention to these things as they write the first draft. Either way, an awareness of the macro- and microlevels of theme can provide one more tool for thinking about *what* you should write, as well as *how*.

Suppose, for instance, you know you're writing a traditional kind of book, in which a major point is that people who hold fast to their ethical convictions ultimately end up happier than those who sell out. You've created a large cast of characters to illustrate this. Some are ethical, others merely expedient. Knowing the pattern you want to weave, you can help yourself plot by asking such questions as:

- What challenges might my ethical people have to face?
- What values will this call on them to live up to? At what cost?
- Will they immediately do the right thing, or will they thrash around for a while, trying to evade the problem? How will they try to accomplish this? Why won't it work?
- What price will they eventually pay for their ethics? How can I dramatize that?

- What will they gain? How can I dramatize that?
- How do my unethical people meet the same challenges?
- What will *they* gain? How can I dramatize that?
- What price will they eventually pay for their lack of ethics? How can I dramatize that?

Answering such questions should certainly help you get a firmer grip on both characters and plot.

If thinking about theme in this way is helpful, do it. If not, then skip this particular approach and concentrate on others that you *do* find congenial. There are all kinds of ways to think about plot and characters; use whichever ones ignite that creative spark for you.

SUMMARY: WAS THAT WHAT YOU MEANT?

- Every work of fiction has a theme, if *theme* is taken to mean an implied view of the world.
- Theme is created from your choice of plot and characters (the "what" of your book) and the novel's tone (the "how").
- One difference between commercial and literary fiction is that in commercial fiction, almost everything relates to the main plot (a "tightly woven" worldview). In literary fiction, subplots, characters and incidents may relate only to theme (a "loosely woven" worldview).
- If you know your theme before you begin the first or second drafts, you can use it to clarify the purpose of existing plot incidents and/or to generate additional incidents.

chapter twenty-five

THE CHARACTERS
AND THE WRITER

Carol Burnett used to do a very funny skit on her old television show. The skit had several versions. There was always a writer (Burnett), typing away at a story, changing her mind often about the plot. (*In despair, Jane jumped over the side of the rowboat*—No. *Jane gazed at the water, thinking about jumping*—No. *Jane shuddered and closed her eyes, unable to look at the water for fear she might give in to the temptation to jump*—No.) At each change, the writer would pull the paper out of the typewriter, wad it up and toss it on the floor. And at each change the character (also Burnett), who existed on the other half of a split TV screen, would dutifully carry out the new version of the action: jumping into the water, climbing back into the boat (dripping wet), gazing at the pond's surface, not gazing at the pond's surface. . . . Finally, at the end of the skit, the harassed and bedeviled character would step out of her frame and attack the writer who was causing her all this messy vacillation.

To people who are not writers, the Burnett skit was funny. To writers, it was utterly hilarious, in the way that only truth can be utterly hilarious. Oh, yes, yes! I've been there! Yes!

Characters *do* come alive to their creators. Writers do come to know their characters, to feel for them and with them, to experience their breathing presences. Purely fictional people take on solidity and substance, distracting us during dinner and cluttering up our study when we're supposed to be doing accounts. Don't take my word alone for this. Listen to the following writers, as diverse a group as possible in every other way, but united in this:

> Your characters must become as real to you as your neighbors—if they are not real to you, it's for damned sure they will not be real to your neighbors. If they are real to you, you will be able to see the world through their eyes in addition to your own.
>
> —Tom Clancy

> I suppose I am a born novelist, for the things I imagine are more vital and vivid to me than the things I remember.
>
> —Ellen Glasgow

> Usually if I just let the characters take over, I do better than if I sit down and calculate and try to plot the thing . . . this thing happens, where the characters take over and you almost want to look behind you to see who's writing your story.
>
> —Joseph Wambaugh

> The suspense of a novel is not only in the reader, but in the novelist, who is intensely curious about what will happen to the hero.
>
> —Mary McCarthy

> But ideas run away with every writer, and it's amazing how you can start out with something and find yourself grappling with a minor character and you never intended to do so.
>
> —James Michener

Characters, if imagined well, are people. And people, as everyone knows, can be ornery.

THE CHARACTER WITH A MIND OF HER OWN

So what do you do when your characters start to drive the story, instead of the other way around?

Sit back and go along for the ride.

More specifically, explore along with your wandering characters. If a scene you never intended to write occurs to you, and keeps occurring to you . . . write it. Even if it seems to wrench the book in a different direction. It will take only a day or two (scenes that nag at you that powerfully usually write very fast). If you don't like it, you can always discard it. If you do like it, and if you keep an open mind while writing the scene, it may suggest all kinds of marvelous directions, subplots or complexities that will enhance your novel.

If a character keeps wanting to do something very much out of character, try to analyze why. Is it because the action is required by the plot? In that case, you need to either rethink the basic characterization or rethink the plot.

Or, is it because the character has another side you hadn't realized? An internal contradiction, an intriguing complexity. Different facets of his personality show themselves at different times. In that case, write a scene or two of this value-added character and see if you want to change who he really is. Depending on how much of the book you've written, this may mean a lot of revising. It may also be worth it.

If the character seems a little flat, you can even induce the Carol Burnett phenomenon deliberately. Hold a dialogue with your protagonist. Set him down and play interrogator about your mutual plot:

- What did you do in the last scene?
- Why did you do it?
- What is your perception of how things are going?
- What are you pleased with so far in this plot? What are you disgruntled with?
- What would you like to see happen next? What will you do if you don't get your way? To whom will you do it?
- What will you do if I do give you what you want? What's it worth to you?

- What are your current feelings about the action so far? About the other people sharing the action?
- Where were you on the night of the crucial last event? Where do you think you'll be for the next major event? How do you feel about that?
- What don't the others know about you? Go on, tell me, you can trust me. Tell me in your own words.

If this exercise seems silly to you, don't do it. Which brings me to an important caveat for this whole chapter:

DIFFERENT-STROKES DEPARTMENT, LITERARY DIVISION

Some authors say their characters never "run away with them." Such writers invent the characters to fit the plot, *period*, and the characters behave as they were invented to do. These writers find the whole idea of out-of-control characters something between hilarious and irritating. As writer Connie Willis has said, "*I* control the characters. How could it be otherwise? These people don't even exist!"

If this is your approach, fine. Whatever works is valid. Ignore the preceding part of this chapter and carry on as you choose: plot first, characters designed to carry it out. And don't worry about it.

FAVORITE CHARACTERS: MOM ALWAYS LIKED YOU BEST

No matter which kind of writer you are, however, you will probably at some point develop personal feelings about your characters. You may like some, dislike others. You may fall in love with one of them. You may become obsessed with one, or more. Ayn Rand, to take an extreme example, become so involved with the characters of *Atlas Shrugged* that when the very long book was finally finished, she spent the next several months just reading it over and over, unwilling to be separated from the world she had created.

In this vein, how you feel about your creations leads to an important question: Is it true that the closer and more attached you are to your characters, the more effective and real they will seem to your readers?

No. In fact, the opposite is often true. Characters you don't love or identify with may come across as *more* real than your favorites.

If you think about it, this makes sense. It's always easier to describe someone standing a short distance away, rather than someone pressed tightly against you. You can see more. And when the person is, say, a suspicious-seeming neighbor rather than a beloved child, you are more likely to observe more accurately, instead of seeing only what you wish to see. Love can be very blind.

Including love for one's characters. In *Atlas Shrugged*, for example, the hero, John Galt, is a blurry and ultimately not very interesting figure. A number of critics have commented that he seems more a walking ideology, in which Ayn Rand was passionately interested, than a real human being. Rand did much better in creating characters whom she did not like so much: Lillian Rearden, Jim Taggart.

Similarly, Nobel Prize winner Sinclair Lewis succeeded in *Dodsworth* far better with his character of an unlikable wife than with her foil and successor. Fran Dodsworth is vividly, achingly real in all her spirited selfishness. Edith Cortright is an idealized blur.

What does all this mean? That you must stand apart from even your most cherished characters, so that you can see them more accurately. Admire your heroes, but hold yourself back from the kind of dazzled love that blurs perspective. You're a writer, not an acolyte.

UNFAVORITE CHARACTERS: YOU'RE A TERRIBLE WASTE OF PRINTER INK

For some writers, however, the opposite is true. They dislike some characters so much that dislike, not love, erases perspective.

Stephen Vincent Benét warned a young writer about this decades ago. In 1935 Benét, a generous mentor, wrote to fledgling novelist George Abbe:

> Parts of the book are real and moving—certain parts and certain characters, to me, very unreal. The office, for instance, seems to me overdone and fantastic. Your personal dislike for it and its people gets in the way of your representing it to the reader. . . . The office people, in the main, don't live—they are dummies set up to be knocked down.

Nothing has changed since 1935. Writers still sometimes fail to see that even horrible people are people: human beings with their own complexities, motivations, desires, fears, loves and—yes—virtues. Be sure you are not letting your distaste for some characters prevent you from making them vivid. Ask yourself the same kinds of questions about dreary types (see chapter fourteen) as about interesting ones, so that you don't end up making them blurry clichés.

REVISING CHARACTERS:
WHEN SOMEONE ELSE WANTS TO PLAY GOD

In one sense, this entire book has been about revising both characters and plot: thinking about them more deeply, changing them throughout the story, changing your ideas about them as the writing progresses. However, all this revision has been assumed to be the writer's idea. What about when the revision suggestions come from the outside—as, for instance, from an editor?

Many writers are particularly sensitive about editorial requests about characters. Such writers will unresistingly reconsider plot, objectively weigh questions of pace or setting, amiably consider cutting out exposition or adding scenes to clarify. But touch their characters and all hell breaks loose. My offspring! My living and breathing child! How dare you suggest I amputate his limb, decrease his precocity, change the color of his eyes!

This attitude is self-defeating. Your protagonist may indeed lie at the very heart of your novel (indeed, he'd *better*). But that does not mean that revving him up (or damping him down) won't result in a stronger and more believable character—and a stronger and more believable novel. It may be that in that perilous passage from the person in your head to the person on the page, something has been lost in the translation. A second opinion on characterization should be considered with the same thoughtful care as other editorial criticism.

On the other hand, your editor's suggestions may amount not to a clearer translation but to an entirely different text. If she wants revisions that profoundly change the nature of main characters, there is no way you can write them without also profoundly altering the book itself. Your aging police captain trying desperately to hide a hearing loss cannot become a gruff journalist in the prime of his career. Not without eviscerating the plot. Unless this strikes you as the most interesting idea you've ever heard, resist. An editor may be much more knowledgeable than you about fiction, but you are still the creator of this particular piece of fiction. You're the writer.

Will such an attitude lose you a sale? Maybe. Only you can judge what price is worth sticking by your original character. Although you might suggest to the editor that you keep the police captain as he is, and write a different book about the gruff journalist.

POLITICAL IMPLICATIONS: YOUR CHARACTER ON THE SHIFTING SANDS OF SOCIAL PERCEPTION

There's one other important emotional relationship that you the writer may have with one of your own major characters, and it's an uneasy relationship: political incorrectness.

You are Jewish, and you've written an insecure, materialistic Jew— as did Philip Roth.

You're female, and you've written a scheming, man-exploiting, other-woman-disdaining bitch, the worst nightmare of male chauvinists in divorce court.

You're religious, but your religious protagonist is hypocritical and self-serving.

Your first name is *Mohammed*, and you never want to see the words *Arab* and *terrorist* as an automatic coupling—but your international terrorist cartel includes at least one Arab.

You're black, and so is your fictional drug-using pimp.

Or—for another kind of sensitivity dilemma—you're not Jewish, female, religious, Arab or black. And you're uneasy because your character, in all his glorious negativism, is.

But you want to write this character. Because, first, the character is vivid and compelling and *good*. And second, because your observations of the world have convinced you that such politically incorrect people do exist. Certainly they're not the majority of a given group, but they *do* exist. Should you write about them, and reinforce destructive stereotypes? Or should you not write about them, and portray either only positive members of such groups or, at least, members who are negative in ways different from the stereotypes? Which should prevail: fiction as description of everything that *can* be perceived in the real world, or fiction as description of what *should* be perceived?

There is no easy answer to this one, and I'm not going to try to insist on one. So many factors are involved: what your novel is trying to accomplish. The tone of the book. Your implied attitude toward the characters. The treatment you give all the other characters. The book's overall theme.

Sometimes even the use of stereotypes is devastatingly effective.

Terry McMillan and Toni Morrison have both been criticized for perpetuating the stereotype of the feckless, irresponsible black man—yet both authors claim they write, in their different ways, of the world they actually know. Mark Twain's *The Adventures of Huckleberry Finn* has been accused of demeaning blacks—yet Jim, the runaway slave, is the most compassionate and moral character in the book. The same contradictions could be advanced about various novels about various other ethnic, racial, religious or sexual groups.

The only guideline here that makes sense to me is to be aware of what you're doing. Give your flirting-with-the-stereotypical character considerable thought. Does he really seem true to you, or just a reflection of secondhand TV and dated potboilers? Do you know enough about his world to render it fairly? Have you looked deeply into the motivations, social conditions and background that surround him? Do you genuinely understand witchcraft, or homosexuality, or Hasidism, or black street culture, or feminism, or whatever other minority group your protagonist belongs to?

Most important, what is *your* motivation for creating this character? Truth, or personal anger? Observation for its own sake, or prejudgment masquerading as observation?

Once you've wrestled with these particular angels, go ahead and write the character. And be prepared for the inevitable criticism.

THE FINAL WORD: RESPECT

Ultimately, how effective your characters are depends on how much you respect them.

Think about it. When you respect a real-life person—friend, spouse, neighbor, teacher, public figure—you treat her in certain ways. You let her have her say, even if you disagree with the content. You listen, even if you dislike what you hear. You ponder her reasons, even if they seem wrong. You grant her the dignity of a separate existence, apart from how she fits into your own.

The writer who respects his characters does the same. He tries to see them clearly, to listen to them, to ponder what they are. He may not fully understand the character, but he grants her the dignity of having her own existence, of which he is observer and recorder and judge—but not oppressor. Even a satirist who laughs at his creations laughs at a person's pattern of behavior, not an isolated and disembow-eled trait. At least, if he's a good writer, he does.

Consider the ridiculous Mr. Collins in Jane Austen's *Pride and Prejudice*—an ignorant buffoon, self-serving and bootlicking. Yet Mr. Collins has his author's respect in the sense that Austen portrays him as a member of a functional community, with his own concerns and goals. He has some minor virtues: thrift, fidelity, hospitality. He is not a straw man for the author to rip apart; he is a ruefully observed sample of what a foolish man can become. Foolish, but a man, not merely an object. Mr. Collins lives, he breathes, he has been endowed by his creator with life, liberty and the pursuit of his own venal happi-ness. Mr. Collins is the butt of Jane Austen's wit, but he is not dimin-ished by it. He is treated with derision, perhaps, but he is treated as a human being.

This is the meaning of *respecting your characters*. They don't need to respect each other, but they do need your respect to become people to us, not didactic tools.

Because, ultimately, characters succeed by how much we are inter-ested in them. If the fiction they inhabit offers an entertaining plot, we will be entertained only if we can suspend disbelief and accept that this plot is happening *to someone*. If the fiction carries metamessages about the world—and it does—these will get through to us only if we believe the characters. If the fiction enlarges our perceptions of life— how we think, or feel, or both—it is only because the characters en-gage us. Fiction happens to fictional people, who become, in readers' minds, real people.

Go create some.

> The most influential books, and the truest in their influ-ence, are works of fiction. They do not pin the reader to a dogma which he must afterwards discover to be inexact; they do not teach him a lesson which he must afterwards unlearn. They repeat, they rearrange, they clarify the les-sons of life itself.
>
> —ROBERT LOUIS STEVENSON

Genre, essential descriptions within, 71-72

Home, details of, 14-15

Idea, creating characters from an, 162

Image
creating characters from an, 162-163
visual, creating a, 9-18

Libel, 75-81
Love, 163, 166-168

Mannerisms, using, to indicate personality, 15-16
Metaphors, using, to replace descriptions, 16
Motivations, 108, 169-170, 221-222, 237
leaving out, 72-73

Names, 19-23, 69-70
Narrative, balancing, with dialogue, 60
Narrator, 177-179
Newscasts, using, 107, 115-121
Novel, situation-change, 198-199
See also Character-change story; Reader-change story

Pacing, 64-65
Personality, indicating, 9-17, 31, 79, 95-96
See also Character; Characters
Plausibility, 172, 189, 194
Plot
archetypal, 225-246
based on real-life events, 219-224
development, 43, 155
dream-as-, 108
elements, 86-88
getting to, from character, 158-167
problems, 186-196
skeleton, 242
using background to generate, 29-34
See also Subplot
Plot forms
atonement, 239
basic, 229-230

chase, 230-231
competition, 234-235
defeat, 243-244
losing-by-winning, 244-245
pyrrhic victory, 244
quest, 231-234
rescue, 230
revenge, 238-239
rise-and-fall, 240-242
romance, 235-237
sacrifice, 237-238
transformation, 239-240
underdog, 234
victory, 242-243
winning-by-losing, 245-246
Point of view (POV), 91-96
character, 126, 128, 134-135, 175
chart, 179
first-person, 92-93, 180
third-person, 91-96, 180
Protagonist, 178-179
unsympathetic, 132-138

Reader-change story, 199-200
Relationships, 16-17

Senses, using, to indicate personality, 17
Setting, 24-34
creating characters from, 162
Situation-change novel, 198-199
Situations, temporary, describing, 12-14
Social circumstances, 40
Socioeconomic structure, 38
Stereotypes, 26-27, 126, 260-261
Subplot, 194

Tension, 62, 222-224
Theme, 247-253
Thoughts, presenting character, 90-98
See also Attitude
Timing, 169

Viewpoint. *See* Point of view
Villains, 122-132
Violence, 168-174

Worldview, 115, 248-253